W9-AQJ-608

00741981 5

Also by CHRISTOPHER LASCH

The Agony of the American Left
(1969)

The New Radicalism in America, 1889–1963
(1965)

THESE ARE BORZOI BOOKS,

PUBLISHED IN NEW YORK BY ALFRED A. KNOPF

THE
WORLD OF NATIONS

THE WORLD
OF NATIONS

*Reflections on American History,
Politics, and Culture*

CHRISTOPHER LASCH

New York / Alfred·A·Knopf / 1973

THIS IS A BORZOI BOOK

PUBLISHED BY ALFRED A. KNOPF, INC.

Library of Congress Cataloging in Publication Data:

Lasch, Christopher, date.   The world of nations;
reflections on American history, politics, and culture.

CONTENTS: Preface.—The limits of liberal reform: Origins of the
asylum. Two "kindred spirits": sorority and family in New England,
1839–1846. Divorce and the "decline of the family." The woman
reformer's rebuke. The Mormon Utopia. The anti-imperialists, the
Philippines, and the inequality of man. The moral and intellectual
rehabilitation of the ruling class. [etc.]

1. Social history—Modern. I. Title.

HN15.5.L37   309.1'04   73–4309

ISBN 0–394–48394–4

Manufactured in the United States of America

FIRST EDITION

Portions of this book originally appeared in *Atlantic Monthly*, *The
Columbia Forum*, *The Nation*, *The New York Times*, *New York Review of Books*, and *Katallagete*.

Grateful acknowledgment is made for permission to reprint the following material:

"The Anti-Imperialists, the Philippines, and the Inequality of Man"
by Christopher Lasch, from *Journal of Southern History*, XXIV
(August, 1958). Copyright 1958 by the Southern Historical Association. Reprinted by permission of the Managing Editor.

Excerpt from *The New American Revolution* by Roderick Aya and
Norman Miller. Copyright 1971 by the Free Press, a division of the
Macmillan Company. Reprinted by permission of the Macmillan Com-
pany.

"The Gates of Eden" by Christopher Lasch, from *The Yale Law
Journal*, Vol. 80. Reprinted by permission of the Yale Law Journal
Company and Fred B. Rothman & Company.

"The Social Thought of Jacques Ellul" by Christopher Lasch, from
Introducing Jacques Ellul, by James Y. Holloway, published by William B. Eerdmans Publishing Co. Used by permission.

TO CHRIS

But in the night of thick darkness
enveloping the earliest antiquity, so
remote from ourselves, there shines the
never-failing light of a truth beyond all
question: that the world of civil society
has certainly been made by men, and that
its principles are therefore to be found
within the modifications of our own human
mind. Whoever reflects on this cannot but
marvel that the philosophers should have
bent all their energies to the study of the
world of nature, which, since God made it,
He alone knows; and that they should have
neglected the study of *the world of
nations* or civil world, which, since men
had made it, men could hope to know.

—VICO

CONTENTS

Preface

SINCE THESE ESSAYS DEAL WITH A WIDE VARIETY OF SUBJECTS, ANY AT-
tempt to order them was bound to be somewhat arbitrary. The
essays in the first section treat a number of themes in the social
and cultural history of the nineteenth and early twentieth centuries, exploring, among other things, the strengths and weaknesses of traditional liberalism. A second series attempts to bring
historical data and theory to the analysis of more contemporary
issues, in particular to the claim of various kinds of radicalism to
offer a convincing alternative to liberalism.

The essays in the last section deal more broadly with contemporary problems, again from a historical point of view. They
attempt to analyze certain central aspects of advanced industrial
society—neo-imperialism, the educational structure, the dominance of technology—that seem to me to be inadequately explained either by liberal or by radical traditions of social
thought. Although I reject the contention that we live in a "post-
industrial" society to which the older criticism of capitalism
formulated by Marx and other nineteenth-century critics is now
hopelessly irrelevant, it does appear to me that the rigidity of
Marxism and of the socialist tradition generally has helped to
create the theoretical vacuum such "theories" seek to fill. The
weaknesses of a purely economic interpretation of American
imperialism invite an interpretation of American foreign policy
as "post-imperial." The failure to come to grips with theoretical
problems presented by modern technology—the ritualistic repe-
tition of the tired old cliché that what matters is the economic
system, not technology itself (which is "politically and ethically

neutral")—invites interpretations of the "technological society" in which visions of a technological apocalypse alternate with visions of technological utopia. The left's failure to provide a satisfactory analysis of the modern educational system, of the university in particular, leaves unchallenged the idea that the emergence of the "multiversity" helps to define the transition from capitalism to post-industrial society—one of the alleged characteristics of the new order being the dominance of what Galbraith calls the "scientific and technical estate." The essays in this last section eschew the crude determinism that so often passes for Marxism, while at the same time attempting to show the continuity between the nineteenth and twentieth centuries, between advanced industrial society and earlier forms of capitalism, and thus to refute the notion that contemporary life rests on new and unprecedented forms of social organization.

Disparate as they are in their subject matter, most of these essays, even the earliest in point of composition, reflect a long-standing antipathy to Whiggish or progressive interpretations of history. I have never found very convincing those explanations of history in which our present enlightenment is contrasted with the benighted conditions of the past; in which history is regarded as "marching," with occasional setbacks and minor reverses, toward a better world; and in which moral issues appear unambiguous and reform and radical movements are seen as a straightforward response to oppression—outpourings of humanitarian sympathy. There are some signs that this kind of historical sentimentalism may be coming back into fashion in the form of an attack on the conservative historiography of the 1950's, and it is therefore necessary to insist that a radical or socialist version of these "enlightened prejudices," as Engels once called them, is no more acceptable than a liberal version. If these essays help to discourage a revival of historical progressivism, or even to put a few obstacles in the way of its triumph, they will have justified their publication in this form.

THE LIMITS
OF LIBERAL REFORM

[I]

Origins of the Asylum

IN THE OPENING PAGES OF *The Princess Casamassima,* HENRY James records the visit of Amanda Pynsent and her young ward, Hyacinth Robinson, to the penitentiary in which Hyacinth's mother lies dying. James's description of the prison —"that huge dark tomb"—evokes an unforgettable impression of the early industrial age, the monuments of which still stand in the older sections of our cities: grim factories, crumbling fortress-like schools and reformatories, prisons and poorhouses, asylums of every kind, faceless and forbidding.

. . . [T]hey saw it lift its dusky mass from the bank of the Thames, lying there and sprawling over the whole neighbourhood with brown, bare, windowless walls, ugly truncated pinnacles and a character unspeakably sad and stern. It looked very sinister and wicked, to Miss Pynsent's eyes, and she wondered why a prison should have such an evil air if it was erected in the interest of justice and order—a builded protest, precisely, against vice and villainy. This particular penitentiary struck her as about as bad and wrong as those who were in it; it threw a blight on the face of day, making the river seem foul and poisonous and the opposite bank, with a protrusion of long-necked chimneys, unsightly gasometers and deposits of rubbish, wear the aspect of a region at whose expense the jail had been populated. . . . As she hung back, murmuring vague ejaculations, at the very goal of her journey, an incident occurred which fanned all her scruples and reluctances into life again. The child suddenly jerked away his hand and, placing it behind him in the clutch of the other, said to her respectfully but resolutely, while he planted himself at a considerable distance:

"I don't like this place."

"Neither do I like it, my darling," cried the dressmaker pitifully. "Oh, if you knew how little!"

The nineteenth century has been called, with reason, the age of the asylum. For while many of these ruins date from an earlier period, it was only at the beginning of the nineteenth century that confinement acquired positive values—that is, came to be seen as a cure. Owing largely to the efforts of humanitarian reformers, confinement for the first time came to be associated not simply with the preservation of justice and order but with the general improvement of society. Until then the house of confinement had been a place where people were detained while waiting trial, not a place to which they were sentenced for "correction"; or else it was a workhouse, a place of forced labor; or yet again a "hospital," paradoxically, for those conditions, like madness, that were held to be irremediable. The reformers insisted that confinement could cure. They saw it not simply as a "protest against vice and villainy" but as a means eventually of eliminating vice and villainy altogether, first from the patient, eventually from society as a whole. Yet the visible remains of their well-meant labors cannot fail to inspire not hope but apprehension and fear. Instead of asserting the latent possibilities of the human spirit, the asylum seems implicitly and forcefully to deny them. The asylum as we know it, however, was conceived in hope and charity. What went wrong?

The usual answer is that the good intentions of reformers have consistently been thwarted by legislative indifference or penury and by the popular conception of confinement that lies behind them: the conception of the prison, for instance, as a form of punishment, detention, and deterrence, as opposed to the more enlightened conception of confinement as "rehabilitation." Penologists regularly complain that while progressive administrators may understand the need for correction, the general public is more concerned with keeping prisoners behind bars and with making imprisonment as painful as possible, presumably in order to deter others from a life of crime. Enlightened administrators point out that imprisonment has never acted as an effective deterrent and that the principal justification for confinement is to replace anti-social impulses with the spirit of cooperation and sociability; in other words, to create good citizens. Popular ignorance nevertheless persists, denying needed funds and periodically demanding stricter discipline in prisons where the men are allegedly being "coddled"; and these pressures, administrators and penologists argue, prevent the penitentiary from effectively devoting itself to correction.

What makes this controversy relevant to an inquiry into the origins of the asylum is that historians of social reform have generally adopted the point of view of the penologists. Thus Gerald N. Grob, in his recent history of the Worcester State Hospital in Massachusetts, emphasizes the tension between custody and rehabilitation, between the humanitarian ideas of the hospital's first superintendent, Samuel Bayard Woodward, and the state legislatures with which Woodward had to deal. Conceding that Woodward's Yankee background may have caused him "to make the standards of his own class applicable to all of society," Grob nevertheless blames public indifference for his failures. Whereas Woodward wanted "a hospital for the insane [to] look as much like a private residence as possible" and thought inmates should be treated as "children and kindred"— "respect them," he maintained, "and they will respect themselves"—the Massachusetts legislature cared more about custody than about cure. It authorized only the cheapest construction, "unwisely conclud[ing]," as a contemporary critic put it, "that every subordinate object might be disregarded, provided the principal one—the custody of the patient—were secured." In 1832 the legislature passed an act removing all dangerous lunatics from the jails and confining them to mental asylums, while ignoring mental patients not classified as dangerous. "Thus the hospital, like most other state institutions," in Grob's judgment, "gradually became custodial in nature."

This perspective blinds us to the underlying ambiguity of nineteenth-century humanitarian reform. By taking the side of the reformers in their continuing contest with public apathy and ignorance, historians of reform have seen only one side of their work, namely, the effort to win acceptance of the view that criminals and madmen were human beings entitled to human treatment. What they miss is the way in which this very humanization of madness and crime created new forms of repression. The ambiguities of egalitarian reform begin to emerge only when one makes a determined effort to escape the Whiggish view of history as a continuous progress from the barbarism of the past to the enlightenment of our present age. When Alice Felt Tyler writes that the prison reformers of the late eighteenth century were "already . . . groping toward" the modern conception that "society itself is responsible for many nonsocial actions," she takes it for granted that the achievements of the past are to be valued in the degree to which they seem to anticipate the wisdom of the present. The abandonment of corporal punishment in favor of imprisonment appears, in her eyes, as a step away from barbarism. Frederick Engels once spoke of the "enlightened prejudice that since the dark Middle Ages a steady progress to better things *must* surely have taken place." It is this prejudice that I object to in the historical literature on reform, on the grounds that it prevents us from seeing what Engels called "the antagonistic character of real progress." It prevents us, that is, from seeing not only that progress comes through conflict but that it gives rise to as much suffering as happiness. The process by which humanitarian reform gave rise to the total institution is a notable example of the antagonistic character of moral progress.

One of the objections to the view of prisons and mental hospitals that I have been criticizing is that, while it may tell us something about prisons and mental hospitals, it omits from consideration a whole series of analogous institutions in which the same tension between popular ignorance and administrative sophistication cannot so easily be cited as an explanation of the repressive character of those institutions, but in which repression is equally obvious. The theory of total institutions, as worked out by Erving Goffman and Gresham M. Sykes, helps us to see that "what is prison-like about prisons," in Goffman's words, "is found in institutions whose members have broken no laws." In other words, prisons, insane asylums, orphanages, and other institutions as different from each other as concentration camps at one end of the spectrum and convents at the other, nevertheless share certain common features. Different as they are in many respects, they obey an internal dynamic of their own that has little relation either to the stated purpose of the institution or to the particular pressures to which the public may try to subject it. Considered from this point of view, what is prison-like about prisons is not first and foremost the conflict between administrators and the public over how prisons should be run. The essence of the prison is seen instead to lie in certain characteristic social relations within the prison itself, which grow out of the very nature of total institutions. In order to maintain effective control and to assure the orderly operation of the daily routine, the custodians of total institutions are forced to deal with inmates in ways that defeat the purpose of therapy. The daily routine becomes at once an instrument of custodial control and the test of its effectiveness. Healing is necessarily sacrificed to the requirements of bureaucratic control. Thus it is possible to argue that mental asylums, for instance, not only do not cure the "mentally ill" but make them sicker.

It is important to note that prisons and other places of confinement are not total institutions by their very nature. They acquired the characteristics of total institutions at a particular point in history—ironically, at the very point at which they came to be associated with therapy. The total institution may be defined as "a place of residence and work where a large number of like-situated individuals, cut off from the wider society for an appreciable period of time, together lead an enclosed, formally administered round of life." It will readily be seen that this definition does not apply to all types of confinement. It describes a special kind of confinement that could emerge only when two decisions had been taken: to separate "like-situated individuals" from other individuals with whom they had previously been confined, and to subject them to a "formally administered round of life." The contribution of humanitarian reform lay precisely in the introduction of these principles into the administration of asylums, which until then had been organized along quite different lines. Before the last quarter of the eighteenth century, the only places that conformed to the modern definition of total institutions were convents and monasteries, which had been consciously organized around the central concept of discipline at a time when prisons and insane asylums were still an anarchic bedlam. In effect, the humanitarian reformers applied certain principles of the monastery to secular institutions: humiliating rituals of initiation, designed to strip away the identity which the inmate brings to the asylum from outside; mortification of the flesh; sexual deprivation; submission to a discipline that extends to the smallest details of daily life. In the early penitentiaries built on the Auburn model, absolute silence was enforced, even when the prisoners were eating or working together, just as in certain monastic orders speech is strictly proscribed. The penitentiary, like the monastery, was a place to make people penitent. Similarly in the case of the mental asylum; Samuel Tuke called his asylum at York a retreat. The humanitarian reformers consciously or unwittingly took over from the cloister the principle that withdrawal from the world is a necessary condition of spiritual cleansing. The results, however, were unexpected: a principle that served very well the needs of an institution into which entrance was voluntary and residence expected to be permanent took on quite different meanings when transferred to places people were forced to enter for a time in the expectation that they would emerge once again into the world, fully prepared for the burdens of citizenship. Whereas the purpose of the monastery was to teach one to live as a monk, the asylum could not very well claim that its ideal product was the ideal inmate of an asylum, tractable, amenable to arbitrary discipline imposed from above, and unable to function outside systems of total control; yet such was in fact the person asylums tended to create.

The case of madness shows with particular clarity the steps by which the older type of confinement gave way to the new-model asylum organized around the principles of the total institution: segregation of "like-situated individuals" and the imposition of formal discipline or "moral treatment," as it was called in the nineteenth century. Before that time, madmen were either "treated" at home or confined indiscriminately with paupers and criminals in "hospitals" like Bicêtre or prisons like Newgate. The promiscuous character of confinement was exactly the feature of the older system that first drew the criticism of John Howard, Philip Pinel, Samuel Tuke, Benjamin Rush, and other reformers. When these men rediscovered the houses of confinement built in the seventeenth century and then for a long time more or less ignored by the general public, they found an appalling condition, one that proved peculiarly shocking to the moral sensibility of the emerging bourgeois order. They found madmen locked up together with the sane, hardened criminals with youthful offenders, and men with women, so that the inmates "contaminated" each other and "corruption" became universal. In the barrage of criticism the reformers directed against existing prisons and hospitals, one image recurs again and again, the image of contagion. In his introduction to Beaumont and Tocqueville's survey of American prisons, Francis Lieber complained that although "prisons have been called hospitals for patients laboring under moral diseases," in most cases they resembled rather "the plague-houses of the East, in which every person afflicted with that mortal disorder is sure to perish, and he who is sent there without yet being attacked, is sure to have it." A French observer said of Bicêtre: "These wards are a dreadful place where all crimes together ferment and spread around them, as by fermentation, a contagious atmosphere which those who live there breathe and which seems to become attached to them." Mirabeau wrote of the same asylum: "I knew, as did everyone, that Bicêtre was both hospital and prison; but I did not know that the hospital had been built to nurture sickness, the prison to nurture crime."[1] This obsession with contamination shows how closely the concept of cure, introduced into philanthropy at this time, was bound up with the concept of "classification," as it came to be known among penal reformers —the segregation of criminals, madmen, sick people, and indigents in their own special institutions; and within those institutions, the segregation of different categories of offenders.

If therapy demanded segregation, it also demanded the presence of an army of administrators, custodians, doctors, and other healers, who were expected to supervise very closely the lives of the inmates. The two principles, "classification" and discipline, were closely related. Thus the movement to abolish imprisonment for debt reflected, among other things, a belief that this practice had been "one of the chronic factors in prison disorder," as Sidney and Beatrice Webb noted in their history of English prisons. "No place of confinement could, as we now see, possibly have been maintained in a decent state so long as the law required the admission of a whole class of inmates to whom the common prison discipline could not be applied. The mere presence, in nearly all the local prisons, of persons detained only for nonpayment of debts, rendered nugatory all attempts at a uniformity of regimen."

The introduction of discipline—of "a uniformity of regimen" imposed by professional experts and administrators—had two

1. A hundred years later the same charges were leveled against local jails in America, particularly in the South. "They are so constructed as to compel the promiscuous association of the young and old, the convicted and the unconvicted, the hardened villain and the novice in crime, and in some cases—but this is rare—even of the sexes. In none of them is there provision for the employment of their inmates; and there are comparatively few where any attempt is made, officially at least, either at moral or mental culture. Their condemnation may be pronounced in a single sentence—they are an absurd attempt to cure crime, the offspring of idleness, by making idleness compulsory. The moral atmosphere of these prisons is foul—no fouler exists anywhere. It is loaded with moral contagion. The contact of the inmates is close, their intercourse unrestricted, their conversation abominable, the corruption of the innocent certain, while that of the depraved must be augmented." E. C. Wines, *The State of Prisons* (1880), pp. 115–16.

consequences, not only in mental asylums but in asylums generally. In the first place, as Michel Foucault points out, it had the effect of defining madness, and deviance in general, as nothingness or non-being, as the absence or degeneracy of "normal" attributes. The older methods of treatment, or non-treatment, implied a very different theory of insanity: possession by evil or, somewhat later, bestiality. As such, madness was expelled, beaten, chained, or "cured" by means of frightful tortures. Horrible as these methods were, however, they kept alive a sense of the terror and mystery of madness. Tortured and abused, madness nevertheless retained some trace of its former power to offer a commentary on existence, on the precarious distinction between madness and sanity, and on the pervasiveness of "folly" in the world. The act of humanizing madness, whereby madness was released from its chains and subjected instead to moral discipline, had the effect of defining the madman as an empty vessel waiting to be filled with moral responsibility. The reformers dwelled incessantly on the resemblance between madness and childhood. Woodward insisted, as we have seen, that inmates of the Worcester State Hospital be treated as "children and kindred." In the course of drawing the same analogy, a passage from Samuel Tuke shows how these premises led to certain conclusions concerning discipline. Mental patients, Tuke said, should be regarded "as children who have an overabundance of strength and make dangerous use of it. They must be given immediate punishments and rewards; whatever is remote has no effect on them. A new system of education must be applied, a new direction given to their ideas; they must first be subjugated, then encouraged, then applied to work, and this work made agreeable by attractive means." Thomas Eddy, another Quaker reformer, made the same point: treating madmen like children meant that the authorities had to make it clear to the inmates that their treatment in the asylum depended on their conduct, especially on the compliance with which they submitted to the discipline of work.

Thus the second effect of the new moral discipline was the establishment of the unwritten rule so characteristic of total institutions in general, that "good patients" enjoy better living conditions and more privileges than "bad" ones. The humanizing of the asylum made it possible, as it had not been possible before, to confuse the health of the inmates with the health of the institution itself. So long as the asylum was no more than a place of detention and physical punishment, there was little pretense either of therapy or of efficient administration; administration, in the absence of therapy, being almost entirely unnecessary. Once therapy became the object of confinement, however, and once therapy had been defined as learning to submit to moral discipline, efficient administration came to be so closely identified with treatment that in practice the distinction between them was almost impossible to maintain.

At his "retreat" near York, Samuel Tuke instituted social ceremonials which he thought would encourage "self-restraint," but which at a deeper level of meaning can be seen to have implicated the madman in a kind of charade, a pretense of sanity the object of which was to persuade him to renounce madness and accept the burden of moral responsibility. The assumption of responsibility, however, though it was ostensibly intended to prepare the patient for his re-entry into the outside world, in the meantime served also to render him susceptible to the internal discipline of the asylum itself. "It rarely happens," Tuke observed in connection with these ceremonies, "that any unpleasant circumstance occurs; the patients control, to a wonderful degree, their different propensities; and the scene is at once curious and affectingly gratifying." Gratifying, that is, to a therapist who sincerely believed that the welfare of his patients demanded a willed renunciation of madness; but gratifying, in a more immediate sense, to administrators whose duties pulled them almost irresistibly toward an identification of "mental health" with the administrative requirements of the institution— self-control, the absence of any "unpleasant circumstance."

As with madmen, so with criminals. Indiscriminate confinement, at the end of the eighteenth century, gave way to the penitentiary, which has the same significance for crime as the insane asylum for madness. Like the insane asylum, the penitentiary represented the culmination of a long process through which the idea of crime gradually dissociated itself from related ideas like vagabondage, pauperism, and madness itself—just as madness, in turn, had been gradually dissociated from the more generalized concept of "folly." In both cases, the process of differentiation revealed itself at the level of treatment as well. The treatment of madness and crime, running closely parallel, can be broken down into three periods. In the first of these—the period approximately from 1400 to 1650—the central features in the treatment of both conditions were ritual and publicity. Madmen were ritually expelled in "ships of fools"; criminals subjected to public punishment, which in serious cases took the form of mutilation or death. Mutilation served to identify the dangerous man among strangers, but it was at the same time a form of ritual expulsion. The criminal, publicly and ceremonially branded, became a pariah. One effect of the public ceremony connected with these remedies was to implicate the whole community in its own decisions. Beginning around 1650, however, the community began to withdraw from the process of law enforcement, delegating the care of criminals and madmen to specially constituted authorities. Yet the public executions on Newgate Hill and the pillory and stocks in colonial New England remind us that mass ceremonial, even during the period of what Foucault refers to as the great confinement, still remained an important element of the system. Ceremony and publicity were not eliminated altogether until the reformers began to insist that the therapeutic effectiveness of confinement depended precisely on the asylum's ability to isolate itself from the world. The advent of the penitentiary and the insane asylum seems among other things to signal a decline in the sense of collective responsibility and to manifest a desire, on the part of respectable people, to insulate themselves from the spectacle of suffering and depravity and to avoid the contamination of the lower orders. The theme of contamination, in the rhetoric of reform, corresponded to this deeper "revulsion" of the middle class, which according to the French historian Philippe Ariès became general toward the end of the eighteenth century. A declining tolerance of variety and of separate systems of honor, together with an emerging class consciousness in societies organized around production, created a situation in which the middle class, in Ariès's words, "could no longer bear the pressure of the multitude or the contact of the lower class. It seceded: it withdrew from the vast polymorphus society to organize itself separately, in a homogeneous environment, among its families, in houses designed for privacy, in new districts kept free from all lower-class contamination." The origins of the asylum suggest that the self-segregation of the middle class had its counterpart in the forcible segregation of criminals and of deviants of all types, including finally even children, who in this period came to be thought of as a special class of persons requiring special "asylums" of their own.

The segregation of children, running in so many ways parallel to the segregation of criminals, madmen, and other outcasts, suggests that the new-style confinement originated not simply in a concern for public safety but in a deeper and more elusive change of sensibility, which expressed itself in part in a new concept of childhood. According to this view, which took shape very gradually and did not achieve definitive form until the 1830's, the dependence and vulnerability of the young justified the prolongation of childhood and demanded that even adolescents, previously treated as young adults, be sheltered, like children, either in their homes or in schools designed for that purpose. Otherwise, it was feared, premature exposure to the adult world would irreparably ruin their morals. What gave these fears particular urgency, in the middle of the nineteenth century, was the new problem of child labor—or rather the new forms child labor was beginning to assume. Industrialism, while it did not introduce child labor into the world, drastically altered its content. The employment of children no longer meant farming them out to another family as servants or apprentices; it meant sending them into the factory or the mine. The moral revulsion against the horrors of the new system was the immediate precipitant of the reform of the school, just as a similar revulsion precipitated the asylum. Here too revulsion came to focus on the moral contamination that allegedly resulted from the promiscuous contact between people of different sexes, ages, and social stations. The factory gave rise to something of the same criticism that was leveled against the old-style house of detention, that promiscuous confinement led to promiscuous corruption. The same solution commended itself in the case of child labor as in the case of the houses of confinement: the creation of a special institution, the common school, designed to meet the special requirements of children and adolescents, and organized internally around the principle of "classification." In the school this took the form of the graded curriculum, the separation of students by ages and sometimes also by sex.

Like other asylums, the school, once it had been divorced from other institutions (like the church) and from other purposes extraneous to its newly defined objective of sheltering the young *in loco parentis,* developed an administrative bureaucracy more concerned with order and discipline than with education. No other institution, in fact, so clearly illustrates the ambiguity of humanitarian reform. Fired with an admirable sense of the liberating possibilities of education, the nineteenth-century reformers created an institution which in the twentieth century has become increasingly authoritarian and repressive. The "fundamental pattern" of the American high school, in the words of Edgar Z. Friedenberg, is "one of control, distrust, and punishment." "The passes, the tight scheduling, the reliance on threats of detention or suspension as modes of social control—are nearly universal. The complete usurpation of any possible *area* of student initiative, physical or mental, is about as universal." As in other total institutions, "the administration is accepted without deference, as a part of the way things work," and the students spend much of their time trying to defeat it in small ways, to beat the system at its own game; while for the administrators, the smooth functioning of the system and the apprehension of "troublemakers" have become ends in themselves. The same configurations reveal themselves even more clearly in grade schools, as is shown by the recent studies of Jonathan Kozol and Herbert Kohl. Yet the outlines of the present system were already discernible in Horace Mann's conception of "good citizenship" as the aim of the public school. "If we do not prepare children to become good citizens—if we do not develop their capacities, if we do not enrich their minds with knowledge, imbue their hearts with the love of truth and duty, and a reverence for all things sacred and holy, then our republic must go down to destruction, as others have gone before it." Just as the repressive features of the insane asylum and the penitentiary seem to be latent in the very premise of confinement as cure, so the repressive features of the public school follow almost inevitably from the initial concept of the school as a refuge from the world—a place to which children are sentenced, in effect, although ostensibly for their own good, until such time as they are judged worthy of admission into the adult world. The basic assumption of the modern public school system, as Friedenberg points out—an assumption so deeply rooted that it is easy to miss, but which more than any other determines the character of the system—is that

> the state has the right to compel adolescents to spend six or seven hours a day, five days a week, thirty-six or so weeks a year, in a specific place, under the charge of a particular group of persons in whose selection they have no voice, performing tasks about which they have no choice, without remuneration and subject to specialized regulations and sanctions that are applicable to no one else in the community nor to them except in this place.

The point of this discussion can now be stated in a more general form. The rise of egalitarianism in western Europe and the United States seems to have been associated with a heightened awareness of deviancy and of social differences of all kinds, and with a growing uneasiness in the face of those differences—a certain intolerance even, which expressed itself in a determination to compel or persuade all members of society to conform to a single standard of citizenship. On the one hand, egalitarian theory and practice insisted on the right of all men (and logically of all women as well) to citizenship and to full membership in the community; on the other hand, they insisted that all citizens live by the same rules of character and conduct. The articulation of a single standard of honor—of which the principal ingredient, in a bourgeois society, was the duty of self-reliance and self-support—instead of uniting men with their brothers tended to divide them and to widen the distance between those who conformed to the dominant definition of citizenship and those who did not.

The humanitarian reformers of the nineteenth century not only reflected the changing sensibility of the period—this growing consciousness of differences of all kinds—they played a central part in the process whereby this consciousness came to be embodied in various forms of institutionalized segregation. The modern asylum is only one, though in many ways the most striking, of these forms. Another is the modern family, an institution that was also redefined in the nineteenth century as a kind of asylum or refuge; and it would be possible to show, if it did not take us too far from the subject of the present essay, that the reform of the family, like the reform of the asylum, originated in the same process of differentiation—in this case, from an exaggerated consciousness of sexual roles, as well as from the new idea of childhood to which I have already alluded.

We might see yet another manifestation of the same tendencies in the changing attitudes and practices regarding race that provoked, in the United States, the deepest moral crisis of the century. It is a striking fact that the idea of the Negro sorted itself out from related concepts of nationality and religion—from the concepts of African, heathen, and savage—at the very point in time when large numbers of men and women were beginning to question the moral legitimacy of slavery. The simultaneous rise of antislavery feeling and the notion of race—the latter often accompanied by elaborate theories of racial inferiority—lends strong support to the contention that there is a close historical connection between egalitarianism and intolerance.

Two "Kindred Spirits": Sorority and Family in New England, 1839–1846

L IFE IS SHORT, AND KINDRED SPIRITS ARE FEW, THE CHANCES OF their meeting are fewer still, and poor human nature has so many jarring strings, that, after all, friendship is something more to be worshipped as an ideal good, than a real, and possible thing, something that *may be,* rather than something that *is*." So wrote one New England lady to another in 1839. The writer, Mrs. Luella J. B. Case of Lowell, Massachusetts, was the wife of a preacher, newspaperman, and entrepreneur. She did not count her husband as one of those "kindred spirits" whose ideal friendship she craved. She had in fact met only one such person, a woman twenty years older than herself, whom she had known, significantly, in her childhood—that golden time in the life of the American girl, the time of innocence before the onset of adolescence. But before her death she was to find one other: Sarah Edgarton of Shirley, Massachusetts, the recipient of this letter. It was on the tremulous brink of that encounter that Mrs. Case wrote the resigned yet (in the context) hopeful words quoted above.

But Sarah in 1846 married a clergyman, and her intimacy with Mrs. Case came to an end. Two years later she died at the age of twenty-nine. In the year of Sarah's marriage, Mrs. Case left her husband; she spent the remaining ten years of her life at her girlhood home in Kingston, New Hampshire.

That, in its bare outline, is the uneventful history of Mrs. Case and Sarah Edgarton. The fact that Mrs. Case happened to be a granddaughter of Josiah Bartlett, one of the signers of the Declaration of Independence, may lend the story some slight additional interest, but it will hardly engage our attention for very long. The significance of the story for the social historian lies rather in the fact that Mrs. Case and her friend were writers, or aspired to be. They were among that growing number of American women who were beginning at that time to seek fulfillment in literature—a fulfillment which they evidently could no longer find as wives and mothers. These particular women, in short, were representatives of a general cultural phenomenon. It is this phenomenon—the longing of women for literary careers—that needs to be explained, and the friendship of Mrs. Case and Sarah Edgarton may help to explain it.

It was in the 1830's and 1840's that women in America first began to be spoken of as "restless"; and as everybody knows, they have been restless ever since. They may have been so before, but they did not talk about it; nor did their behavior seem to suggest it. On the contrary, they seemed contented with their "place." But about 1830—a time of general stirring, of widespread restlessness—they seemed all at once to resent the role they were expected to play. They began to campaign for "equality." They talked with passion of ending the tyranny of masculine domination. They demanded to be educated. They undertook literary careers; nor was this last activity, though it seemed on the surface less threatening to masculine prerogatives, any less alarming to men. If literature was not safe from feminine intrusion, what was? Hawthorne's complaint still reverberates: the "damned female scribblers," as he was moved to call them, seemed in his time on the point of monopolizing the profession of letters in the United States.

What explained all this activity? Why, in particular, did women show such a sudden affinity for the literary life? Were women in fact oppressed? Even those of them who held aloof from the crusade for equal rights, even those who, like Sarah Josepha Hale, confined themselves to literature and to the demand for "female education," acted as if they were; and to read the histories of the movement for "woman's rights," one would imagine that they were justified in doing so. As these histories point out, women had "many duties, but few rights," in Miss Flexner's phrase. Not only were they deprived of the vote, but when they married, women surrendered their property—surrendered, indeed, their legal existence—to their husbands. What better proof of subordination?

We cannot here embark on a review of a difficult and complicated subject. But we should note, in passing, certain indications which do not square with the theory of feminine subordination. The accounts of European travelers, for instance—and these travelers almost invariably commented on the matter—stressed the unprecedented freedom enjoyed by American women. It is possible that the position of women in the United States appeared attractive only in comparison with the position of women in Europe. Yet even this is hard to reconcile with the notion that the agitation for woman's rights was nothing more than a protest against women's degradation. For if this were so, one would expect to find an even greater agitation in Europe and in particular on the continent, where the position of women was presumably worse than it was in the United States. Only in England and in America, however, did agitation for woman's rights reach notable proportions, and as late as 1914 American observers were surprised at the relative absence of such agitation on the continent.[1] If feminism was simply a response to existing evils, why did it seem to flourish precisely where the evils were least acute?

It is true that even in the United States women labored under a variety of legal disabilities. But it would be a mistake to assume that the laws which seemed to consign them to a position of social inferiority—the laws governing property, for instance—

1. Randolph Bourne attributed the weakness of the feminist movement in France to the fact that "here, though women have not the vote, yet they are 'citoyennes' and are taken with extreme seriousness, whereas in England one feels they are quite superfluous, and in America occupy a highly artificial position, adored and—despised, at once. . . ."

really reflected an existing state of affairs, any more than the laws governing primogeniture in the eighteenth century (to take an analogous example) tell us anything about the actual distribution of property in the colonial South. The laws could be circumvented by private understandings between couples, and the evidence suggests that such arrangements were not at all uncommon. Thus when Antoinette Brown married Samuel Blackwell, they agreed "to be joint owners of everything," as she put it, "—each holding the undivided half of the whole." If either died, half of the property was to go to the other. This arrangement was better, they agreed, than for each to retain his separate earnings—a solution they also considered. Their deliberations hardly support the accepted view that marriage in the nineteenth century meant "legal death" for the woman.

The Blackwells were social reformers and feminists. It may be that other women submitted meekly to their fate. But Elizabeth Dwight Cabot, who was certainly no reformer, gave her husband detailed instructions as to the disposition of her "small sum," even though it was legally her husband's. It was impossible for the feminists to impress upon such women a sense of the injustices which were daily inflicted upon them. Elizabeth Cabot, when she had finished John Stuart Mill's *The Subjection of Women,* threatened to send a copy to her husband, "that you may see how very dreadful my position is compared with yours & what a slave I really am however I may appear." Was her complacency merely the final proof of her degradation?

There is reason to doubt, therefore, that the "restlessness" of the American woman was nothing more than the slave's determination to be free. What remains is to suggest an alternative theory that will explain what the present theory does not explain.

The movement of women into literature may not at first appear to be part of the feminine "revolt" at all. For that very reason, it may reveal something about the sources of women's discontent that studies of feminism have ignored. There has been less temptation to talk about women's literary activities in the terms in which discussion of their political activities has become imbedded. In the field of literature it is possible, therefore, to begin without the preconceptions that have long obscured the real nature of the changes that were taking place in American social life in the middle of the nineteenth century.

It is necessary here not only to ignore the more obvious aspect of the feminist movement but even within the realm of literature to ignore the more prominent of the women writers of the period. This may seem doubly perverse. But it is necessary to confine ourselves to the obscure and the undistinguished if we are to see that the impulse that drove women to literature was widespread, and not confined to a few brilliant and daring women. It is from such superficially unpromising materials that social history must sometimes be written.

Certainly there was nothing either brilliant or daring about Sarah Edgarton and Mrs. Case. Nor were their social origins unusual. They were members of the comfortable middle class in New England, but hardly representatives of an intellectual élite or an avant-garde. They were quite ordinary women who nevertheless felt a strange and powerful compulsion to embark on literary careers. Sarah was the daughter of a manufacturer, the tenth of fifteen children. Like most women of her class, she was educated at home. She was brought up in the Universalist religion. So, presumably, was Mrs. Case. At any rate the latter was a Universalist by the time she met her husband, and it was possibly through her influence that Eliphalet Case abandoned Methodism—he had earlier been a popular revivalist, and it was said that he won his wife's heart with his preaching—for the more rationalistic and humanitarian creed of the Universalists. (He shortly left preaching altogether and became a journalist. Eventually he plunged into a series of speculations which led to his ruin.)

Both Sarah and Mrs. Case were active in the affairs of their church. They attended Universalist conventions and wrote for Universalist publications. They commiserated over the tendency of New Englanders, especially in the rural sections, to cling to older, less enlightened faiths. When Mrs. Case went to visit her ailing mother in Kingston, she noted that "there is nothing here, but Calvinist, and Methodist preaching, and whenever I attend, which is necessarily but seldom, I invariably hear the denomination, which I believe the right, villified [*sic*], and abused, in the coarsest terms." It was through the church that the two friends first met. In 1839 Sarah assumed the editorship of a Universalist annual, *The Rose of Sharon,* and asked Mrs. Case, who had evidently been recommended to her by a friend, for a contribution.

Yet though a devotion to the Universalist faith inspired both their literary efforts and, initially, their friendship itself, both soon transcended religious concerns. Mrs. Case urged her friend to write for a larger audience, to submit pieces to the *Knickerbocker* and the *Democratic Review.* "I hope you will not understand me," she wrote, "as wishing you to leave the object of your present efforts, that of raising, and refining the standard of taste in our own denomination, and of spreading farther, and beautifying our holy, and sublime faith." But publication in periodicals of more general interest would "bring you before the literary world," she insisted, ". . . and give you the place to which those talents entitle you."

Those talents, Mrs. Case was convinced, were of a high order; they far excelled her own. Her attitude toward her friend was that of a patroness toward an unusually gifted protégée—an attitude made all the easier to hold by the fact that Sarah was not only several years younger than herself but unencumbered by the "domestic entanglements" which she felt impeded her own literary career. Were it not for those, she wrote to Sarah, "so much should I like your vocation, and its duties, with all your prospects of success, that . . . I should forthwith take in good earnest your jesting hint about being assistant 'editor' [of the *Rose of Sharon*], and jump on board your barque, content to let the wind that would fill your sails, carry along my humble self, down the unreturning current." As for her humble self, she could justify her inclusion in such a partnership only by reminding herself that it required more than genius, after all, to "reform the age." "God works by lesser, as well as mighty agents, and the coral-worm throws up a surer foundation, from the bottom of the deep, than the heaving volcano; and all the reforms in science, and morals, have been effected by individual efforts of many, and sometimes lowly agents." But she confessed to scribbling "for a more selfish reason, *'pour me amuser* [sic],'" and though she had "somewhat of a dread of criticism, yet let it once come, heavy, and savage, and I should be the very last to die of a review. The spirit of resistance, once aroused, would be strong, and unsleeping."

Sarah had misgivings about her own work—many "falterings and doubts," as she put it, "in my inward way." It is a difficult lesson for me," she confided, "to learn to be content with my feebleness. I have no desire to be great, but I wish I might do good, and bless everything I love,—my religion, and all who come within its brotherhood, and through them, the world. . . . [B]ut though these self-reproaches are not the best comforters in the world, they will doubtless work their good; they at least incite me to perseverance." Mrs. Case would not be put off, however, with such modesty; her reply took account of the possibility of her friend's "greatness" as well as the fact of her "goodness." "Do not fear, do not be discouraged. The path before you is one of light, all light . . . [W]hen the failing spirit comes over you, think who is there among our celebrated American lady authors, who has been as favorably received by the public at your age . . . as yourself." It was these reflections which prompted her desire to "jump on board your barque."

Much more was involved, however, than "goodness," or "greatness" either, for that matter. It was one of the ironies of the literary life that the esthetic ideal tended eventually to crowd out the didactic and religious impulse which had first called it into being. The conflict between the poet's commitment to beauty and "the more important subject for which we came into this world a passport to a better," as another female scribbler put it—this conflict could no longer be resolved by means of platitudes. If it could be resolved at all, it was only by a more and more liberal construction of religion itself; if art conflicted with religion, it was religion which had to yield. Thus by a queer process the injunction to disseminate God's truth among the multitude, if one took the injunction seriously, led one in the end away from God; away, at any rate, from the god of John Calvin.

But it was finally not so much an esthetic ideal which these lady writers were pursuing as an ideal of the literary life—an ideal of pure friendship between women, based on a shared sensitivity; and this, not even Universalism could accommodate. It was not so much beauty itself as the common pursuit of it that interested Sarah and Mrs. Case—which may help to explain, incidentally, why they were not better writers. What they sought in literature was not so much craft as companionship, and their most eloquent flights—expressed in the amorous language which was the characteristic style of feminine friendship in the nineteenth century—were addressed not to the muse but to each other. But the ideal of pure friendship, given the peculiar moral atmosphere of the period, grew quite logically out of a devotion to literature. With whom after all, could a woman converse, assuming that she was endowed with the refinement which qualified her in the first place to write of the beauties of the "spiritual" life, except with other women so endowed?

In the same letter in which she set down her "falterings and doubts," Sarah suggested—not "jestingly," as Mrs. Case rather coyly insisted—that Mrs. Case become assistant editor of the *Rose*. She continued in the best manner of the age of sentiment.

Will you accept? How I would like it and how light would be the labor thus shared! Come to me when the flowers and birds are come, and we will dwell with them in greenwood bowers—and our papers and books shall be with us and we will read and talk, and form plans and be the happiest editorial wood-nymphs that ever watched over the flowers and *our* flower, the dear little "Rose," shall be the sweetest and purest that ever blest a dryad's care, and we will—Oh, dear, why should I sketch so bright a picture? Can it ever be a copy from nature—a scene from history—*our* history, my beloved friend? Would, indeed, that it might be, but life is for the most part made up of darker views, and *perhaps* higher pursuits. Nevertheless, I cannot but often dream of hours like these—they seem so soft, and sweet, and unalloyed—so like a fairy life, in which, invisible dwellers in Nature's holy sanctuaries, we should quietly work unseen blessings for the race of man, and bless ourselves in our deeds. You see how *self* predominates in these dreams, how I would draw you from all your domestic ties, and make you a very girl with myself. I am very foolish, I know—a perfect *natural,* for in my baby-days I had the same wild fantasies floating in my brain, and the same dreamy desires for gipsy freedom. I would be one of Diana's maids of honor, and if it be true that she condescended to kiss Endymion, who knows but she would allow me to love some shepherd—pastoral or divine? Pardon me, I will cease.

It becomes clear in such a passage as this—stylized as it is—that the work of "reforming the world" was not at bottom what chiefly concerned these women. The importance of reform, for Sarah and Mrs. Case as for Henry James's Olive Chancellor, lay rather in the fact that it furnished the setting for a friendship which had very little to do with reform—a friendship founded, in fact, on a very different ideal, the dream of "gipsy freedom." James understood the process perfectly, and it is *The Bostonians,* in fact, more than any work of history, which teaches us how to understand the passion of nineteenth-century women for literature and reform—for uplifting activities of every kind. In that novel he portrayed, with an uncanny sense of the psychological origins of the movement for women's rights as well as of its social setting, exactly the kind of relationship being discussed here: a young girl of poetic temperament (Verena Tarrant) falls under the spell of an older woman (Olive Chancellor), who we are given to understand is motivated by what Mrs. Case would have called "destructive" instincts rather than by the zeal for reform which she professes and which manages for a time to conceal them. To attach to the relationship between Olive and Verena the label "Lesbian," as some critics have done, does violence to its subtlety and complexity, if only because such labels—at least as they are ordinarily used—carry with them the suggestion of perversity and abnormality, the suggestion that when one uses them one is describing a "case." For that reason we have not used such a term here any more than James would have used it in *The Bostonians* even if he had had such a term at his disposal. Our point throughout this discussion is that in such a society as nineteenth-century America the kind of behavior we are concerned with here may have been normal rather than perverse. Were it not for that possibility, the social historian would find very little of interest or significance about the instance at hand.

What interests us especially are the social conditions which drove women into such relationships. A thorough analysis of these conditions would of course fill volumes. Here we can only note what seems the obvious, though necessarily the most immediate and superficial, explanation: that women no longer found in the family (or, one should add, in the church) a source of affection and understanding, of meaningful contact with other people. The reasons for this are to be found in the transformation of the family itself, not so much as a result of industrialization, as has been suggested, as because of the dispersal of settlement—from Europe to America, then from the seaboard into the interior. Migration and dispersal eroded all agencies of social cohesion—not merely the family but church, state, and social classes. The family lost its economic and even its educational functions; extended kin groups broke down; and as a result the family was driven in upon itself: man, wife, and children held together not by mutual dependence, as formerly, but by affection. But affection was not enough to hold either the family—even this remnant that remained—or society together.

Mrs. Case and Sarah Edgarton may be numbered among the innumerable victims of this remorseless process, though in Sarah's case the process was only beginning. She came, as noted above, from a large family, and there, as her husband later observed, she was "permitted to spend a great portion of her time; for, until a recent period, the family circle has only widened by the marriage of its inmates;—all the married sons and their families living near their father's house." In contrast, there is something very modern about the marriage of Mrs. Case—whatever her early life may have been like. She and her husband lived for the most part in boarding houses rather than "keeping house" for themselves. They had no children. Both their families were scattered about the country. They themselves moved three times during their married life—from Lowell to Portland, Maine, to Cincinnati. Their lives totally lacked whatever stability comes from living in one place among a multitude of brothers and sisters and aunts and uncles and cousins. It is hardly any wonder that Mrs. Case sought a sister in Sarah.

For a time such women may have found solace—not specifically religious—in the church. Organized religion in eighteenth- and nineteenth-century American history may be understood in part as a substitute for the family, as the language in which it clothed itself—"brethren," "sisters," etc.—suggests. It is significant, in this context, that both Sarah and Mrs. Case devoted themselves with such zeal to their religion. Both of them, moreover, married ministers. But it is quite clear that for Mrs. Case especially religion had lost its power to bind together its devotees in a community of sympathy and understanding. Mrs. Case and Sarah therefore turned to the sorority as their model of the ideal society—the sisterhood of sensibility. They turned to the sorority for the same reasons that men, in the same period, turned to the Masons or immigrants to their national and fraternal orders—as an alternative to emotional anarchy.

What remains to be explained is why the sorority—or for that matter the fraternity—became the peculiar recourse of men and women in search of the society of kindred spirits. Why did these organizations (if one can call them that), so often achieve exclusiveness by excluding members of the opposite sex? The answer seems to lie in the myth of the purity of women, so deeply cherished by the nineteenth century. The myth itself was yet another product of social disintegration, of the disintegration of the family in particular. It represented a desperate effort to find in the sanctity of women, the sanctity of motherhood and the Home, the principle which would hold not only the family but society together. In a society that felt itself on the verge of chaos—a "frontier" in the broadest sense of the term—women came to represent cohesion, decency, and self-restraint; and the cult of the Home, over which they presided, became the national religion.

But the cult of women and the Home contained contradictions that tended to undermine the very things they were supposed to safeguard. Implicit in the myth was a repudiation not only of heterosexuality but of domesticity itself. It was her purity, contrasted with coarseness of men, that made woman the head of the Home (though not of the family) and the guardian of public morality. But that same purity made intercourse between men and women at last almost literally impossible and drove women to retreat almost exclusively into the society of their own sex, to abandon the very Home which it was their appointed mission to preserve.

It was as a sister, then, that Sarah Edgarton begged Mrs. Case to dwell with her in "greenwood bowers," in an Eden of eternal adolescence. Her language was appropriate to the sentiment. Her references to Diana called up a vision of a world without men, of the perfect friendship of women unalloyed by baser and coarser natures. And in her reference to her desire to draw Mrs. Case from her "domestic ties"—a desire she spoke of as selfish and therefore reprehensible—the point became explicit: "I would . . . make you a very girl with myself."

Mrs. Case replied with a fantasy of her own—the "barque" conceit referred to above. She characterized herself, in the language of phrenology, as "destructive"—a word which was probably more descriptive of the state of her mind than the shape of her head. She seems to have been conscious throughout of depending more on Sarah than Sarah depended on her. Sarah, after all, had friends of her own, to whom she wrote long letters, though none of them so ardent as her letters to Mrs. Case; but Mrs. Case, as she once confessed, wrote only to her brother and sister and to Sarah. It was precisely this disparity of dependence that compelled her to make light of her friend's earnest entreaties, with which her impulses must have been so thoroughly in accord. "A nice couple of voyagers we would make," she wrote, "with my *destructiveness,* of which I have plenty, and to spare, to offset your *benevolence,* and *adhesiveness,* of which you might lend me occasionally from your superabundance. We would brush away all the noisy mosquitoes with our handkerchiefs, and, if now and then, a wasp exhibited his disposition to break the peace of our commonwealth, we would give him such a blow as would teach him better manners for the future." There is evidence elsewhere in the correspondence that Mrs. Case may have had a specific "wasp" in mind—with whom, to mix a metaphor, were associated those "domestic entanglements" which she felt impeded her literary career, and from which her friend so guiltily longed to free her.

Sarah shared her friend's aversion to insects. ". . . If we could live and work together," she wrote back, "if you would guide the 'barque,' and let me merely dip the oars; if you would suffer me to brush away the musquitoes [*sic*] that vex your ears, while you are kissing away the venom of some angry hornet from my lips, why, then, I should be ever very happy, let what evils would assail us. But can we ever be voyagers thus together?" It is difficult to know just how literally to take these suggestions. It seems unlikely that Sarah was actually urging Mrs. Case to leave her husband. Yet it is conceivable that Mrs. Case was already considering such a course, for she eventually followed it.

Her references to her husband, in her letters to Sarah, are almost always satiric. Usually she does not even use his name but refers to him as "the good man," "dearly beloved," "my liege lord," and so forth. It is the sentimental cliché of the Home, and woman's place in it, that she is deliberately mocking; and it is against this conception, with everything it implies, that she is in rebellion. Yet that very rebellion—the dream of a waspless society—is a curious affirmation of the notion on which the whole cult of the Home rested: the notion of women's innate purity. If Mr. Case were rejected by his wife, he was rejected as exactly what the myth made him out to be (and, no doubt, what he was convinced he was)—unimaginative and insensitive, a man of "affairs" incapable of responding to the flights of feminine fancy. No wood-nymph, he.

In fact he must have been the most accommodating, the most enlightened, the most modern of husbands—even allowing for his "imperiousness." Certainly he did nothing—as one might imagine from Mrs. Case's letters—to discourage his wife's literary efforts. Instead he encouraged them by printing her contributions, as well as Sarah's, in the Lowell *Star* and later in the Cincinnati *Enquirer*. It was simply that Mrs. Case, for whom "an association with cultivated minds of differing orders of intellect" when combined with "a friendly feeling" was "something to be prized above all else," evidently never considered that she might find such an association with her own husband. "Life is short," she could only conclude, "and kindred spirits are few. . . ."

The world in which Sarah and Mrs. Case enjoyed the fleeting hours, at infrequent meeetings, of their friendship was a world of women: the point needs no reiteration. Mrs. Case speaks highly of only one man, and he was a minister and therefore not involved in the world of affairs—A. C. Thomas, who boarded for a time with the Cases in Lowell. She describes him as "elegant in his general appearance," "fascinating in his manners," "kind," "amiable," and "good." She may even have considered him a good match for Sarah; in one letter she went out of her way to disavow any "designs" on the latter's "peace." "I am no match maker, but I sincerely respect Mr. Thomas."

Respect, however, was not the same thing as a romantic attachment such as one might conceive for any of the several women who are so admiringly described in Mrs. Case's letters—some of whom Mrs. Case had not even met. Thus she could fall "half in love" with Mrs. Seba Smith after reading her novel *Western Captive;* "she must have a beautiful soul," Mrs. Case imagined. She "fell quite in love," on another occasion, with "a most delightful, fascinating woman," a Mrs. Sawyer of Boston—"or my admiration would take that name, were I a gentleman." "She is as graceful, and interesting, as her own beautiful German translations." Again, she wrote a long paragraph in praise of "a sweet flower" of her acquaintance—a woman whom Sarah would be sure to admire "for her beauty, and for the true womanly character of her mind—so pure, and so full of all the holy, domestic affections."

Of all these women the one whose friendship Mrs. Case cherished most—aside from Sarah herself—was a woman twenty years her senior, now dead, whom she had known when a girl herself. "She was gentle, and refined, and spiritual in every impulse, and though . . . believing a sterner faith than she knew mine to be, I cannot recall one word, or look, that does not fall softly, and pleasantly on my recollection. To her society, I owe much of the cultivation of those tastes, and the power of living within myself that after experience has found so valuable. . . ." It was on that earlier relationship, in all likelihood, that Mrs. Case unconsciously modeled her own with Sarah, though not without misgivings as to her "destructiveness." Nor was Sarah at twenty unwilling to accept the role of Mrs. Case's tutee; she depicted herself, as we have seen, as a "perfect natural," a moonstruck adolescent—"am I not lunatic?" she punned.

Inevitably a relationship so delicately poised came abruptly to an end. In 1844 Sarah, now twenty-five, became engaged to a young man of twenty, a divinity student named A. D. Mayo. Mrs. Case's feelings on that occasion may be easily enough imagined; but her words are worth quoting. She wrote bravely from Portland:

And so you are engaged, are you Sarah? Well, I am much flattered by your confidence in the matter, and thus far, though *sorely tempted,* have told no individual being of it, not even my liege lord himself. . . .

From your description, I like your lover very much, and do not wonder you have been taken "captive, hand and heart" . . . I like the name of your intended—like all you say of him, but I wish he were a little *older,* dear Sarah. Do not mistake me—I am not foolish enough to think a year or two of seniority on the lady's part can have any influence on married happiness, but young gentlemen of twenty rarely have the character fixed, and are sometimes addicted to inconstancy, especially if of an ideal and loving temperament.

But there may be traits of the heart and mind that can over-
balance the temptations of youth. . . .

What followed, intended to be reassuring, ended in a sigh of
resignation.

> Your last letter gratified me very much, and so far from being
> disposed "to laugh at your childishness," I was much interested in
> the minutiae of your description, and half inclined to fall in love
> with him myself. Dont [sic] be frightened. Falling-in-love-days are
> all over with me *now,* besides, I have plenty else to do. . . . It
> would be a beautiful and blessed thing if we could keep the fresh-
> ness, and glory of our youthful feelings all along our journey to the
> grave—even to its verge—but it may not be. Life has its autumn as
> well as its spring, and we look to *immortality* alone for the un-
> sealing of the frozen fountains and the awaking of the perished
> flowers.

It was a curious letter to write to a young friend who had just
become engaged. In the circumstances, however, nothing could
have been more natural than Mrs. Case's elegiac mood. The fact
of Sarah's engagement was enough by itself to bring to an end
her special relationship with Mrs. Case, but her lover's youth and
"poetical" temperament must have seemed to Mrs. Case doubly
to be deplored—must have seemed almost a betrayal: of herself, of the dream of a world without wasps. It might also
have appeared—from a point of view more altruistic—an unwise
attempt, bound to fail, to combine in one alliance domestic
duties and an association with "cultivated minds." Her own
experience could hardly have enabled Mrs. Case to imagine such
a thing as possible or even desirable.

In any case, the friendship seems not to have outlived Sarah's
engagement. Only a few brief letters survive, either in manuscript or in Mr. Mayo's memoir of his wife; and it seems likely
that no others were written. The last of these was sent by Mrs.
Case in 1846, after the Cases' removal to Cincinnati; the year
before had put physical as well as emotional distance between
the correspondents. For the rest, the story is quickly told. Sarah
and Mr. Mayo were married in July 1846 and settled in Glouces-

ter, where he became pastor of the Independent Christian Society. In September 1847, Sarah bore a daughter. In July 1848 she died very suddenly and without warning—of what sickness, her husband does not say.

Mrs. Case left her husband in 1846 and went back to Kingston, where she died ten years later. Eliphalet Case played out the rest of his life in series of futile speculations; nor could anything have been more characteristic of the period—unless it was the friendship between his wife and Sarah Edgarton—than his rapid progress from riches to rags. He died of pneumonia in December 1862 at the age of sixty-six, childless, "poor and not beloved." No epitaph, not even his name, marked his grave. The anonymity of his death suggests that he too, no less than his wife, was the victim of the relentless American environment, which ripped men and women from the safety of a predefined social context and cast them out into a world where a man was defined only by his own efforts—where every man and woman was obliged to become, in a sense more profound than those who coined the phrase may have intended, "self-made."

[III]

Divorce and the "Decline of the Family"

THE PRESENT AGE, BELIEVING ITSELF PECULIARLY ENLIGHTENED in its sexual ethics, greatly exaggerates the moral distance between its own practices and those of the Victorians. The "twentieth-century sexual revolution" is supposed to have dispelled puritanical superstitions and inaugurated an era of unprecedented sexual freedom. The evidence for this proposition seemingly lies all about us: bikinis on the beach and skirts above the knee; nudity and obscenity on stage and screen; increasing license among adolescents; and what used to be referred to, by critics of modern depravity, as "the rising tide of divorce." The fact that divorce is no longer novel or shocking merely testifies further, presumably, to the decay of the old order, the attitudes and institutions of an earlier time, which now evoke mingled nostalgia and contempt.

Most discussions of divorce take for granted that the rising divorce rate is part of the "sexual revolution" and that it reflects, more specifically, the decay of the patriarchal family. Arthur W. Calhoun, in his still standard *Social History of the American Family* (1919), set the style for treating divorce as part of "the passing of patriarchism and familism" and of the revolt of women. He thought it highly significant that two-thirds of all divorces over a forty-year period (this tendency continues) were granted on demand of the wife. "The new ideals of woman are in conflict with the old despotism of the husband." According to this commonly held view of the history of the family, the Victorian family was a "patriarchal" arrangement, resting on a double standard of sexual morality according to which fidelity was demanded of the wife while the husband pursued his extramarital career of sexual escapades among prostitutes or expensive mistresses, depending on his social class. People did not marry for love so much as for the convenience of the families concerned; all marriages were in this sense "arranged." Divorce or annulment, when they rarely occurred, took place at the pleasure of the husband, the wife having no recourse in the face of her husband's indifference, infidelity, or brutality except the solace of religion and the sewing-circle society of women, fellow victims of a system which consigned them, it seemed, to perpetual subordination.

Such is the picture of Victorian marriage to which the modern family is held up in striking contrast. Nowadays, even a President's daughter marries for love, a fact of which it is one of the functions of journalism ritually to remind us. The affectional basis of marriage presumably works to make the partners equals. The growing divorce trend, whether one attributes it to romantic illusions surrounding marriage or to sexual difficulties or to any number of other explanations, must therefore reflect, in one way or another, the new equality of the sexes. The fact that most divorce proceedings are now instituted by women would seem to confirm the suspicion that the relaxation of old taboos against divorce represents still another victory for woman's rights. As a recent historical study observes, "Whereas divorce in earlier periods of history had been primarily a prerogative demanded by men to rid themselves of unwanted wives and open the way for new marriages, nineteenth century American divorce was becoming more and more a right demanded by women on humanitarian grounds." Considered in isolation, this statement is certainly correct; but it does not follow that the reform of the divorce laws, together with the relaxation of Victorian taboos, more effective methods of contraception, and changing standards of premarital and extramarital sex, constitutes a "revolution" that has weakened the "patriarchal" family and placed the relations between men and women on a new footing of equality.

The history of the family needs to be seen much more broadly than we have been accustomed to see it. There are good reasons to think that the decisive change in the character of the family occurred not at the beginning of the twentieth century but at the end of the eighteenth, and that the Victorian family, therefore, which we imagine as the antithesis of our own, should be seen instead as the beginning of something new—the prototype, in many ways, of the modern household.

If we forget for a moment the picture of the Victorian patriarch surrounded by his submissive wife, his dutiful children, and his houseful of servants—images that have come to be automatically associated with the subject—we can see that the nineteenth-century conception of the family departed in important respects from earlier conceptions. Over a period of several centuries, the family had gradually come to be seen as preeminently a private place, a sanctuary from the rough world outside. If we find it difficult to appreciate the novelty of this idea, it is because we ourselves take the privacy of family life for granted. Yet as recently as the eighteenth century, before the new ideas of domesticity were widely accepted, families were more likely to be seen "not as refuges from the invasion of the world," in the words of Ariès, "but as the centers of a populous society, the focal points of a crowded social life." Ariès has shown how closely the modern family is bound up with the idea of privacy and with the idea of childhood. Before these ideas were securely established, masters, servants, and children mingled indiscriminately, without regard for distinctions of age or rank.

The absence of a clearly distinguishable concept of childhood is particularly important. The family by its very nature is a means of raising children, but this fact should not blind us to the important change that occurred when child rearing ceased to be simply one of many activities and became the central concern— one is tempted to say the central obsession—of family life. This development had to wait for the recognition of the child as a distinctive kind of person, more impressionable and hence more vulnerable than adults, to be treated in a special manner befitting his peculiar requirements. Again, we take these things for granted and find it hard to imagine anything else. Earlier, children had been clothed, fed, spoken to, and educated as little adults; more specifically, as servants, the difference between childhood and servitude having been remarkably obscure throughout much of Western history (and servitude retaining, until fairly recently, an honorific character which it subsequently lost). It was only in the seventeenth century in certain classes—and in society as a whole, only in the nineteenth century—that childhood came to be seen as a special category of experience. When that happened, people recognized the enormous formative influence of family life, and the family became above all an agency for building character, for consciously and deliberately forming the child from birth to adulthood.

These changes dictated not merely a new regard for children but, what is more to the point here, a new regard for women: if children were in some sense sacred, then motherhood was nothing short of a holy office. The sentimentalization of women later became an effective means of arguing against their equality, but the first appearance of this attitude seems to have been associated with a new sense of the dignity of women; even of their equality, in a limited sense, as partners in the work of bringing up the young. The recognition of "woman's rights" initially sprang not from a revulsion against domestic life but from the cult of domesticity itself; and the first "rights" won by modern women were the rights of married women to control their own property, to retain their own earnings, and, not least, to divorce their husbands.

Until the middle of the nineteenth century in England and the United States, grounds for divorce were pretty much confined to adultery and cruelty. Divorces, moreover, had to be granted by legislative enactment. These provisions, making money and political influence requisite to divorce, effectively limited divorce to members of the upper classes; and except in rare cases, to upper-class men, eager for one reason or another to get rid of their wives. The new laws, still in effect today in most places, substituted judicial for legislative divorce and broadened grounds of divorce to include desertion. Both of these provisions, particularly the second, show that women were intended to be the principal beneficiaries of the change. That was certainly the result. Ever since the liberalization of the laws in the mid-nineteenth century, divorces have been easier and easier to obtain, and more and more of them, as noted earlier, have been granted to women.

But those who see in these statistics a general dissolution of morals and a threat to the family misunderstand the dynamics of the process. The movement for earlier divorce owed its success to the very idea that it is supposed to have undermined, the idea of the sanctity of the family. Indeed, it is somewhat misleading to see divorce-law reform as a triumph even for woman's rights, since the feminists could hardly have carried the day if their attack on the arbitrary authority of husbands had not coincided with current conceptions of the family—conceptions of the family which, in the long run, tended to subvert the movement for sexual equality. It was not the image of women as equals that inspired the reform of the divorce laws but the image of women as victims. The Victorians associated the disruption of domesticity, especially when they thought of the "lower classes," with the victimization of women and children: the wife and mother abused by her drunken husband, deserted and left with children to raise and support, or forced to submit to sexual demands which no man had a right to impose on virtuous women. These images of oppression wrung ready tears from our ancestors. The rhetoric survives, somewhat diluted, in the form of patriotic appeals to home and motherhood, and notably in the divorce courts, where it is perfectly attuned, in fact, to the adversary proceeding.

Judicial divorce, as we have seen—a civil suit brought by one partner against the other—was itself a nineteenth-century innovation, a fact which suggests that the idea of marriage as a combat made a natural counterpoint to the idea of marriage as a partnership. The combat, however, like the partnership itself, has never firmly established itself, either in legal practice or in the household itself, as an affair of equals, because the achievement of legal equality for the married woman depended on a sentimentalization of womanhood that eroded the idea of equality as easily as it promoted it. In divorce suits, the sensitivity of judges to the appeal of suffering womanhood, particularly in fixing alimony payments, points to the ambiguity of women's "emancipation." From the husband's point of view, the whole thrust of the divorce law is unmistakably punitive: the wife is assumed to be an innocent victim, the husband a tyrant, lecher, or playboy bent on evading not only his matrimonial obligations but the alimony payments that a minimal sense of decency would prompt him cheerfully to assume. Nobody on the side of the law questions that the wife—whatever the real reasons behind the divorce—has a right to whatever she can get; the burden of proof falls on the husband to show, in detail, why he should *not* be obliged to pay, as the least he can decently do, what his wife asks him to pay. The divorce courts, far from posing a threat to the family, thus constitute one of the last strongholds of Victorian sanctimoniousness. To speak of the rising divorce rate as evidence of "a new freedom for women" misses the point: this "freedom" derives from the very myths that effectively discourage women from aspiring to a life beyond domesticity.

The sexual "emancipation" of women, in divorce as in other areas, does not rest on a growing sense of the irrelevance, for many purposes, of culturally defined sexual distinctions. It represents, if anything, a heightened awareness of these distinctions, an insistence that women, as the weaker sex, be given special protection in law.

From this point of view, our present divorce laws can be seen as faithfully reflecting ideas about women which, having persisted into the mid-twentieth century, have shown themselves to be not "Victorian" so much as simply modern, ideas that are dependent, in turn, on the modern obsession with the sanctity of the home, and beyond that, with the sanctity of privacy. Indeed, one can argue that easier divorce, far from threatening the home, is one of the measures—given the obsession with domesticity—that has been necessary to preserve it. Easy divorce is a form of social insurance that has to be paid by a culture that holds up domesticity as a universally desirable condition: the cost of failure in the pursuit of domestic bliss—especially for women, who are discouraged in the first place from other pursuits—must not be permitted to become too outrageously high.

We get a better perspective on modern marriage and divorce, and on the way in which these institutions have been affected by the "emancipation" of women and by the "sexual revolution," if we remember that nineteenth-century feminism, at its most radical, passed beyond a demand for "women's rights" to a critique of marriage itself. The most original and striking—and for most people the least acceptable—of the feminists' assertions was that marriage itself, in Western society, could be considered a higher form of prostitution, in which respectable women sold their sexual favors not for immediate financial rewards but for long-term economic security. There was "no sharp, clear, sudden-drawn line," they insisted, between the "kept wife," living "by the exercise of her sex functions alone," in Olive Schreiner's words, and the prostitute. The difference between prostitution and respectability reduced itself to a question not of motives but of money. The virtuous woman's fee was incomparably higher, but the process itself was essentially the same; that is, the virtuous woman of the leisure class had come to be valued, like the prostitute, chiefly as a sexual object: beautiful, expensive, and useless—in Veblen's phrase, a means of vicarious display. She was trained from girlhood to bring all her energies to the intricate art of pleasing men; showing off her person to best advantage, mastering the accomplishments and refinements appropriate to the drawing room, perfecting the art of discreet flirtation, all the while withholding the ultimate prize until the time should come when she might bestow it, with the impressive sanction of state and church, on the most eligible bidder for her "hand." Even then, the prize remained more promise than fact. It could be repeatedly withdrawn or withheld as the occasion arose and became, therefore, the means by which women learned to manage their husbands. If, in the end, the respectable husband had to seek satisfactions elsewhere, that merely testified to the degree to which women had come to be valued, not simply as sexual objects, but precisely in proportion to their success in withholding the sexual favors which, nevertheless, all of their activities were intended to proclaim.

The defenders of the conventional types of prostitution, meanwhile, did not fail to see the connection between prostitution and respectability. In the words of William Lecky, the historian of European morals, the prostitute was "ultimately the most efficient guardian of virtue" because she enabled virtuous women to remain virtuous. "But for her the unchallenged purity of countless happy homes would be polluted, and not a few who with the pride of their untempted chastity think of her with an indignant shudder, would have known the agony of remorse and despair." The same reasoning, as we have seen, led to the nineteenth-century reform of the divorce laws. The purity of the home demanded just such outlets as prostitution and divorce if it was to survive intact and "untempted."

The central features of this system of sexual relationships persist into the twentieth century essentially unchanged. Courtship is more than ever a "sex tease," in Albert Ellis's words, and marriage remains something to be managed—among other ways, by the simultaneous blandishment and withdrawal, on the part of the wife, of her sexual favors. Let anyone who doubts the continuing vigor of this morality consult the columns of advice which daily litter the newspapers. "Dear Abby" urges her readers, before marriage, to learn the difficult art of going far enough to meet the demands of "popularity" without "cheapening" themselves (a revealing phrase); while her advice to married women takes for granted that husbands have to be kept in their place, sexually and otherwise, by the full use of what used to be called "feminine wiles." These are prescriptions, of course, which are not invariably acted upon; and part of the "sexual revolution" of the twentieth century lies in the increased publicity which violations of the official morality receive, a condition which is then taken as evidence that they are necessarily more frequent than before. Another development, widely mistaken for a "revolution in morals," is a growing literal-mindedness about sex, an inability to recognize as sexual anything other than gross display of the genitals. The sexual advances of the respectable woman, accordingly, have come to be more blatant than they used to be, a fact predictably deplored by alarmists, themselves victims of the progressive impoverishment of the sexual imagination, who erroneously confuse respectability with the concealment, rather than the alternating offer and withholding, of sexuality. We should not allow ourselves to be misled by the openness of sexual display in contemporary society. The important thing is the use to which sexuality is put. For the woman, it remains, as it was in the nineteenth century, principally a means of domestic management; for the man, a means of vicarious display.

[IV]

The Woman Reformer's Rebuke

THE NINETEENTH CENTURY PRODUCED A NEW AND DISTINCTIVE social type: the woman as reformer. Defying convention, she was nevertheless the product of one of the most popular conventions of the period, the sexual division of labor, which assigned commerce and politics to men and "culture" to ladies. In the orthodox version of the Victorian social myth, this same division of labor justified women's confinement to the home. But in the 1830's, the reformers began to draw a different conclusion: if women were more "spiritual" than men, as the prevailing sexual stereotypes so clearly implied, to restrict their influence to the home was a criminal waste of resources.

Critics of feminism complained that exposure to the masculine world would unsex women, causing them to lose that fresh-eyed innocence which was the pride and pinnacle of Western civilization; but their solicitude, it turned out, was singularly inappropriate to the women on whom it was lavished. *Their* innocence, when put to the test, proved to be invulnerable. Nor did they lose the consciousness of themselves as women. On the contrary, they based their claim to be heard on the superior virtue of their sex, as well as on various communications received directly from God—and these, unpredictable as they were, were not likely to be communicated, it seemed, to anyone so indifferent to spiritual appeals, so immersed in the sordid business of making money, and so besotted with the world's enjoyments, as a man.

Although they rejected the advice to stay at home, nineteenth-century women reformers did not reject the view of women on which this advice was based. Given the kind of family experiences that most of them seem to have undergone, both as daughters and as wives, they might pardonably have washed their hands of the whole business. In Europe, a certain kind of feminist reacted to domestic distress by trying to live as a "free woman." The feminism of Mary Wollstonecraft sprang from a squalid childhood, and George Sand's from a bad marriage, but neither proposed to reform the male sex, nor did they come to equate the subjection of women with sexuality itself. Instead they tried to free sexuality from the conventions that stifled it.

In America, however, unhappy homes commonly left a passionate sense of the wrongs of woman, a sense of the sisterhood of suffering which in turn nourished a tradition, handed down from mother to daughter, of masculine brutality. The female reformer, taking quite seriously her role as the custodian of official morality, threw herself into public causes in the belief that the influence of women would purify politics, abolish slavery, stamp out the demon rum, and lead to a general revival of religion. Finding themselves discriminated against even in such advanced circles as the abolitionist and temperance movements, American women, meeting at Seneca Falls in 1848, organized their own movement for "independence." From then on, feminism in the United States was solidly aligned with the civilizing mission of women, even more than it had been before. It represented, among other things, a translation into political emotions of the whispered grievances that women confided to each other in their parlors—dark tales of sexual exploitation, of wives used up by repeated pregnancies, of wives abandoned, of infidelity, of indifference and neglect.

Some of this still survives as an undercurrent in American society, but for reasons that are far from clear, it no longer produces reformers like Carry Nation, the saloon-smashing temperance agitator who terrorized the drinking public from 1900 until her death in 1911. Mrs. Nation attacked alcohol in general, but she specifically attacked the saloon, symbol of masculine independence and irresponsibility. (The general problem to which she was addressing herself was finally "solved," in a manner of which she could hardly have approved, by the integration of the saloons.) Mrs. Nation's taste of domestic life, as a recent biographer makes clear, was of the most discouraging sort. Her father, though "an angel on earth" in his daughter's eyes, was "an incorrigible migrant," "happiest," Robert Lewis Taylor writes, "when the furniture was being piled into the wagons and carts." A failure in the classic American tradition of failure, he moved from Kentucky to Missouri and then to Texas in search of a windfall that would retrieve the family's declining fortunes. His wife believed she was Queen Victoria and conducted herself accordingly. Carry's first husband, who died shortly after she left him, was a drunkard. Her second husband, David Nation, divorced her after years of bickering.

It is not surprising that Mrs. Nation, surrounded by such a babble of strife and madness, began to be visited with more congenial voices, hearing which she would sometimes fall on all fours and gallop about her house barking like a dog. (She once described herself, in another connection, as "a bulldog running along at the feet of Jesus, barking at what He doesn't like.") On June 6, 1900, following one of these visitations, she sallied forth into the streets of Kiowa, Kansas, armed with rocks and brickbats, and smashed the interiors of three saloons, telling the startled customers, "Men! I have come to save you from a drunkard's grave!" Some years later, a journalist, after explaining unnecessarily that Mrs. Nation "was no glamour girl"—"she wore layers and layers of long full black skirts, capable of concealing any sort of weapon"—characterized her as "the motherly type gone wrong."

Mr. Taylor, the author of *The Travels of Jaimie McPheeters* and several biographies, makes the most of the comic possibilities in his material—material which suggests, once again, that life is stranger than fiction, even if its meaning is sometimes a little obscure. Mr. Taylor does not linger over the meaning of Mrs. Nation. He gets on with the story, narrating with numerous witticisms, some good and some bad, the singular career of the Kansas crusader; her abandonment of brickbats in favor of the hatchet, thereafter the approved tool of her trade; her memorable assault on Wichita's Hotel Carey Bar, with its unspeakable painting of "Cleopatra preparing for her bath"; her innumerable jail sentences; her visit to Yale, where she pronounced the students "the toughest proposition I ever met." "I never saw anything," she wrote in her memoirs, "that needed a rebuke, or exhortation, or warning, but that I felt it my place to meddle with it."

Mr. Taylor admires this astuteness about herself, as well as "her warm, down-to-earth gift for making herself companionable with people of diverse origins." He makes a good case for the presence of these qualities in his subject. But in the end he is as puzzled by Mrs. Nation as he was in the beginning. It is disconcerting to find him, after 308 pages, still describing her as "a paradox of fury wrapped in an enigma of love." His final judgment is hardly a judgment: "With all her faults [the "extremism of her methods," etc.] . . . she fought what thousands considered to be the good fight." Does Mr. Taylor himself think it was a good fight? A few years ago, a reviewer of an ostensibly political play noted that American writers, in dealing with political material, almost invariably reduce it to the level of the personal—a habit of mind, it is hardly necessary to add, that characterizes the attitude toward politics of Americans in general. Mr. Taylor has dealt with Carry Nation, a political figure, by ignoring the political questions raised by her life: What was gained and what was lost by making alcohol a political issue— an issue, moreover, in which the element of sexual antagonism was the principal component? She appeals to Mr. Taylor, obscurely, because she showed "a resolve that makes one wonder if today's willingness to give in, compromise, cringe before an enemy, gear progress to the weakest and worst, can assure the country's survival." Americans tend to admire "resolve" and "survival" for their own sake (while ritually deploring "extremist methods"), regardless of the values to which they happen to be attached; and Mr. Taylor is no exception.

· · ·

The same uncertainty of judgment, and the same ineptitude in handling political material, can be seen in the most recent biographies of Victoria Woodhull, one of the most dashing of nineteenth-century feminists, now almost forgotten. Johanna Johnston confesses, rather disarmingly, that she hasn't even been able to establish whether Victoria could read and write. M. M. Marberry's *Vicky* arrives at this feeble conclusion: "What the ultimate judgment of posterity on Victoria C. Woodhull will be, no one knows. Yet surely few people today will deny that she was *sui generis.*" The only thing Mr. Marberry is really sure of is that Victoria was beautiful—an opinion with which no one is likely to quarrel. The most impressive thing about his book is the frontispiece, a photograph that shows to good advantage Victoria's elegant profile, her clear eyes, and the trace of condescension in her expression—the expression of a woman conscious not merely of her beauty but of her general superiority among members of her sex.

Born in Ohio in 1838, Victoria Woodhull grew up in a large, migratory family of eccentrics. Her father, "Buck" Claflin—a notable ne'er-do-well—left Ohio when his neighbors began to suspect that he had set fire to his barn in order to collect the insurance in which he had prudently invested. The Claflin family resembled the Nations—shiftless father, mad mother—except that Buck Claflin was not only shiftless, he was a charlatan who advertised Victoria and her sister Tennessee as clairvoyants and toured the country with them. This early exposure to show business, together with their good looks, helps to explain why the Claflin girls turned out to be "adventuresses," as they were known among their contemporaries, instead of saloon-smashers. Eventually they both married English gentlemen and lived, as wicked people often live, to a ripe old age. Henry James described Victoria's "Conquest of London" with understandable relish, and he made use of her early career as a medium in *The Bostonians,* in which Victoria appears, distantly, as Verena Tarrant.

Victoria was married at fifteen and divorced ten years later. With her lover James Blood (whom she also married and divorced) and her sister Tennessee (sometimes, by her own preference, known as Tennie C.), she drifted to New York in 1868, followed by the rest of the family, and launched herself, with the help of the infatuated Cornelius Vanderbilt, as America's first female stockbroker. In 1870 the enterprising sisters founded *Woodhull and Claflin's Weekly,* from which they preached both woman's rights and sexual freedom, a novel combination in the 1870's. It was through the efforts of these journalists that a scandalized world first learned of the Beecher-Tilton affair. (With fine impartiality, Victoria hinted that she herself had enjoyed sexual relations with both of the principals in the case.) It is proof of her genius for public relations that she managed to convert the affair into another battle in the sex war—an interpretation, it should be noted, which the leaders of organized feminism readily accepted, in spite of the doubts some of them entertained about Victoria's commitment to the cause.

Among American feminists, Victoria Woodhull and her sister Tennessee Claflin were exceptional not only in their beauty but in the effective use to which they put it. Their lives show how, in special cases, the new ideology of feminism grafted itself onto an older type of feminine careerism. An unusually efficient and clever courtesan might, on occasion, put on the disguise of a "new woman." The remarkable thing about Victoria Woodhull is that she not only captivated lecherous old vulgarians like Commodore Vanderbilt, who besides dandling the lovely sisters on his knee took their spiritualism seriously (which must have amused them; but then the National Association of Spiritualists took it seriously too, twice electing Victoria president); she also captivated the official leaders of American feminism. Nothing could have been further from these ladies' thoughts than free love. Yet at the annual convention of the National Woman's Suffrage Association in 1871, Victoria dazzled the austere assembly, overcame the suspicions of Isabella Beecher Hooker (who lost no time in confiding to Victoria the details of her brother's relations with his pious convert, Elizabeth Tilton), and even won the hearts of Elizabeth Cady Stanton and Susan B. Anthony. A biographer of Victoria Woodhull, one might suppose, would attempt to explain how this unprecedented feat was possible. What was it in American feminism that capitulated so unexpectedly, and for a time so completely, to Victoria's charm? The feminist, however strait-laced, shared with the courtesan a contempt for the opposite sex which might furnish the basis for temporary and rather shaky alliances. James caught the essence of this relationship in the curious friendship between the high-spirited Verena and the heartless Bostonian reformer, Olive Chancellor; and although *The Bostonians* hardly says the last word about the feminist movement, it tells us a great deal more than the standard histories of the subject, and a great deal more than biographies written for a public that craves facts even more than it craves "color," and for which novels make too great an imaginative demand.

There seems to be no reason to doubt that Victoria was liter-ate, except on the general principle that since she lied about practically everything else, she may have lied when she pre-sented herself to a credulous public as an accomplished editor, lecturer, and pamphleteer. Yet words were Victoria's real talent, even more than the bed. She had the wit to see that respectable society not only craves sensations but relishes the kind of attacks on itself which treat forbidden subjects with apparent candor without threatening established conventions. Victoria's cele-brated address in Steinway Hall in 1873, in which she replied to the heckling of one of her sisters in the audience (the Claflins, although a close-knit family, were continually feuding with one another in public) by boldly declaring, "Yes, I am a free lover! I have an inalienable, constitutional, and natural right to love whom I may; to love as long or as short a period as I can; to change that love every day if I please!"—this speech was a stroke of genius, worthy of a great showman like Barnum or Jim Fisk. "Free love" shocked and titillated people while leaving uncriti-cized the one feature of conventional sexual relations that was vulnerable to radical attack—the use of sex (on both sides of the sexual barrier) as an instrument of domination. Since Victoria herself used sex in this way, she was hardly in a position to criticize it; nor did she intend to. She made her mark; she created a sensation, won fame and fortune, and eventually achieved even respectability, for which she yearned far more than she yearned for the excitements of the carnival.

The nineteenth century expected women to marry and live happily ever after. Women who failed to find husbands or, worse, found the wrong ones had to choose between two almost equally unsatisfactory careers: resignation and eccentricity. Today little remains of the resigned, except for bitter thoughts written in diaries or in occasional letters to fellow sufferers. Eccentric women at least made themselves heard. Neither Victoria Woodhull nor Carry Nation could easily be ignored. Like all eccentrics, they defied convention by carrying convention beyond its limits. Were women made for love?—Victoria Woodhull proposed that love become truly "free." Did women guard the morals of society?—Carry Nation provided an unforgettable demonstration of woman's moral custodianship in action.

Another Victorian convention assigned religion to the care of women, in accord with the sexual division of labor that defined practical life as masculine, and "spiritual" affairs—the ornamental and decorative arts—as belonging to the domain of the "weaker sex." What an imaginative and unhappy woman could make of this assignment is shown by the work of Mary Baker Eddy, who took it more seriously than most of her sisters. Ailing and despondent, she sought spiritual consolation from the noted healer, clockmaker, and animal magnetist Phineas P. Quimby, quickly absorbing and then transforming his doctrines, purging them of all trace of "magnetism." Later she insisted that Quimby himself "was growing out of mesmerism" at the end of his career. Like psychoanalysis, to which it otherwise bears only the most superficial resemblance, Christian Science had to repudiate its shady past and claim for itself scientific standing. Mrs. Eddy's latest biographer, Robert Peel, feels impelled to argue that Christian Science in its beginnings had nothing to do with mesmerism—an assertion no more convincing than the assertion that psychoanalysis owed nothing to Freud's early experiments with hypnotism.

In any case, recognition of a thinker's debt to earlier influences does not detract from his originality, provided his own work has some intrinsic claim to our attention. Freud's contributions speak for themselves. There is some question whether the same can be said of Mrs. Eddy's. It is precisely in Peel's handling of her relation to Quimby that we detect the hand of the apologist, who always ends by claiming more for his subject than a strict construction of the evidence will allow. This is not to say that Peel's book is unreliable. But it does little to locate Christian Science in American history, since Peel the apologist (as distinguished from Peel the historian) is less interested in making connections with other material than in breaking them down.

What explains Mrs. Eddy's extraordinary success? To a Christian Scientist, the answer is self-evident. Mrs. Eddy's writings became the basis of an important religion because they embodied Truth. Neither the historian nor the sociologist, however, can accept such an answer even for Christianity. They must ask what it was about this particular version of truth (if that is what it was) that commended itself to so many people at this particular time. Donald Meyer, in *The Positive Thinkers,* has shown that Christian Science addressed itself to a phenomenon which in the late nineteenth century was agitating doctors, psychiatrists, and clergymen, the problem of "modern nervousness." It was no accident that Christian Science made healing the core of its doctrine; nor was it an accident that a woman founded Christian Science. Women—women of the genteel class—were the chief victims, it seemed, of "nervousness." Feminists identified neurasthenia with "underemployment" and demanded that women find useful work. Mrs. Eddy identified it with loss of faith and self-discipline and proposed—self-discipline. She might have recommended, with William James (who shared her interest in "mind cure"), a relaxation of superconsciousness. But "far from letting-go into the subconscious," Meyer notes, "in order to escape the cage of consciousness mind cure aimed at still greater control over the subconscious." The feminist solution was equally self-defeating in the long run. If commerce corrupted, as it did by the feminists' own reckoning, how could women save themselves by entering the realm of commerce?

The lives of Carry Nation, Victoria Woodhull, and Mary Baker Eddy share a number of common features which seem to be rooted in the social conditions of the middle and late nineteenth century. Each of them had a father of whom it could be said, as Mrs. Eddy's brother said of theirs, that he was "the least qualified to *make money* of any man that I ever saw of his natural abilities." Each married a ne'er-do-well from whom she was subsequently divorced. The combination of these experiences was not calculated to leave a high opinion of men, either as partners or as providers. The failure of their marriages, moreover, typically threw women of this class into the superfluous and despised category of widows and spinsters—people who were forced to live, like orphans, in other people's families, and to move from one place to another with tedious regularity. Between 1866, when her husband deserted her, and 1870, when she finally settled in Lynn, Massachusetts, Mrs. Eddy changed her place of residence more than thirteen times. During the first fifty-four years of her life she had more than twenty different homes, not counting her lengthy visits to Dr. W. T. Vail's Hydropathic Institute and to Dr. Quimby in Portland, Maine.

These patterns in the lives of women reformers—and one could point to many other examples—do not explain why women became reformers (for every divorcée or widow or spinster who threw herself into reform, there were presumably dozens who did not), but they help to explain why feminine reform took one shape instead of another—why the woman reformer, in the nineteenth century, became a sort of universal maiden aunt, "the motherly type gone wrong." The reformer's censoriousness, her need to rebuke and exhort (as Mrs. Nation put it), was the censoriousness of the outsider in the family circle, born of deprivation but also of a certain primness, a sense of superiority to one's immediate environment. "It was an unfortunate fact," said one of her disciples, "that Mrs. Eddy with her small income was obliged to live with people . . . who were without education and cultivation." Such people, he explained, seldom appreciate the more sensitive spirits with whom it is their privilege to come into contact. "Simple-minded people who take life as it comes from day to day find any one with so fixed an object in life a rebuke to the flow of their own animal spirits." This rebuke—the rebuke of the "lonely woman past her prime" (as another contemporary described Mrs. Eddy) to *l'homme moyen sensual* with whom she finds herself obliged to live—it was the historical mission of the female reformer to institutionalize. Mrs. Nation used a hatchet, so that no one would mistake her meaning. In Mrs. Eddy's case, the rebuke took a more rarefied form, as befitted a daughter of New England—a magisterial assertion, breathtaking in the sweep of its condemnation, that once and for all put sensuality in its place: "What is matter? Nothing."

The rebuke turns up, in still another guise, in the movement for woman suffrage. Thanks to an excellent study by Alan P. Grimes, *The Puritan Ethic and Woman Suffrage,* we can now see that suffrage triumphed in the western states not because it was associated with radical democracy but because it was associated with "civilization" as represented by Aunt Polly—the civilization from which Huckleberry Finns have always found it necessary to light out. Grimes takes up one of the hoary clichés about feminism—that feminism was a product of the "frontier" —and subjects it to sustained and devastating analysis. His main thesis, which he demonstrates convincingly, is that woman suffrage in the West, far from springing from frontier conditions, came about after the frontier stage had already passed and was part of an effort, in which women were prominently involved, precisely to subvert frontier conditions and to re-establish order and refinement. Conceptually, the great value of Grimes's study is that it draws a clear distinction between the feminist movement, which originated in England and in the eastern United States, and the triumph of woman suffrage in the West, which came about for reasons having little to do with feminism.

In this sense *The Puritan Ethic and Woman Suffrage* does for American feminism what J. A. and Olive Banks, in a very different way, did for English feminism in their *Feminism and Family Planning in Victorian England*—it enables us to distinguish between two things that are usually confused, the feminist movement on the one hand and the "emancipation" of women on the other. "Emancipation," coming about for reasons that had very little to do with feminism, gradually freed women from unrelieved domesticity, excessive child-bearing, and the extreme sexual reserve which a fear of "consequences," together with other influences peculiar to the Victorian period, imposed. None of these changes struck at the confusion of sex with power, which feminism at its most radical attacked; nor did they even make it possible for women to compete more effectively for jobs. They merely gave women time to be ladies.

Feminism itself was ambiguous on some of these points. It too associated itself with the civilizing work of women. That is one reason why the feminists did not clearly perceive that "emancipation" of women did not necessarily equalize the relations between men and women. Grimes shows how the feminist movement gradually departed from its early egalitarianism and embraced the "puritan" values that were associated with the coming of woman suffrage in the West—prohibition, racism, opposition to immigration. (Aileen Kraditor makes a somewhat similar point in her study, *The Ideas of the Woman Suffrage Movement*.) *The Puritan Ethic* would be a better book if its two themes—the irrelevance of feminism to woman suffrage in the West, and the growing conservatism of eastern feminism itself—were more carefully distinguished, and if both were dissociated from the concept of puritanism, which, strictly speaking, has very little to do with the censoriousness of female reformers. Aunt Polly was a Victorian, not a Puritan. The Puritans would have been appalled by her.

In spite of these conceptual flaws, Grimes has written one of the few studies of women and woman suffrage that advance beyond guesswork and anecdote to real historical analysis. It contains no "color" but is worth a stack of colorful biographies.

[V]

The Mormon Utopia

THE MORMONS, ONCE A PERSECUTED SECT, HAVE BECOME A world religion, with temples from Norway to Chile, from Düsseldorf to Tokyo. They number more than 3 million members, 2 million of whom have been added since 1947. But when Wallace Turner, in *The Mormon Establishment,* writes with some alarm that "in widening waves, this religious force in American life is felt across the nation," he loses sight of the conditions on which all this growth has been predicated. It is not as a *religious* force that Mormonism now makes itself felt. It makes itself felt precisely in the degree to which the Mormon influence has ceased to be distinguishable from any other vested influence. As long as the Mormons were different from their neighbors, their neighbors hounded them mercilessly. Only when they gave up the chief distinguishing features of their faith did the Latter-day Saints establish themselves as a fixture of the ecclesiastical scene, another tolerated minority. This may well be the most important fact of Mormon history.

Mr. Turner, a journalist, has a muckraker's instincts, useful equipment when joined to the proper subject. In this case his efforts are misplaced. The Mormons have been exposed so many times, and with such telling effect, that there is nothing left to expose. Alarmed by the disclosure that these bearded sectarians were living in "licentiousness, lawlessness, and all evil," God-fearing Americans long ago demanded that the federal government, guardian of liberty and virtue, take action against "that sink of iniquity"; and the Mormons, in the face of unremitting harassment (and as the price of statehood for Utah), eventually capitulated. Polygamy, which fascinates Mr. Turner, is about as relevant to Mormonism today as an exposé of simony is relevant to Catholicism. Mr. Turner insists that polygamy is still practiced widely, but since the people who practice it are all apostates from the Church of the Latter-day Saints, it is not clear what their activities have to do with Mormonism. Nevertheless, Turner deems the details worth two chapters in his book. He gets equal mileage out of the Mormons' antipathy to blacks, which is a scandal, but a scandal not peculiar to the Mormons.

The trouble is that Turner does not distinguish between Mormonism as a religion and the Mormons as the dominant social class in the state of Utah. The Mormons' present conservatism, which Turner tries unsuccessfully to read into the teachings of Joseph Smith and Brigham Young, has to be understood as the conservatism of an economic élite, not as something intrinsic to Mormon doctrine, which in its original form pointed to an egalitarian rather than a conservative form of social organization. Turner is so indifferent to such distinctions, and in general so imperfectly acquainted with the early history of the church, that he makes the mistake of saying that the Mormons have "historically" set a low value on women. One might infer a contempt for women from polygamy, but it would be an erroneous inference. In nineteenth-century Mormon society there was none of that pious cant about the sanctity of motherhood, the sanctity of home and hearth, which was the real mark of women's degradation elsewhere. Mormon polygamy cannot be understood if one thinks of it as an alien institution, a form of "Oriental" debauchery, as anti-Mormons have always believed it to be. That polygamy could co-exist with a high respect for women is precisely what was distinctive and interesting about Mormon polygamy.

The prominence of Mormons in politics—Ezra Taft Benson in the Eisenhower cabinet, his son in the John Birch Society, George Romney a leading candidate for the presidency in 1968 —disturbs Mr. Turner, as it vaguely disturbs a great many other people. An interview with Romney "reassured" the author that Romney's Mormonism would not influence his actions as President. This inquiry was as unnecessary as similar inquiries, a few years ago, into John Kennedy's Catholicism. The political prominence of Mormons and Catholics testifies not to the growing power of those religions but to their assimilation into American society. Mormons as a religious group have no reason to seek national political office, especially now that they have nothing to fear from the federal government. Even when they did so in the past, they had no wish to govern a country which they believed was doomed to moral destruction. "We do not intend to have any trade or commerce with the gentile world," said Brigham Young. ". . . I am determined to cut every thread of this kind and live free and independent, untrammeled by any of their detestable customs and practices." If George Romney shared these sentiments, he would never have sought federal office. The larger implications of this fact, however, if one considers them carefully, are dismaying, because they show how far religion has lost its power to influence the world of affairs, politics in particular. Elsewhere we find Quakers leading the cry for war. It is not a question of hypocrisy. What has happened is that religious questions have been arbitrarily defined as questions of private belief that have no application to public life.

When the Mormon Tabernacle Choir made a triumphal tour of Europe in 1955, the church engaged a public relations consultant, Robert Mullen, to blaze the trail. How was it possible, a hundred years ago, for the Mormons to reach Utah, many of them walking the entire distance pulling their families' goods in handcarts, without benefit of a press agent? Mr. Mullen, a non-Mormon, was so taken with the Saints that he wrote a book about them, which has been published for reasons that are not entirely clear. The best that can be said for the book is that it is no worse than the books Mormons write about themselves; but why do we need still another uncritical account of Mormonism?

The book contains no glaring errors of fact, although it glosses rather uncomfortably over the race issue. It is true that Utah (which has few blacks) has complied with federal civil rights legislation. But it is also true, as Turner points out, that the Saints have no missions anywhere in Africa except in the

Union of South Africa, and that efforts to start one in Nigeria collapsed because the Nigerian government refused to give visas to Mormon missionaries. (On the other hand, Negro priests have been ordained by missionaries in Brazil, in violation of the official dogma which bars Negroes from the priesthood.) In general, however, Mr. Mullen does not have to evade the truth, because unless one has strong feelings about polygamy, the truth about the Mormons—at least about their history—contains nothing particularly scandalous. The absence of falsehoods, however, does not necessarily add up to historical truth.

If the history of the Mormons is to mean anything, it has to be referred to larger patterns in Protestantism and in nineteenth-century society as a whole. Neither Turner nor Mullen is much concerned with historical context—a fact that is not surprising, since their books deal principally with the contemporary Mormon church. One turns to Robert Bruce Flanders's *Nauvoo,* on the other hand, in the expectation that a book on Nauvoo, Illinois, where the Mormons lived from 1839 to 1846 and where many of the distinctive features of their communal life first took shape, will do what the other books do not—relate Mormonism not only to other religious developments of the period but to other utopian experiments, both religious and secular. It says a great deal about contemporary scholarship that Professor Flanders shows so little interest in these matters. His historical account is no more historical, in the true sense, than the books by Turner and Mullen, which do not pretend to be historical in any but the most perfunctory way.

Flanders has ransacked all the relevant sources and has meticulously described the settlement of Nauvoo, the financial difficulties which attended the purchase of land and which helped to bring about the failure of the settlement, the internal struggles within the leadership, and the harassment of the Mormons by other settlers—culminating in the murder of Joseph Smith by a local mob—which completed the destruction of Nauvoo. Flanders has also described, in detail, the Mormons' highly successful mission to England, where between 1837 and 1856 they made more than 75,000 converts, of whom 25,000 migrated to America. But when all these things have been said, the history of the Mormons remains as puzzling and as obscure as it was before. From what source, what reservoir of superstition, paganism, hope, and frustration, did Mormonism, in the midst of the most "enlightened" civilizations of the age, suddenly spring, with its grotesque theology, its ancestor worship, its polygamy, its social program at once authoritarian and egalitarian, and its inspired, crazy messiah, Joseph Smith, whose accounts of visions and voices not only affronted credulity but consistently contradicted themselves? An effort to understand the Mormons, one would suppose, could not possibly stop with the Mormons themselves. In the history of Anglo-American society, the Mormons are so clearly a pathological symptom that a historian could not address himself to the Mormons, it would seem, without asking himself what kind of society could have produced them. Too much historical "research" consists of detaching a subject from its surroundings, thereby draining away whatever was interesting about the subject in the first place. In this way historians avoid the intractable questions their materials raise, but they also forfeit their claim to attention. Why should anyone but a specialist wish to read about the Mormons, when their history remains an isolated episode, a narrative detached from any larger questions beyond whatever topical interest attaches to the prominence of the Mormon governor of Michigan—itself, it may be, no more than an ephemeral phenomenon?

It is admittedly difficult to make sense of a movement as eccentric as Mormonism. The theology of the Latter-day Saints was the creation of its founder, "shiftless," "indolent," "prevaricating," "cunning" Joe Smith, Jr., as he was known to his neighbors in Palmyra, New York. Smith's father, a native of Vermont, farmed, kept store, did odd jobs, moved his family nineteen times in ten years, joined the Universalists, joined the Methodists, joined the Presbyterians, and "had what he called visions," Alice Felt Tyler notes, "which seem to have made some impression on his family." He and his son spent much of their time hunting for buried treasure with a divining rod. In 1823, "young Joe" had a vision of the angel "Moroni," who after a four-year period of trial showed him the golden tablets (Smith first described them simply as a book that had been buried in the ground, but in later versions they became metallic), buried by the angel 1400 years earlier. On them was recorded, in cryptic signs which it was given to young Joe to read, the history of the Nephites, last survivors of the lost tribes of Israel—their migration to the New World, the civilization they built in the wilderness, and the eventual destruction of this civilization by the American Indians. The record of these revelations, set down by Smith in the Book of Mormon (Mormon, he explained, was the father of Moroni), contains passages borrowed from the Christian Bible, but it can be considered a Christian document only in a very general sense. It requires adherents to believe that Christian history is mostly a fraud, a monumental miscarriage, and that not the Christians but the Nephites and their successors the Mormons are the chosen people of God.

Mormon theology bears something of the same relation to Christianity as the doctrines of the Black Muslims bear to Islam; nor does the similarity end there. The fierce exclusiveness of the Mormons, coupled with a formidable talent for proselytization, their search for a territorial base of their own, which drove them from New York to Ohio to Missouri to Illinois and finally to Utah, their rejection of the feminine component in Christianity in favor of an explicitly patriarchal style of life, and above all, the amazing capacity of the new religion to inspire the poor, the restless, the down-and-out with a sense of their own importance—Joe Smith, "the most ragged, lazy fellow" in Palmyra, being himself a principal case in point—all these things, together with their outlandish, trumped-up, pseudo-historical myth of themselves as the chosen people, strongly remind one of the Black Muslims. Both theologies are excrescences of larger systems of thought, as much pagan as they are Christian or Mohammedan, synthetic constructs invented on the spot by men whose careers continually invite the suspicion of outright imposture—Smith, like Elijah Muhammed, seems always to have had one eye on the main chance—yet which for all their artificiality make a genuine appeal to the outcasts and underdogs of the world, the class of people to whom Christianity itself was first addressed but whom in its triumphs it learned, with the rest of the world, to despise.

Mormonism, even in the history of Protestant sectarianism, was eccentric; but it was a recognizable product, all the same, of the evangelical revival of the early nineteenth century. Taking first root in the "burned-over district" of western New York, it was the product, more specifically, of a peculiar set of circumstances which made that part of the country so fertile a source of enthusiasms of every kind. Successive waves of revivalism rendered the people of the burned-over district peculiarly susceptible to intense religious emotions. (In England too Mormonism grew in ground already fertilized by Methodism.) While fierce competition among proliferating sects produced a chronic state of religious excitement, it gave rise at the same time to uncertainties and doubts which turned some men away from dogmatic religion altogether while driving others into a search for ultimate religious truth, a dogma to end dogmas. "In the midst of this war of words, and tumult of opinion, I often said to myself, What is to be done? Who, of all these parties, are right? or, are they all wrong together? If any one of them be right, which is it? and how shall I know it?" Thus Joseph Smith described his youth in the burned-over district; and if he finally worked out for himself answers to these questions that were highly idiosyncratic, the search itself, grounded in the assumption that the answer, whatever it was, would reveal itself in some definitive system of belief, grew out of expectations shared by other inhabitants of that part of the world. Even the imagery of Mormonism was rooted in local superstition. A mania for treasure-hunting had seized the district a few years before. And as Whitney Cross has shown in *The Burned-Over District,* legends of the lost tribes of Israel flourished here years before Joseph Smith turned them to his own account.

The people of the burned-over district also experienced, more distantly, the lingering force of Puritanism, which had given way to Congregationalism in the more settled parts of the country but lived on in the rural districts of New England from which many of the settlers of western New York had originally migrated. David Brion Davis has explained how the Puritan legacy predisposed the settlers of western New York to a set of religious expectations quite at odds with the prevailing liberalism. "The descendants of farmers from isolated valleys in Vermont and Connecticut instinctively thought of one church, *the* church, with a definite logical creed and reassuring covenants." Moreover, they expected religion to provide not only spiritual guidance but a set of principles around which to organize the social order. The essence of Mormonism was the attempt to create a community of "saints," in which every "secular" activity should be governed in accordance with a religious conception of the good society. It was in this respect that the Mormons showed themselves most fully the descendants of the New England Puritans and of the Calvinists at Geneva. More broadly, their ideas reflect what Philippe Ariès has called the moral "rehabilitation of the lay condition"—a belief in the perfectibility of secular life, which stands in sharp contrast, at one historical extreme, to the medieval view that the only truly religious life consisted in the renunciation of the world and the pursuit of the religious vocation within the church itself, and, at the other extreme, to the modern conception of secular activities as sufficient ends in themselves. Part of the originality of early Protestantism lay in defining work and marriage as "callings" no less Godly—in Protestant eyes, a good deal more Godly—than priesthood or monasticism; and although these ideas gave way in time to an easygoing acceptance of the world as it is, they regularly reappeared in those periodic revivals of moral enthusiasm that marked the history of Protestantism down to the nineteenth century.

If it is important that the Mormons were originally sons of New England, it is equally important that they were poor people— poor farmers, unsuccessful mechanics, industrial workers (in

England); in short, the dispossessed. The point is not so much that, lacking education, they fell easy prey to superstition. More important, their lack of education prevented them from being exposed to liberal culture. Thus an earlier religious tradition was able to survive in the working class after it had disappeared, leaving hardly a trace, from the middle class. In this respect as in many others—their family organization, their sexual practices, their taste for paternalistic modes of social organization which elsewhere were giving way to laissez-faire—the nineteenth-century poor lived in a culture that had become a storehouse of pre-industrial archaisms. Of these, Mormonism was one of the most vivid and poignant examples.

The Mormons' utopianism, expressing itself in the wish to found model communities, reflected the survival of a powerful, obsolescent pattern of religious thought. It also reflected the utopianism of the immediate historical period in which Mormonism took shape. Alice Tyler, in *Freedom's Ferment,* argues that utopianism grew directly out of the logic of sectarianism: "The leaders of these new sects emphasized their separateness and the need for close association of all members. The more peculiar the tenets of their faith, the more necessary became the intensive instruction, criticism, and supervision that community living could make possible."

The tenets of the Mormons were "peculiar" enough, particularly after the adoption of polygamy in 1853, after a period of perhaps ten years during which it had been secretly practiced by the Mormon leaders. Yet even here, at what appears to be their most idiosyncratic, the Mormons had more in common with other sects than one might suppose. None of the others adopted polygamy, but all of them in one way or another repudiated the conventional family (even while adopting some of its values): the Shakers, Rappites, and others practiced celibacy; the Fourierists instituted cooperative housekeeping and child-rearing; the Perfectionists set up " complex marriage" accompanied by what John Humphrey Noyes, their leader, called "male continence" (*coitus interruptus,* designed to liberate women from the tyranny of constant childbearing). Noyes himself pointed out the connection between communitarianism and sexual experiments: communal living dictated the abandonment of exclusive possession not only of goods but of women. "Thus Mormonism," wrote Noyes, "is the masculine form, as Shakerism is the feminine form, of the more morbid products of Revivals"—that is, of the well-known tendency of revivalism to excite the sexual as well as the religious impulse.

In defense of his own system of "free love," Noyes appealed not only to the logic of communism but, more concretely, to the bad effects of the conventional system. Monogamy, by giving "to sexual appetite only a scanty and monotonous allowance," contributed to "the peculiar diseases of women, of prostitution, masturbation, and licentiousness in general." The Mormons justified polygamy on similar grounds. The advantages for men are obvious enough; what surprised nineteenth-century visitors to Utah was that Mormon women, whom they had expected to find groaning under intolerable oppression, defended polygamy with some enthusiasm. They argued that it prevented bad marriages and forestalled the evils, for women, of the unmarried state.

The alleged excess of spinsters was a general concern of the early nineteenth century, at least in America, perhaps because diminishing employments for women rendered single women increasingly dependent on their families. This alarm about spinsters, together with the hazards single women faced on the frontier, may help to explain, not why the Mormon leaders introduced polygamy (a matter which it is probably impossible to settle) but why it was accepted with so little resistance by their followers, who after all had been raised in the same monogamous culture as other Americans. Polygamy was one response to a general set of conditions—a response quite in keeping with the values peculiar to the Mormons. Monogamy, a Mormon woman told the French traveler, Jules Rémy, "compels a number of women to their lives in *single blessedness,* without husband, without children, without a friend to protect and comfort them; or still more, it condemns them to a life of poverty and loneliness, in which they are exposed to temptations, to

culpable connections, to the necessity of selling themselves."
Polygamy among the Mormons was another aspect of their
insistence on the life of the community as opposed to private
satisfactions.

The communal idea appears most clearly in the economic
policies of the Mormons, particularly those carried out by the
organizing genius of Brigham Young after the death of Joseph
Smith. The idea of the Christian commonwealth now acquired
an egalitarian emphasis which had been missing from earlier
manifestations of the same impulse except as a minor strain—in
the career, for instance, of Roger Williams. The union of communitarianism with the idea of equality, however, came too late;
in American society as a whole the idea of equality—insofar as it
displayed any real vitality at all—tended increasingly to manifest
itself in the form of economic individualism. Rationalistic religion, meanwhile, more and more removed itself from any
responsibility for the social order. From the point of view of
liberal Christianity, the Mormon experiment was impossible to
understand. A Universalist visiting a Mormon settlement in
Ohio complained in 1837 that the Mormons had "too much
worldly wisdom connected with their religion—too great a
desire for the perishable riches of this world—holding out the
idea that the kingdom of Christ is to be composed of 'real estate,
herds, flocks, silver, gold,' as well as of human beings." These
uncomprehending observations show the degree to which the
idea of the religious community had already fallen into general
disarray.

In Utah, under Young's leadership, the Mormons created a
self-sufficient, cooperative, egalitarian, and authoritarian economy devoted not to individual enrichment but to the collective
well-being of the flock. Leonard Arrington in his very useful
study of the Mormon economy, *Great Basin Kingdom,* shows
how the Mormons accomplished, through a system of cooperative and compulsory labor, impressive feats of planning and
development—irrigation, roads, canals, sugar beet factories, iron
works—without generating the institutions or the inequalities
elsewhere associated with industrial progress; indeed, without

even developing a money economy. Cooperation and planning caused the desert to bloom, in marked contrast to the exploitive patterns of agriculture which on other frontiers exhausted natural resources and left the land a smoking waste. These practices of the Mormons, however—so successful both from a human and from a technological point of view—ill accorded with the prevailing drift toward laissez-faire. More broadly, "the theocratic economy," as Arrington notes, "interfered with the spread of capitalistic institutions." Beginning with the "Mormon War" of 1857–58, when federal troops tried unsuccessfully to break up the Mormon settlements, the government harried the Saints by a combination of military, legislative, and judicial action. Finally, in 1887, Congress passed the Edmunds-Tucker Act, named in part for a respected liberal senator from Vermont, which effectively deprived the Mormon church of its secular powers by stripping polygamists of their civil and political rights. (It also abolished woman suffrage in Utah Territory.) In 1890, the Supreme Court upheld the law. Four months later the president of the Mormon church, Wilford Woodruff, declared that the Mormons would abide by the decision. The capitulation of the church did not remove it altogether from the economic life of Utah, but its role was now reduced to that of an investor in companies the management of which, Arrington observed, "has been left free to pursue normal business policies. . . . Church investments, which were mostly promotional and developmental in the ninteenth century, often became, in the twentieth century, such income-producing investments as rural and urban real estate and stocks and bonds in established industrial and commercial enterprises." Arrington's book ends on a wistful note: "The remarkable thing about Mormon economic policy over the century is not that it varied to meet changing circumstances and conditions, which it did, but that it held fast as long as it did to the original program."

The destruction of the temporal powers of the church put an end, for all practical purposes, to the Mormon enterprise; the enterprise had no meaning apart from the effort to create a community integrated and controlled by religious rather than by economic sanctions. After that, the church became an appendage of the economic oligarchy which grew up following the intrusion of capitalism into this last remaining enclave of precapitalist institutions—just as, two centuries before, Congregationalism had become the official religion of the slave-trading descendants of the Puritan founders of Massachusetts Bay. Present-day Mormonism bears the same relation to nineteenth-century Mormonism as Congregationalism to Puritanism; which is to say, hardly any relation at all, beyond a certain pride of ancestry. It does not surprise us to read, in Turner's book, that contemporary Mormons take an unusual interest in genealogy. The need to establish genealogical links with the past, characteristic of newly arrived élites in every period, testifies to the weakness of more substantial connections.

Similarly the appearance of a book on Mormon history by a public-relations consultant—a book stressing the "colorful" aspects of the "Mormon experience," as it will no doubt come to be called—suggests that Mormon history has already become part of the generalized myth of the American West and of the triumph of American enterprise. The Mormon church continues to grow. It grows because it can offer special attractions of its own—more community sense, more social discipline, more mystique than other churches competing for lower-middle-class converts, a combination that is appealing to those reared strictly who find things falling apart. But the growth of the Mormons, like the growth of the other churches, has been achieved by sacrificing whatever features of their doctrine or ritual were demanding and difficult. In the case of the Mormons, what was demanding and difficult was the conception of a secular community organized in accordance with religious principles. Accordingly the utopian elements of Mormonism were abandoned while the absurd theology remains, leaving the monstrosity of a church which is fundamentalist in most respects but which has nevertheless come to share the central feature of religious liberalism, the comforting illusion that religion is an affair of the spirit alone having nothing to do with the rest of life. From posing a challenge to the American way of life Mormonism has become a defense of its most reactionary aspects.

Meanwhile the spread of federal power throughout the continent—the imposition of uniform laws, economic practices, and institutions—reduces religious, ethnic, and regional minorities to the level of tolerated and "privileged" corporations—privileged in the sense that they enjoy a quasi-official relationship to the body politic which allows them to wear their colorful and distinctive cultural dress on the understanding that these garments shall be reserved, as it were, for ceremonial occasions, to be put off, on working days, in favor of the plain garb of the American citizen. Ethnic eccentricities, harmless and quaint, not only contribute to our amusement but add to our flattering self-portrait of ourselves as a "pluralistic" society. The ultimate fate of American minorities is to become tourist attractions. Mr. Mullen points with pride to the increase of tourism in the Salt Lake Kingdom of the Saints. But the tourist boom means the same thing in Utah that it means in Vermont, the same thing it means wherever the past has been piously "restored," roped off, and put on display—not the vitality but the decadence of a way of life.

[VI]

The Anti-Imperialists,
the Philippines,
and the Inequality of Man

THE CESSION OF THE PHILIPPINE ISLANDS TO THE UNITED STATES precipitated a great debate on the nature of American foreign policy and national destiny. While the arguments in favor of the imperialist policy have been studied at length, the anti-imperialist side of the debate has largely been ignored, perhaps because historians have tended instinctively to sympathize with it and to assume that the anti-imperialists of 1898–99 were voicing objections to colonialism now commonly accepted.

The position of the anti-imperialists does at first appear to have been sensible and straightforward: imperialism was not only inexpedient but unjust, a departure from the historic principles of the Declaration of Independence. But a closer examination of certain facets of the anti-imperialist argument may require us to see the anti-imperialists in a rather more critical light. Their argument did not foreshadow the liberalism of the Good Neighbor policy. It was in fact no more liberal than that of the expansionists. Indeed, it resembled the expansionist rationale, against which it appeared to be a protest, far more closely than it does any of the objections we might today raise against a colonial policy, or for that matter than it resembled the theories of Thomas Jefferson. It was a product of the late nineteenth century, not of the eighteenth or twentieth centuries.

The anti-imperialists, like the imperialists, saw the world from a pseudo-Darwinian point of view. They accepted the inequality of man—or, to be more precise, of races—as an established fact of life. They did not question the idea that Anglo-Saxons were superior to other people, and some of them would even have agreed that they were destined eventually to conquer the world. They did not quarrel with the idea of "destiny"; they merely refused to believe that destiny required such strenuous exertions of the American people, particularly when they saw in those exertions the menace of militarism and tyranny. There were important differences of opinion, of course, between those who favored and those who opposed the annexation of the Philippines, but for the moment it is perhaps more important to dwell on the matters on which they agreed. Most Americans in the 1890's agreed in attaching great importance to the concept of race, and that agreement gave the cultural life of the period its peculiar tone.

It is characteristic of the period that neither side in the debate over the Philippines was content to rest its case on considerations of expediency alone, although the expansionist clique on whom defense of the "large policy" devolved tried to rouse the business community, which was apathetic toward the whole question of expansion, with visions of glittering markets in China. But economic arguments could too easily be attacked as sordid, and the expansionists preferred to stand on higher ground. They appealed to "manifest destiny," an old idea, and to the newer, post-Darwinian idea that it was the manifest *duty* of higher civilizations to displace lower ones, either through outright elimination (as the white man had eliminated the Indian) or through a process of uplift and "Christianization." It was as carriers of civilization, they argued, that the American people were obliged to annex the Philippines, however disagreeable the obligation might appear.

The anti-imperialists, largely ignoring the economic and strategic arguments for annexation, replied with a moral argument of their own. They admitted that American history, as the expansionists were fond of showing, was a record of territorial expansion, but they fixed the limits of the nation's westward destiny at the shores of the Pacific. The United States, in their view, was destined to be a continental, not a global power. All of the areas previously acquired by the United States had been on the North American continent, and all except Alaska had been contiguous to the old states. Because they were contiguous and because they were thinly populated, they came to be settled by citizens from the older states, by white, Protestant, English-speaking people—by a population, in short, indistinguishable from that of the older states. The new territories, therefore, could be, and were, admitted to statehood. (Alaska, again, was the single exception.)

But to annex distant islands already heavily populated by racial aliens, the anti-imperialists maintained, would be a momentous and disastrous departure from the past. The Filipinos, for any number of reasons, could not become American citizens; they would have to be governed as subjects. But how could a republic have subjects? For the United States to acquire the Philippines without admitting their people to full citizenship would amount to government without the consent of the governed—a flat contradiction of the cardinal principle of American democracy, the principle over which the United States had separated from England, the principle of the Declaration of Independence. Nor was this all. As a result of the initial injustice, others would follow. A large standing army would have to be created in order to defend the new possessions not only against foreign powers but against the natives themselves, who were already in revolt against American rule; and an army called into being for the purpose of crushing freedom abroad would ultimately be used to destroy it at home. The administration had already begun to censor news from the Philippines, in order to create the impression that the hostilities there were purely defensive in character, and the anti-imperialists saw in this an evil omen—proof that if the United States persisted in imperialism, it would eventually go the way of Rome.

The exponents of annexation could offer no satisfactory answer to all this. Instead, they attempted to create a dilemma of their own—to show that there was no satisfactory alternative to annexation. Accordingly they argued that the Filipinos were not "ready" for self-government and if left to themselves would fall into the hands of a native dictator or a foreign conqueror. Not a single expansionist, however, proposed that the privileges of citizenship be extended to the Philippines. They assumed that the Filipinos would have to be governed as second-class citizens, and with that assumption they departed from the natural rights philosophy of the Declaration of Independence, exactly as their antagonists accused them of doing. Senator Henry M. Teller, an expansionist, confessed that to hold the islanders as subjects would be "rather objectionable in a republic"; but there seemed no choice. Not all the expansionists had similar reservations, but almost all of them recognized and admitted the implications of their policy for the doctrine of natural rights. In effect, they substituted for the Jeffersonian proposition that the right to liberty is "natural"—hence universal—the proposition that rights depend on environment: on "civilization," of which there were now seen to be many stages of development; on race; even on climate. A pseudo-Darwinian hierarchy of cultural stages, unequal in the capacity for enjoyment of the rights associated with self-government, replaced the simpler and more liberal theory of the Enlightenment, which recognized only the distinction between society and nature. "Rights," as absolutes, lost their meaning by becoming relative to time and place. Rights now depended on a people's "readiness" to enjoy them.

It is not surprising that the anti-imperialists accused the expansionists of abandoning the Declaration of Independence. What is surprising is that their own arguments were no closer to the spirit of that document than the ones they denounced with such fervor. The anti-imperialists were in fact no more Jeffersonian in their essential outlook than Theodore Roosevelt or Henry Cabot Lodge or Alfred T. Mahan was, for they did not challenge the central assumption of imperialist thought: the natural inequality of men. The imperialists at least had the merit of consistency; they made no professions of Jeffersonianism. The anti-imperialists, on the other hand, invoked the name of Jefferson at every opportunity.

Some light on the anti-imperialists is shed by the high proportion of Southerners among them. In the Senate, only four of twenty-eight Southern senators favored unconditional ratification of the treaty with Spain, and Southerners led the attack on the treaty in debate. Their arguments against ratification clearly reflected the lingering bitterness of Reconstruction, as well as more recent movements to exclude Negroes from the benefits of citizenship. Annexation of the Philippines, they argued, would merely compound the race problem by introducing into the country what Senator John W. Daniel of Virginia called a "mess of Asiatic pottage." Benjamin R. Tillman of South Carolina was especially active in the anti-imperialist cause, playing ingenious variations on the racial theme. At times he gave it a distinctly Darwinian note: ". . . we [referring to the South] understand and realize what it is to have two races side by side that can not mix or mingle without deterioration and injury to both and the ultimate destruction of the civilization of the higher." At other times he gave it a pro-labor bias: ". . . here are 10,000,000 Asiatics who will have the right as soon as the pending treaty is ratified, to get on the first ship that they can reach and come here and compete in the labor market of the United States." In a more somber mood, he appeared to speak more in sorrow than in anger: ". . . coming . . . as a Senator from . . . South Carolina, with 750,000 colored population and only 500,000 whites, I realize what you are doing, while you don't; and I would save this country from the injection into it of another race question which can only breed bloodshed and a costly war and the loss of the lives of our brave soldiers." More often, however, he spoke with biting irony which revealed the Negro, not the Filipino, as the real source of his anxiety and, further, which showed that he was more interested in embarrassing the North —in forcing its senators to admit to a contradiction—than he was in preventing the acquisition of the Philippines. When Knute Nelson of Minnesota, once an abolitionist, declared that the Filipinos were incapable of self-government, Tillman replied: "I want to call the Senator's attention to the fact, however, that he and others who are now contending for a different policy in Hawaii and the Philippines gave the slaves of the South not only self-government, but they forced on the white men of the South, at the point of the bayonet, the rule and domination of those ex-slaves. Why the difference? Why the change? Do you acknowledge that you were wrong in 1868?"

It is unnecessary to insist that such arguments did not spring from a deep-seated attachment to the Declaration of Independence. But it would be manifestly unfair to judge the whole anti-imperialist movement on the basis of its Southern wing, particularly when many Northern men of the persuasion were clearly uncomfortable at finding themselves in the company of men like Tillman. An examination of their own arguments, however, discloses no important difference from that of the Southerners, except that Northern anti-imperialists did not dwell on the parallel with the Southern Negro problem—something they were by this time eager to forget. One is left with the impression that it was not the Southern argument as such that disconcerted the Northerners, but the use to which the South put it. When it came to giving reasons why the Philippines should not be annexed, North and South found themselves in close agreement.

Anti-imperialists contended that the Filipinos, unless they were given their independence, would have to be held in subjection, since they could not be admitted as citizens. What is interesting is the manner in which they arrived at the latter conclusion. A brief study of the process reveals a racism as thorough-going as that of the imperialists themselves.

In the first place, the anti-imperialists argued, if the Filipinos became citizens, they would migrate to the United States and compete with American labor—a prospect especially alarming in view of the racial composition of the islands. As Samuel Gompers declared: "If the Philippines are annexed, what is to prevent the Chinese, the Negritos, and the Malays coming to our own country?" This was more than an economic argument. It implied that those people were accustomed to a low standard of living and, what is more, that they were incapable, by virtue of their race, of longing for anything better. It implied that Orientals, in short, would work for low wages because they could not, and never would, appreciate the finer things of life which money alone could buy. This view had already come into vogue on the West Coast, where it was particularly popular with organized labor; it is not surprising, therefore, to find Gompers appealing to it.

If cheap Filipino labor would compete unfairly with American labor, cheap Filipino goods could be expected to compete unfairly with American goods. If the United States took over the islands, it could neither prevent immigration nor levy protective import duties. Annexation would therefore injure both capital and labor.

The Filipinos would also be given the vote. Considering, again, the racial composition of the islands, the results would clearly be ruinous. Carl Schurz declared:

> If they become states on an equal footing with the other states they will not only be permitted to govern themselves as to their home concerns, but will take part in governing the whole republic, in governing us, by sending senators and representatives into our Congress to help make our laws, and by voting for president and vice-president to give our national government its executive. The prospect of the consequences which would follow the admission of the Spanish creoles and the negroes of the West India islands and of the Malays and Tagals of the Philippines to participation in the conduct of our government is so alarming that you instinctively pause before taking the step.

The same sentiments were expressed by James L. Blair of St. Louis, the son of the old Free Soil leader Francis Preston Blair. "History," Blair said, "shows no instance of a tropical people who have demonstrated a capacity for maintaining an enduring form of Republican government." To admit such a people into a share in the government of the United States would be self-destructive. David Starr Jordan warned his countrymen: "If we govern the Philippines, so in their degree must the Philippines govern us." Or as Champ Clark put it even more forcefully in the House of Representatives: "No matter whether they are fit to govern themselves or not, they are not fit to govern us [applause]."

But if it was undesirable for the Filipinos to come to the United States or to take part in American government, was it not still possible that Americans would emigrate to the Philippines and gradually displace the native culture? The anti-imperialists denied that any such outcome was possible. In the first place, "the two races could never amalgamate"; "the racial differences between the Oriental and Western races are never to be eradicated." Suppose the Filipinos were eliminated by force or herded into reservations, like the American Indians. Even then, the anti-imperialists insisted, annexation would be unwise, for the fact was that neither the "northern" (or "Anglo-Saxon" or "Germanic") race nor democratic institutions could survive in a tropical climate. "Civilization," said Jordan, "is, as it were, suffocated in the tropics." On another occasion he explained that the Philippines "lie in the heart of the torrid zone, 'Nature's asylum for degenerates.'" "Neither the people nor the institutions of the United States can ever occupy the Philippines," he said. "The American home cannot endure there, the town-meeting cannot exist." Schurz echoed the same refrain: "They are . . . situated in the tropics, where people of the northern races, such as Anglo-Saxons, or generally speaking, people of Germanic blood, have never migrated in mass to stay; and they are more or less densely populated, parts of them as densely as Massachusetts—their population consisting almost exclusively of races to whom the tropical climate is congenial— . . . Malays, Tagals, Filipinos, Chinese, Japanese, Negritos, and various more or less barbarous tribes. . . ."

Such arguments clearly showed that the anti-imperialists had abandoned the philosophy of the Declaration of Independence for a complicated Darwinian view of the world. According to this view, which appeared to be substantiated by the science of the day and by the writings of historians like Herbert Baxter Adams, geography, race, and political institutions were inextricably intertwined. The temperate zone—specifically the northern part of it—bred the "Germanic" race, from which Americans were descended. Free institutions were associated with the rise of that race; a study of other cultures showed no similar institutions. Because they alone were capable of using liberty wisely, the Germans had already risen to a cultural level far beyond that of any other race and were possibly destined to supplant all others. In view of their inability to survive in the tropics, however, it was not quite clear how this was to be accomplished; and for that reason, perhaps, the anti-imperialists preferred to see the Anglo-Saxons stay at home, in their native habitat. In any case, to mingle their blood with that of Asiatics would be a fatal departure from what Charles Francis Adams, for example, called the "cardinal principle in our policy as a race." He referred to our Indian policy, which he admitted had been harsh; but it had "saved the Anglo-Saxon stock from being a nation of half-breeds." The acquisition of the Philippines would again endanger the purity of the old stock, on which America's very survival depended.

An examination of the arguments against annexation of the Philippines leads to a number of interesting conclusions. In the first place, it is difficult, after having read their writings and speeches, to convince oneself that the anti-imperialists had the better of the argument, as historians have tended to assume. Whatever the merits of the expansionists' contention that the Filipinos were not ready for self-government, the expansionists were at least consistent in the conclusions they drew from it. If it was true that the Filipinos could not govern themselves, the humane policy (although not necessarily the wisest one) was to govern them ourselves. The anti-imperialists, on the other hand, while sharing the expansionists' basic assumption, were perfectly willing to leave the Filipinos to their fate—certainly a most un-Christian policy if they were indeed unable to manage their own affairs. So far as the moral argument had any validity at all, the anti-imperialists were on weak ground; and since they insisted on treating the question as a matter of right and wrong, it seems fair to judge them accordingly.

But it is not possible to condemn anti-imperialists for holding certain opinions on race unless one is willing to condemn the entire society of which they were a part. The fact is that the atmosphere of the late nineteenth century was so thoroughly permeated with racist thought (reinforced by Darwinism) that few men managed to escape it. The idea that certain cultures and races were naturally inferior to others was almost universally held by educated, respectable Americans. The widespread and almost unconscious adherence to it was unmistakably manifested, in the same period, in the national policy toward minorities more familiar to American experience than the Filipinos, and in particular toward immigrants and Negroes. This was the period of the first serious restrictions on immigration; it was the period of the South's successful re-elimination of the Negro from white society. Men who called themselves liberals—survivors of the antislavery crusade and the battles of the sixties and seventies on behalf of the Negroes: liberal Republicans, mugwumps, "independents"—acquiesced in these developments. A study of anti-imperialism makes it a little clearer why they did, for the anti-imperialist movement was dominated by these same men—men like Schurz, Adams, Jordan, and Moorfield Storey.[1] Except for Storey, these men had now receded from their earlier idealism. They continued to speak of their part in the struggle for Negro rights, to refer to it with pride, but by referring to it as a fight that had already been won they indicated their indifference to the continuing plight of the Southern Negro. Indeed, they had abandoned him, as they now proposed to abandon the Filipinos. They had no further interest in crusading; the times, it appeared, called for retrenchment.

---

1. The clear connection between the anti-imperialist movement and earlier movements for liberal reform has never received much attention; and it concerns us here only in passing. It should be pointed out, however, that although the movement received widespread and varied support, it was led and dominated by men like Schurz, Godkin, Storey, Adams, Blair, Edward Atkinson, Erving Winslow, and Gamaliel Bradford, who had at one time or another been active on behalf of antislavery agitation, civil service reform, free trade, and other "liberal" causes. These men regarded party politicians who joined the struggle—politicians like Tillman, Bryan, and even Senator George F. Hoar—with distinctive misgivings, as not wholly sincere in their opposition to the "large policy." This suspicion was not without basis.

[VII]

The Moral
and Intellectual Rehabilitation
of the Ruling Class

I

THE MOVEMENT TO PREVENT ANNEXATION OF THE PHILIPPINES, THE racist overtones of which have been examined in the preceding essay, marks a turning point in the history of the American ruling class. The defeat of the anti-imperialists signaled the triumph of nationalizing and expansionist tendencies within the ruling class over regional and parochial habits of mind. The leaders of the anti-imperialist movement, many of whom were New Englanders, appealed quite consciously to regional traditions in their propaganda. Not satisfied with that, they appropriated the most attractive elements of the national past and identified them with a purely regional heritage; as if the Revolution, the antislavery crusade, and the liberal tradition in general were incidents in the history of New England alone.

The temporary alliance of New England with the South, incongruous as it seemed in many respects, was deeply fitting, since it brought together the two regional traditions most immediately threatened by the expansionist policy and the centralization of political power which that policy reflected. The Southern gentry, like that of New England, faced a crisis of regional identity. It upheld the peculiar traditions of the South with a vehemence inversely proportional to their capacity to influence events. The legend of the Lost Cause took shape—and, it should be noted, won wide acceptance outside the South—at a time when the landed gentry itself, in enthusiastic partnership with Northern bankers and manufacturers, was building railroads, setting up cotton mills, and otherwise transforming the face of the South. Neo-regional literatures, which were just beginning to flourish not only in the South but in other parts of the country as well, celebrated ways of life that were rapidly passing into memory. The neo-regionalist revival became an important influence on letters, on architecture, on the theater, and even on music at precisely the moment at which regionalism had ceased to be an important influence on politics.

The anti-imperialist movement, then—a movement led by New England mugwumps, Southerners, and representatives of such outstanding provincial families as the Blairs of Missouri—was the dying gasp of a regional aristocracy faced with the domination of great national and international corporations, of uncouth outsiders risen to positions of great power (the Rockefellers, Goulds, Harrimans, and Hills), and of such unpredictable renegades from its own ranks as Theodore Roosevelt and Henry Cabot Lodge. Legend has it that the old mugwump aristocracy was simply overwhelmed by raw new men, as the power of money displaced the influence of breeding and character. This version of the social history of the late nineteenth century, deriving from the mugwumps themselves and from the nostalgia associated with the neo-regionalist revival, makes it impossible to account for the persisting influence of old wealth and its traditions. On the assumption of a radical shift in class power or "status revolution" it is difficult to explain why in Philadelphia, for instance, an élite of old families, many of them dating back to the Revolution, still formed the core of the business "aristocracy" as late as 1940. So much has been made of the mugwumps' futility and their predilection for failure that it is easy to overlook their successes: introduction of civil service reform; elimination of the grosser forms of corruption in politics and business; infiltration of the corporations themselves. As a result of the political battles of the late nineteenth century—in which the mugwumps saw themselves as hopelessly outnumbered and overwhelmed by unscrupulous opponents—the old élites not only preserved much of their influence but imposed their own values on the national ruling class that was beginning to emerge. So too in the social counterparts of these political fights, waged in salons and at the best resorts, the *nouveaux riches* forced their way into élite society—Mrs. Vanderbilt at last wresting from Mrs. Astor a grudging recognition of her social existence—but ended by absorbing the outlook of their erstwhile enemies.

In order to survive, however, the older élites had to undergo a moral and intellectual rehabilitation. Two choices confronted them: to fall back on regional traditions, either as a last-ditch defense against modernity or as a bittersweet consolation for defeats in the political realm; or to plunge into the business and political life of the new industrial age, attempting to bend it to their own purposes. Much more was involved than the efforts of a dying élite to retrieve its fortunes by allying itself with new money. With considerable insight into the underlying dynamics of the period, William Dean Howells deliberately eschews this time-honored theme in *The Rise of Silas Lapham,* depicting instead a young Brahmin attracted to the "romance" of money-making and only secondarily to the prospect of marrying it. His father half-humorously demands "an apology" when he discovers the young man's intentions: "I supposed you wished to marry the girl's money, and here you are, basely seeking to go into business with her father." By allying itself matrimonially with "new fortunes," the seaboard commercial élite might have transformed itself into a genuine leisure class, devoting itself to art and learning and even retaining political influence, as in England, through the sheer force of its glittering example. In a country in which "culture" has always been considered somewhat effeminate, it is perhaps not surprising that the upper class chose instead "to go into business with her father"; nor should it amaze us that the internecine battles attendant on its own self-transformation should so often have been conducted in sexual language, as if what was demanded of aristocrats faced with the turmoil of the Gilded Age was above all a demonstration of their masculinity.

2

TWO EXEMPLARY CAREERS SHOW THE CONFLICTING POLES BETWEEN which the older upper classes were repeatedly torn. On the one hand, there is the self-dramatized (and absurdly exaggerated) "failure" of Henry Adams. Endlessly bemoaning the obsolescence of sturdy republican virtues in a time of unprincipled self-seeking, while at the same time unable to sustain the role of an ironic commentator on the general wickedness—lapsing instead into grandiose geopolitical fantasies and "scientific" theories of history—Adams flirts with the self-destructive impulses which under different circumstances produced nihilistic or proto-fascist reactions among disgruntled aristocrats, or yet again the exoticism of the *fin de siècle*. Whatever one makes of the irony with which Adams was careful to hedge statements about his own career, his pessimism was clearly attractive to men of his class and appears without irony in the grumpy reminiscences of Schurz, Godkin, and other spokesmen of the mugwumpish élite.

On the other hand, ambitious members of the upper crust had before them the compelling, if slightly bizarre, example of Theodore Roosevelt—a man who was felt in many ways to have betrayed his class (like his even more illustrious relative three decades later) but whose acrobatics, tasteless as they were, at the same time seemed to point the way to survival. With a talent for self-dramatization unequalled even by Adams—and happily untroubled by any corresponding tendency toward irony or introspection—Roosevelt succeeded in converting his career into a parable of the career of his class. Here was a sickly, pampered child growing up in a household of women; nearsighted; asthmatic; the natural prey of bullies, who by sheer willpower built himself up into a roughrider, big-game hunter, politician, President, wielder of the big stick—the terror of bullies and of "malefactors" in general. ("As I rose, I struck quick and hard with my right just to one side of the point of his jaw, hitting with my left as I straightened out, and then again with my right. . . . When he went down he struck the corner of the bar with his head . . . he was senseless.") Roosevelt had accomplished this amazing transformation of himself and his prospects, he believed, without coarsening himself, without for a moment losing his taste for good books or the company of refined women. Therein lay the moral for all good men who might be tempted to flinch from the rough world of combat. "My plea is for the virtue that shall be strong."

The passage in which these last words appear—from a lecture given on many different occasions—makes it obvious that Roosevelt was not simply addressing American boyhood in general. Drawing on a national myth of masculinity, he nevertheless applied it to the particular circumstances of his own class.

> The worst development that we could see in civil life in this country would be a division of citizens into two camps, one camp containing nice, well-behaved, well-meaning little men, with receding chins and small feet, men who mean well and who if they are insulted feel shocked and want to go home; and the other camp containing robust and efficient creatures who do not mean well at all. I wish to see our side—the side of decency—include men who have not the slightest fear of the people on the other side.

The embodiment of the genteel tradition, Roosevelt reveals himself here as one of its critics as well. We can recognize an echo of his plea for masculinity in politics in the aggressively masculine literature that was taking shape during the years of his presidency—even though Roosevelt himself found the writings of Norris, London, and Dreiser excessive and in questionable taste.

Unless one considers Roosevelt as a spokesman for his own class—a commercial gentry faced with extinction by a new breed of unscrupulous manufacturers and financiers—it is hard to understand the virulence of his attack on the mugwumps, men of his own kind. A crisis in his career occurred in 1884, when the mugwumps tried to persuade the Republican convention to nominate Senator Edmunds, the respectable "independent" from Vermont, in preference to the Plumed Knight, James D. Blaine. Roosevelt and his close friend, Henry Cabot Lodge, can hardly have failed to observe the scorn with which the party regulars greeted this invasion of silk-stocking Eastern prigs, who "had their hair parted in the middle, banged in front," according to Foraker, "rolled their r's and pronounced the word either with the *i* sound instead of the *e*" (a fair description of Roosevelt himself in this period). When the mugwumps bolted to Cleveland after Blaine's nomination, Lodge and Roosevelt made the painful decision to stick with the regulars. The independents denounced them as unprincipled. Roosevelt's unremitting hatred of mugwumpery—unexcelled even by his hatred of populism—dates from this encounter. Again and again he denounces the mugwumps in crude sexual imagery, calling them, for example,

> men of cultivated tastes, whose pet temptations were back-biting, mean slander, and the snobbish worship of everything clothed in wealth and the outward appearance of conventional respectability. They were not robust or strong men; often they felt ill at ease in the company of rough, strong men; often they had in them a vein of physical timidity. They avenged themselves to themselves for an uneasy subconsciousness of their own shortcomings by sitting in cloistered—or rather, pleasantly upholstered—seclusion, and sneering at and lying about men who made them feel uncomfortable.

Repeatedly he urges the forces of decency to rally themselves, to dirty their hands in politics, to marry young and raise large families—lest they be swamped by the immigrant hordes ("race suicide")—above all, to revive the manly art of war. Always mindful of the connections between the "strenuous life" and social conditions in the country as a whole, Roosevelt and Lodge conceived imperialism as a program of moral regeneration, by means of which the ruling class would acquire the courage and ruthlessness needed to govern unchallenged. Addressing a group of businessmen, Lodge tries to overcome their initial reservations about the "large policy" by reminding them that questions of destiny and principle transcend paltry commercial considerations: "Gentlemen, I have seen it constantly stated . . . that we must not deal with anything but business questions. Now, there is a great deal more than that in the life of every great nation. There is patriotism, love of country, pride of race, courage, manliness, the things which money cannot make and which money cannot buy." To be sure, Lodge and Roosevelt also undertook to convince businessmen that imperialism was profitable; but they clearly preferred arguments that appealed to a selfless sense of duty, to the global mission of the Anglo-Saxon race, and to the love of adventure. "The athlete," according to Lodge, "does not win his race by sitting in an armchair. The pioneer does not open up new regions to his fellow men by staying in warm shelter behind the city walls."

Roosevelt and Lodge were not alone, in this period, in articulating a martial ethic or in tying it to the fortunes of their class. Francis Parkman, the Brahmin historian of the West and one of Roosevelt's heroes, had overcome physical disabilities, undergone arduous trials in the wilderness similar to Roosevelt's experience in the Badlands, and made a cult of masculinity, toughness, and pioneering and war seen as forms of class self-discipline. Something of the same syndrome appears in Oliver Wendell Holmes, the jurist: the same self-testing in war, the same military ideal, the same antipathy to reformers and to the mugwumps in particular. Thrice wounded in the Civil War, Holmes came away from it with a lifelong suspicion of causes and crusades combined with a belief in the nobility of the soldier's sacrifice. "The faith is true and adorable which leads a soldier to throw away his life in obedience to a blindly accepted duty, in a cause which he little understands, in a plan of campaign of which he has no notion, under tactics of which he does not see the use." There is a considerable distance between Holmes's skeptical stoicism and Roosevelt's enthusiasm for the Anglo-Saxon "mission," but it is nevertheless clear that both these aristocrats believed in the discipline of war as a regenerative force and distrusted tendencies in their class which they associated with the dominance of "mere" business motives.

The emergence of an upper-class martial ethic in the late

nineteenth century has misled some historians into supposing that men like Roosevelt, Lodge, Brooks Adams, and Mahan were developing a "warrior critique of the business civilization." Roosevelt's actions as President, which consistently favored corporate interests, should alert us to the foolishness of such an interpretation. The importance of the cult of the "strenuous life" is that it helped a provincial élite to transform itself into a national ruling class and to combat certain regressive tendencies within itself—parochial, defeatist, and escapist habits of mind; a distaste for politics; an aversion to imperial adventures. Expansionist in their foreign policy, mildly "progressive" on domestic issues, men like Roosevelt helped to smooth the transition from localism to imperialism and from Manchester liberalism to "political capitalism"—the intervention of the state to enforce order on an anarchic economy. Once the transition was complete, there was no longer any need for Roosevelt's brand of jingoism. Henceforth American imperialism clothed itself in the ideology of Wilsonian internationalism. Its grosser features—racism, militaristic appeals, the rhetoric of heroism and self-sacrifice—dropped away, to be replaced by a new emphasis on efficiency and the modernization of backward countries, ritualistic reassertion of the "right of self-determination," and loud professions of anti-imperialism (well suited to the interests of a nation that came late to the race for imperial spoils). By the time of World War I, Roosevelt had become an anachronism, as was shown by his proposal to raise a cavalry regiment for service in France. He had left his class, however, with vigorous traditions of public service and with renewed determination to impose its will on the nation and the world.

3

MEMBERSHIP IN THE OLDER ÉLITE HAD BEEN DETERMINED AS MUCH by family and "social" considerations as by business connections or even ethnicity. In Philadelphia, according to E. Digby Baltzell, "the inclusion of cultivated Jews within the halls of the Philadelphia or Westmoreland clubs in an earlier day was characteristic of a provincial and familistic age when the men's club was really social, and membership was based on congeniality rather than, as it has increasingly become, an organized effort to retain social power within a castelike social stratum." The new upper class that emerged at the end of the nineteenth century was at once more flexible and more rigid in its admission policies: more flexible, in paying greater attention to money than to family connections (though by no means ignoring the latter); more rigid, in defining itself at least in part through a policy of ethnic exclusiveness. The institutions that now came to play a decisive role in upper-class social life—boarding schools, country clubs, exclusive resorts, Ivy League colleges, the Episcopal church— served two principal functions. They helped to overcome regional particularism by providing upper-class life with common values and a common discipline. They also served to exclude outsiders, particularly Jews, many of whom would have qualified for membership in the upper class on purely economic grounds.

In their eagerness to identify anti-Semitism with populism, historians have paid too little attention to the much more virulent outbreak of upper-class anti-Semitism in the nineties. The "new immigration" from eastern Europe fostered racism in general and anti-Semitism in particular; but the concerted effort to exclude Jews from upper-class institutions suggests that anti-Semitism was by no means directed exclusively against the working class. It seems reasonable to assume that the emergence of a genteel anti-Semitism in this period served the new upper class, in the struggle to overcome its provincial origins, as another means of self-identification.

This assumption is greatly strengthened when we consider that the corporation itself was becoming an Anglo-Saxon ethnic enclave. "Once it became clear that political control of the big cities would inevitably pass into the hands of the immigrant groups, Big Business," according to Moses Rischin, "came to be regarded as a new preserve of the older Americans, where their status and influence could continue to flourish." After 1900 it became increasingly difficult for Jews to find places in business life, particularly since business itself was being rapidly bureaucratized. The corporate bureaucracies readily adapted themselves to the purposes of ethnic exclusiveness because success in the bureaucratic career depends on the accumulation of educational advantages, on family connections, and on other signs of social status. Only in marginal industries still open to entrepreneurial innovation—merchandising, entertainment, mass communications— did Jews and other outsiders manage to secure a foothold.

From the point of view of the new national bourgeoisie, it was desirable to restrict access to business careers not only in order to maintain Anglo-Saxon supremacy but for economic reasons as well—in order to limit competition. By 1900 the merger movement, which had led to the creation of monopolies or near-monopolies in one industry after another, had spent its force. A revival of competition now set in. Because the movement toward consolidation had been dictated by promotional rather than technological considerations, the new combines proved vulnerable to the competition of firms able to operate at lower levels of production and sometimes more imaginatively directed. In the oil-refining industry, Standard's share of the market fell from 90 per cent in 1899 to 80 per cent in 1911 and only 50 per cent in 1921, while that of new companies like Gulf, Pure Oil, and the Texas Company rose correspondingly. In the steel industry, U.S. Steel, created with much fanfare in 1901 and controlling 60 per cent of the market, showed itself to be highly inefficient in many respects. Its profits and dividends declined, and its share of the market fell to 40 per cent by 1920. In general, the number of manufacturing concerns increased by 4.2 per cent from 1899 to 1904 and by 24.2 per cent from 1904 to 1909.

Having failed to eliminate competition through purely economic methods (pools, mergers, reorganization of bankrupt firms, outright industrial warfare), the leading corporations turned to politics, hoping to enlist the federal government on the side of measures designed to enforce "fair competition," to restrict access to industry, and to facilitate further mergers. The drive for a federal incorporation law—one of the favorite measures advocated by corporate reformers during the progressive period—reveals the dominant motives behind the movement. Such a law would have helped to control entry and to eliminate variations from one state to another. Moreover, it would have substituted federal regulation for regulation by state legislatures, many of which were still under Granger and populist influence. As the *Wall Street Journal* put it in 1904: "Now as between governmental regulation by forty-five states and governmental regulation by the central authority of the federal government, there can be but one choice. . . . The choice must be that of a federal regulation, for that will be uniform over the whole country and of a higher and more equitable standard." *Financial America* of New York said bluntly: "The Federal incorporation idea was generally approved by leading corporate and financial interests as a means of affording relief from oppressive State legislation and nullifying the obnoxious features of the Sherman anti-trust law."

Federal regulation, it was hoped, would also force smaller competitors to meet certain standards. In the meat-packing industry, for example, standards were so low that in the 1880's most European countries banned the importation of American meat, much of it diseased. J. Ogden Armour explained why the larger packers supported the Meat Inspection Act of 1905. "No packer can do an interstate or export business without Government inspection." The Food and Drug Act of 1905—another "progressive" measure—resulted from similar pressure from larger firms in the food industry. In the lumber industry, some of the larger companies wished to prevent indiscriminate cutting by smaller competitors; their agitation was one of the sources of the conservation movement. Progressivism, often depicted as a popular uprising in the tradition of populism, was in large part a response to corporate demands for "efficiency"; and although in some cases the movement was undoubtedly directed against real abuses, as in the packing industry, its overriding objective and result was to enhance the position of firms already dominant and to limit the activity of small entrepreneurs.

A parallel movement in the professions—notably in law and medicine—led to the passage of state licensing laws and, in response to objections that state regulations lacked uniformity, to the creation of centralized machinery of certification; for example, the National Board of Medical Examiners, established in 1916 and supported by a grant from the Carnegie Foundation. Here too the dominant voices in the drive for uniformity and regularity claimed to be protecting the public against quacks and charlatans—echoing Armour's insistence that federal inspection offered the public *"insurance* against the sale of diseased meats"—but the most important effect was to drive out marginal elements, solidify the control of the chief certifying agencies, and give to the professions the monolithic structure they have retained ever since.

4

COMPLEMENTING THE MOVEMENT TOWARD CENTRAL CONTROL OF business and professional life—a control exercised by the corporations and professions through their political representatives—was the growth of "scientific management." In part, the theories of F. W. Taylor and his followers merely served to rationalize efforts to extract an ever-greater surplus from the work force— a glorified speed-up. What was new and important about scientific management was that it revealed a determination, on the part of the more enlightened and progressive employers, to master the practical details of production and thus to free themselves from dependence on the technical competence of their workers. Introduction of the factory system had not altogether abolished the techniques of handicraft production. Many of these survived within the factory, and the workers accordingly retained some control over production, supervising the organization and even to some extent the rhythm of their own work. The capitalist only gradually acquired the technical knowledge necessary to oust the workers from control; in the process of doing so, he had to overcome habits of indifference and neglect and to learn to regard business as a profession in its own right, requiring the intervention of trained experts. The founding of graduate schools of business administration and the growth of such specialized fields as personnel management testify to the changing outlook of many employers, as a result of which they succeeded at last in making themselves masters in their own plants.

Capitalists also had to overcome their antipathy to trade unionism in any form. Only after severe struggles within the business community did the more forward-looking corporate spokesmen succeed in winning sizable support for the view that unions were a stabilizing influence in industry, capable of channeling class bitterness into orderly negotiations for higher wages and better working conditions. Organizations like the National Civic Federation played a leading part in this propaganda, holding up trade unionism as an alternative to socialism. The triumph of Gompers's "business unionism" within the AFL lent plausibility to these claims. Many employers remained unconvinced, however, as is shown by the anti-union campaign of the 1920's; and it was not until the thirties that most businessmen grudgingly conceded the inevitability of unionism.

Changing attitudes toward management and toward labor organizations were part of a much more general ideological reorientation. Classical liberalism no longer served the high bourgeoisie as a workable ideology. Free trade, laissez-faire, and rugged individualism ill suited the needs of a social order based on corporations, unions, and organizations of all kinds, in which the pleasant fiction of a self-regulating economy had become untenable. American liberalism, if it was to survive as an appealing doctrine, needed to cut loose from its Jeffersonian origins and to adopt what might be called a neo-mercantilist approach to problems of state policy. This drastic surgery on the body of liberalism was performed by a number of skilled practitioners— the leading theorists of the progressive movement. To place liberalism on a sounder doctrinal basis was the intention, for example, of Herbert Croly in his enormously influential book, *The Promise of American Life,* published in 1910 and almost immediately translated by Theodore Roosevelt into an effective political slogan, the "new nationalism."

Croly's turgid prose covered a simple, not to say simple-minded, formulation of American history, giving it an air of profundity highly appealing to superficial readers. Treating American politics as a continuing dialogue between the Hamiltonian and Jeffersonian traditions, Croly argued for a fusion of the two while confessing that his own preferences lay "on the side of Hamilton rather than of Jefferson." He admired Jefferson's democratic sympathies but distrusted his "amiable enthusiasm." He distrusted Hamilton's aristocratic proclivities but admired his intelligence, his tough-mindedness, and his understanding of the need for strong central power. In a combined version of the two traditions, Croly wanted the Hamiltonian thread to predominate. After years of drift, the country needed mastery.

Walter Lippmann made a similar plea for planning and control in *Drift and Mastery*. His *Preface to Politics,* with its references to Freud, Bergson, and Sorel, shows how liberal theorists, attempting to bring liberalism into accord with modern reality, drew on continental traditions of thought that were often critical of bourgeois society, adapting them freely to their own purposes. Lippmann avails himself of psychoanalysis in order to provide the governing classes with more effective techniques of social control. Particularly interesting is his appropriation of the scathing critique of bourgeois decadence formulated by Georges Sorel. Ideas that were originally advanced in order to demonstrate the need for socialism are now enlisted in the service of bourgeois self-reformation. In the same way, liberal theorists searching for a more viable political economy often turned in this period to the socialist tradition, not in order to transcend liberalism but in order to rescue it from total bankruptcy. Lippmann, Croly, and Walter Weyl—the third founder of *The New Republic,* which became the leading organ of the new liberalism—all flirted with socialism at various points in their careers, while retaining an underlying commitment to liberalism.

The most penetrating and original theorist of the liberal revival was Thorstein Veblen. The fact that socialists have claimed Veblen's work for themselves suggests its complexity (though it also suggests the degree to which socialists have themselves accepted the technocratic emphases of neo-liberalism). *The Theory of the Leisure Class,* published in 1899, satirized upper-class futility, reducing all aspects of bourgeois culture to status mechanisms allegedly designed to satisfy a boundless craving for display, "notoriety," and "repute." Subsequent books elaborated on what was essentially an "attack on culture," in the words of T. W. Adorno, Veblen's ablest critic. According to Veblen, the leisure class, with its grotesquely dysfunctional culture, was increasingly out of touch with modern production and with the skeptical, scientific, "iconoclastic" habits of mind that were required to operate the industrial plant. An inevitable process of historical "evolution" had already made the capitalists obsolete (only "cultural lag" prevented knowledge of this from becoming general); and their place would soon be taken by those who actually ran the machines—the workers, led by an élite of scientifically minded engineers and technicians.

As C. Wright Mills has shown, Veblen's work rests on a naïve equation of technological indispensability with political power. It also incorporates a thoroughgoing functionalism typical of American sociology in this period—typical, indeed, of many other areas of American thought, reappearing in different form in the philosophy of instrumentalism, in progressive education, and in the modernist movement in architecture. Frank Lloyd Wright criticized disfunctional leisure-class styles in Veblenian terms. The progressive educators attacked the very concept of a cultural tradition and tried to base education on the "needs" of children, as somehow defined by themselves.

It is enough to suggest the shallowness of Veblen's critique of the "leisure class" to remind ourselves of a point made earlier in this essay—that a decisive step in the history of the American ruling class was precisely its refusal to become a leisure class at all. Itself sharing Veblen's functionalism, his horror of leisure, and his suspicion of intellectual culture, the "leisure class" rejected the possibility of making culture its vocation and threw itself with renewed vigor into practical life. In its revolt against leisure, it could have appropriated much of Veblen's critique, in order to formulate a managerial and technocratic version of liberalism, in the same way that Lippmann appropriated Bergson and Sorel. Not that Veblen himself became an upper-class hero and received handsome rewards for his services. On the contrary, he was harried out of academic life, became increasingly bitter and cynical, and took to calling himself a socialist. The question is whether Veblen's work can best be considered, half a century later, as belonging to a critical tradition of social thought that is hostile to corporate liberalism or as a contribution to the renewal of liberalism. Without denying either its idiosyncrasy or its genuine difficulty, we can now see that Veblen's thought fits in very well with the dominant currents of neo-liberalism: a functionalist view of society; faith in technology and "scientific method" applied to industry, politics, and government; an uncritical professionalism (such as underlay Veblen's critique of the university); exaltation of managerial over entrepreneurial methods of business; a belief in central planning by experts; efforts to secure a more "cooperative" society while leaving control of production in private hands.

5

EVEN BEFORE HE ANNOUNCED HIS "NEW NATIONALISM" IN 1912, Theodore Roosevelt had proved receptive to the "progressive" demands advanced by businessmen and other advocates of reform. His administration, as noted, instituted regulation of the drug, packing, and railroad industries. The appointment of Gifford Pinchot as chief forester not only gratified the supporters of conservation but embodied the principle of professionalism in government, Pinchot having trained himself in forestry at Yale and in Europe. (Nor is it irrelevant to note that he came from an old and distinguished Pennsylvania family.) A series of informal understandings with various business interests assured them of immunity from antitrust actions. It was Taft's discontinuance of this system of unofficial "détentes," together with his dismissal of Pinchot, that provoked Roosevelt to seek renomination himself and to launch a third-party campaign when it was denied him, thereby assuring the election of Woodrow Wilson.

In the exciting contest between the "new nationalism" and the "new freedom," Wilson seemed the more conservative of the two progressive candidates with his talk of restoring competition and free trade. In office, however, he abandoned his enthusiasm for antitrust suits in favor of a program of centralized regulation serving the interests of a newly nationalized bourgeoisie that had come to recognize in the federal government an alternative to the "anarchy" of state regulation. Remote from popular pressures and controlled in many of its operations by a self-perpetuating administrative élite, the national government had become a powerful ally of the industrial oligarchy and an indispensable support of the corporate system. When the United States entered the world war, the Wilson administration was able to institutionalize the system of corporate planning that had been emerging as an unofficial policy under Roosevelt; and although business interests shortsightedly destroyed much of this machinery after the war, it served a few years later as a model for the New Deal.

Similarly Wilson's enlightened internationalism, taking the place of the unabashed imperialism of the Rooseveltian variety, laid the basis of New Deal diplomacy, in which the United States attempted to create a stable world order in the name of the "four freedoms," self-determination, the rights of man, and other liberal slogans. The transformation of the ruling class was completed under the second Roosevelt. Absorbing and civilizing the new captains of industry, the nineteenth-century commercial élites had overcome their provincial origins, successfully combatted the temptation to become a leisure class, and reorganized themselves as a national ruling class, equipping themselves with an updated version of liberal ideology in the process.

All this represented a formidable achievement—the real achievement of the so-called progressive era. It is important to recognize, however, that it was a limited achievement even on its own terms. Leaving aside the price that the country as a whole had to pay for the continuing ascendancy of the industrial bourgeoisie, even its sympathizers would have to admit that its successes in this period were by no means unqualified. For one thing, its own understanding of events was imperfect. The delusion that it was acting in the common good was not itself remarkable—other ruling classes have shared the same delusion—but the refusal even to admit the class nature of American society seriously weakened the industrial élite's ability to preside effectively over that society. Its political spokesmen consistently maintained that "we do not have 'classes' at all on this side of the water," as Theodore Roosevelt once put it.

Neither Roosevelt, Wilson, nor FDR knew any economics; they were only dimly aware of the momentous changes taking place around them, which their own policies helped to facilitate. The first Roosevelt, regarding himself as an impartial mediator among conflicting interests, believed that he was able to discipline the corporations at will, when in fact they manipulated him for their own purposes. His attitude toward mergers was inconsistent and arbitrary: he allowed U.S. Steel to absorb its chief competitors in 1907 but denied Standard Oil the same privilege, and could explain his policy only by insisting that U.S. Steel was a "good trust" and Standard a "bad" one—an elusive distinction. Roosevelt's presidential campaign of 1912 was so heavily indebted to the Morgan interests, not only in its financing but in its very conception, that Amos Pinchot with some reason explained the whole business as a Morgan plot, with Roosevelt as an unwitting accomplice. As Presidents in a time of radical changes, Roosevelt and Wilson were in a position to interpret these changes to the public and to ease the transition from a primitive capitalist state to a highly organized and rationalized industrial order; instead of which, their public pronouncements were extraordinarily vapid even by the standards of American politics. In the end, both these men were overwhelmed by events; there is a certain poignancy to their last years, in which they struggled without success to understand why history had so rudely shoved them aside.

Unwilling to recognize the existence of classes or the degree to which liberalism itself was rooted in a system of class power, the spokesmen of the new liberalism were equally evasive about the relation between business interests and expansionist foreign policies. They seldom gave explicit expression to the economic content of expansionism, appealing instead, as we have seen, to the mystique of national regeneration or to high-sounding legalistic abstractions. Only a vulgar Marxist would argue that this evasiveness was itself a consummate piece of mystification contributing to the long-range success of the corporate bourgeoisie. A workable ideology must not only justify the claims of the ruling class but provide a coherent and convincing explanation of reality. The failure to admit into public discussion the fact of class or the economic basis of political power—except occasionally in the form of crude conspiracy theories of politics—meant that neo-liberal ideology contained a large admixture of unreality, just as the corporate system itself retained many irrational features.

It does not seem entirely unreasonable to suppose that the weaknesses of upper-class ideology bore some relation to this class's general indifference to cultural questions. Lacking any real aristocratic tradition, the American "aristocracy" had little understanding of the need to establish centers of culture or to support a cultural establishment of national scope that could unify a heterogeneous population and give direction and clarity to the national life. The upper-class conception of culture was essentially promotional—intellect and the arts being seen chiefly as means of advertising the "advantages" of particular localities (to which industry might be attracted) or more generally, the upper class itself. Lacking a center and focus, the intellectual life of the progressive period remained chaotic and unformed, its major achievements the work of brilliant but erratic iconoclasts whose thought was never assimilated into an intellectual tradition or successfully popularized. The founders of *The New Republic* set out quite deliberately to remedy these defects without understanding their origin; like the group of writers and critics around *The Seven Arts,* founded in 1916, they were attempting to invent a public tradition of culture in a country where the absence of such a tradition was so complete that its absence was not even noticed. Their failure meant that politics remained blandly "pragmatic" and public discussion feeble and banal, confusing class interests with private gain, seldom acknowledging what people knew privately, concerning itself with portentous trivia.

ALTERNATIVES TO LIBERALISM

[VIII]

Is Revolution Obsolete?

I

PROBABLY NO OTHER WORD HAS BEEN MORE ABSURDLY INFLATED BY the debasement of political language than "revolution." Even if we eliminate the more obviously fraudulent uses—in which its appearance alerts us precisely to the absence of important change ("revolutionary new styles in swimsuits"; "revolutionary advances in pollution control")—we are still left with many different kinds of counterfeit. Such phrases as "the world-wide revolution of modernization," such allegations as that "in advanced industrial societies, permanent revolution is a fact," deceive us doubly; first by assimilating the idea of revolution to the category of any "unintended, incoherent change" extending over a long period of time, and second by prejudging an important issue about which it is essential to make no *a priori* assumptions at all: Are modern times really revolutionary? or is modern society in some ways remarkably resistant to change?

Let us define revolution, quite conventionally, as an attempt—sometimes successful, sometimes unsuccessful—to seize state power on the part of political forces avowedly opposed not merely to the existing regime but to the existing social order as a whole. This definition has the advantage of distinguishing revolution, not merely from deep and sudden change in general, but more specifically from the *coup d'état* on the one hand and from rebellion on the other. A *coup d'état* is not necessarily revolutionary, since those who carry it out may have no quarrel with the existing order, proposing merely to overthrow "the rule of the politicians" and to run the existing machinery in a more forceful manner. This applies not only to reactionary generals but also to fascists and other "revolutionary" right-wingers, even though the latter may have strong popular support. Rebellions, on the other hand, can express deep social antagonisms and even class conflicts; but they do not become revolutionary so long as they confine themselves to attacks on feudal overlords, the police, or other agents or symbols of oppression. Revolution is a direct attack—not necessarily violent—on the state.

Revolution is a phenomenon of relatively recent times (although it may be already obsolescent). It is associated with the emergence of nation-states. The same centralization of economic and political life that made possible the modern state also exposed the state to revolutionary attack from below. The very strength of the state, its command of a centralized network of political and judicial institutions, proved to be a source of weakness, in times of crisis, particularly since the new administrative bureaucracy often had its center in the capital city of the realm— a vast but delicate organism dependent for its existence on supplies from the surrounding countryside and, more generally, on regular communications with the entire nation. Barrington Moore, Jr., has recently called attention to the close relation between this vulnerability of the city, in societies still overwhelmingly agrarian, and the creation of the revolutionary urban mass, which in turn—as the studies of George Rudé and others have begun to demonstrate—has played a central role in so many modern revolutions.

Twentieth-century radicals, including Marxists, have tended to minimize the importance of the revolutionary crowd in bringing on the final spasms of the state. Louis Boudin, in *The Theoretical System of Karl Marx,* ridiculed those "who imagine the great revolution as the work of a hungry and desperate mob driven to distraction and the destruction by the immediate lack of work, food and shelter." It is true that no mob ever made a revolution. A commonplace of historical analysis is that utterly desperate people lack the will to contemplate or to carry out an attack on the fundamental institutions of society. Moreover, social change on such a scale presupposes a revolutionary class—as distinct from a mass—with an ideology and culture of its own that it perceives to be threatened or hemmed in by the existing order. Without such a class, closely tied to production but radically alienated from existing social and political structures, even a collapse of the state does not necessarily lead to revolution; it may only lead to its replacement by a more efficient regime presiding over a reformed version of the old order. Bread riots do not provide the infallible signal that a revolutionary crisis is at hand. All the same, it is hard to imagine a modern revolution without them. The "hungry mob" may not constitute a revolutionary class, but it provides the troops for class warfare, and "the immediate lack of work, food and shelter" therefore cannot be ignored as an indispensable element of the revolutionary situation—at least as we have known it in the past.

In the same essay in which he calls attention to the vulnerability of the city as a factor in the classic European revolutions, Moore distinguishes another type of revolution characteristic of recent upheavals in backward countries. Here the state is attacked not at its center but on its periphery. Through protracted civil and guerrilla warfare, the revolutionary forces, which can survive for long periods of time because they control and even administer parts of the realm, gradually erode the state's capacity for repression and eventually defeat it. This distinction between urban revolutions in Europe and peasant revolutions in Asia, Africa, and Latin America seems somewhat overdrawn, however, for a number of reasons. In the first place, civil war has also been a feature of the major European revolutions, and usually for the same reason that explains its prominence elsewhere. A successful revolution or a revolutionary movement seemingly on the point of success usually invites the intervention of foreign powers bent on re-establishing the status quo. The French had to defend their revolution against the combined monarchies of Europe, just as the Chinese Communists in our own time have had to defeat the Japanese, and the Vietnamese the United States.

It is possible, moreover, to exaggerate the importance of events in the capital city, in contrasting "urban" revolutions in Europe with peasant revolutions elsewhere. Recent studies of the French Revolution have disclosed a great deal of revolutionary activity in the provinces as well. In seventeenth-century England, the revolution eventually succeeded, in part, because the Puritans had established a secure territorial basis in outlying parts of the country, notably in East Anglia.

Moore stresses the importance, in non-European revolutions, of the revolutionaries' ability to function as an alternative government in those parts of the country that they militarily control. Once again, something of the same pattern can be seen in many European revolutions. Before the Jacobin seizure of power in France, the Jacobin clubs had already begun to exercise many of the functions of local government. The same thing is true of the Russian soviets or, for that matter, of the committees of correspondence in the eighteenth-century British colonies of North America. To be sure, this usurpation of governmental functions by revolutionary organizations is not precisely the same thing as the establishment of liberated areas in recent peasant revolutions. In both cases, however, the revolutionary movement grows because it effectively supplants the state in parts of its jurisdiction.

Even the distinction between urban and rural types of revolutions can be overdrawn. It is probably true, as Moore contends, that during the first wave of modern revolution—which embraced England, America, France, all of western and central Europe in 1848, Paris in 1870, and Russia in 1905–17—the principal source of revolutionary energy came from the urban masses (except in the case of England); while the second wave—China, Algeria, Cuba, Vietnam—reflects the dominant influence of the peasantry. Yet the latter revolutions are no more exclusively rural and peasant movements than the former were strictly urban. Eric Wolf suggests that "peasant" revolutions owe much to "the development of an industrial work force still closely geared to life in the villages." This observation would seem to apply also to the earlier revolutions and abortive revolutions in Europe. E. P. Thompson's work on the English working class demonstrates that in the early nineteenth century the most radical elements in English society were those workers, often artisans, who still retained a lively memory of the village past and consciously appealed to pre-industrial traditions in their agitation. There is reason to think that the same pattern can be found in other European countries undergoing the initial stages of industrialization.

Both European and non-European revolutions, in short, seem to have had a number of things in common, and it may be possible to formulate generalizations broad enough to embrace both. Allowing for national and cultural variations, one might view revolutions in general as a type of historical event peculiar to societies still predominantly rural and pre-industrial, in which traditional social relations, however, are subject to severe stress by the commercialization of agriculture, the introduction of new modes of industrial production, and the centralization of political authority. These changes throw peasants off the land in great numbers, proletarianize many of those who remain, bring about the destruction of artisans as a class, and produce sharp divisions in the ruling class itself. They also create new classes, notably the bourgeoisie and the industrial working class; but these elements, although they furnish leadership and ideology to revolutionary movements and although in the last analysis their presence may account for whatever is progressive and democratic in modern revolutions, do not appear to give them their main impetus. It is the older classes, still rooted in traditions of pre-industrial paternalism but directly exposed to the withering blasts of change, that have given to modern revolutions their explosive power, particularly those strata—"middle peasants" and artisans— whose position in the old order was fairly secure. I find highly suggestive Moore's remark, in *Social Origins of Dictatorship and Democracy,* that revolutions are set in motion not by emerging classes but by classes over whom the wheel of progress is about to roll—classes doomed to extinction partly by the very revolutions they set in motion.

Revolutionary movements articulate new ideas of liberty and equality, but these ideas, it would seem, are rooted in traditional, pre-industrial ways of life. Revolutions are directed against powerful states that have arisen on the ruins of seigneurialism but have not yet perfected the methods of repression and control available to the industrial state. In this transitional stage of its development, the state has achieved a sufficient degree of centralization to render it vulnerable to attack, without achieving anything like the awesome power, both military and ideological, wielded by advanced industrial states today. A further source of the weakness of early modern states is their authoritarianism. Even in Europe, where parliamentary forms had made some headway during the later Middle Ages, the early modern state, as exemplified by the Stuart regime in England and the Bourbon regime in France, ruled not so much through civil institutions—church, schools, courts, parliaments—as through the direct imposition of bureaucratic authority and military force. The same thing is true, to an even greater degree, of right-wing dictatorships in modern China, Vietnam, and Cuba. An important result of this underdevelopment of civil society and authoritarian state control is that opposition to the state and to the existing order—indeed, opposition of any kind—has to take revolutionary form. Absolutism almost inevitably nourishes a revolutionary negation of itself and forces the state to rely more and more on naked force, thus undermining its own pretensions to divine right or, in the end, to any other form of legitimacy.

2

THE FOREGOING CONSIDERATIONS HELP TO EXPLAIN WHY THERE HAS never been a revolution in an advanced country. Industrial society has not eliminated poverty, but it has eliminated the hungry mob as a force in history. The industrial working class no longer constitutes a revolutionary proletariat. Neither does the so-called new working class of clerks, bureaucrats, technicians, and intellectual workers, even if we could agree to call these groups a working class at all. The industrial state represents a far greater concentration of military power than its predecessors.

It rules, moreover, not through force alone but through an elaborate network of civil institutions. Opposition movements, instead of being driven underground, are permitted and even encouraged to struggle for control of these institutions; accordingly, they become reformist rather than revolutionary in character. Through its control of mass communications, the ruling class coopts dissident styles of culture and politics and identifies them with its own version of the good life. Pre-industrial paternalism, which provided an alternative model of community during the early stages of industrialism, survives as a faint memory only in the urban "culture of poverty" and in isolated backwaters of the western world.

Nor does the culture of the ruling class contain elements subversive of itself, as was the case during earlier periods of Western history, when revolutionary movements could appeal not only to the legacy of paternalism but to ideals of human dignity and freedom implicit in ruling-class ideology itself. One of the most important developments of recent years is that the ruling class in advanced countries has largely outgrown its earlier dependence on general culture and a unified world view and relies instead on an instrumental culture resting its claims to legitimacy, not on the elaboration of a world view that purports to explain the meaning of life, but purely on its capacity to solve technological problems and thereby to enlarge the supply of material goods. The ruling class has abandoned its own humanist traditions, which once served not merely to legitimize its own pretensions but, paradoxically, to nourish alternative social visions. As a result, advanced capitalist society, at the very moment it has laid the material basis for a socialism of abundance, more than ever appears to represent, in the eyes of those who live under its sway, the furthest limits of social development.

For all these reasons, revolutions of the traditional type seem a remote possibility in industrial society. Yet the revolutionary tradition persists and exerts a powerful attraction on the left. How is this persistence, in the face of repeated discouragements, to be explained?

In the course of the nineteenth century, and particularly after the failure of the Paris Commune, the socialist movement gradually ceased to regard the insurrectionary seizure of power as the inevitable and proper goal of radical activity. In its earlier stages the movement consciously modeled itself on French revolutionary examples. By 1900, however, it had largely abandoned hope of overthrowing capitalist society by means of a direct assault on the state. Meanwhile the partial democratization of political life opened up the possibility of achieving socialism through trade unionism and parliamentary politics. This does not mean that socialists had come to agree on every detail of strategy and tactics, or even on fundamental issues. Revisionists like Bernstein argued that capitalism had overcome its "contradictions" and that therefore, in effect, socialist objectives could be achieved within capitalism; orthodox Marxists like Eugene Debs, on the other hand, took the position that capitalist institutions would have to be destroyed before socialism could become a reality. But not even the latter any longer advocated the destruction of state power through a frontal assault or questioned the importance of an electoral strategy. They ridiculed the view, still popular among anarchists and other ultra-leftists, that capitalism would end in "a sudden crash" and, indeed, they went so far as to argue that "this cataclysmic conception of the breakdown of capitalism," as Louis Boudin put it in 1907 (in a book largely devoted to an attack on revisionism), "is not part of the Marxian theory." The socialist movement had evolved, in short, from communism to social democracy, but social democracy had not yet become identified exclusively with timid reformism. Many social democrats retained a commitment to revolutionary objectives even after they had implicitly abandoned the revolutionary strategies deriving from early modern revolutions. The latter, they correctly perceived, were based on social conditions that had ceased to exist—ceased to exist, at any rate, in western Europe and the United States.

World War I and the Russian Revolution profoundly altered the history of the socialist movement. The major social democratic parties' capitulation to the war discredited social democracy, while at the same time, the Russian Revolution gave the insurrectionary tradition a new lease on life. The more recent revolutions in China, Vietnam, Cuba, and Algeria have developed ideologies and institutions appropriate to the problems of predominantly agrarian societies, while the social democratic movements have continued to degenerate until in recent years they have become outright accomplices of imperialism disguised as a world-wide crusade against Communist "totalitarianism." The early twentieth century had seen promising steps toward a theoretical synthesis of the insurrectionary and social democratic traditions, particularly in the works of Antonio Gramsci. These efforts, however, have come to nothing. As a result, the socialist movement finds itself lacking either a theory or a practice appropriate to the realities of advanced industrial society. The most militant elements cling to an antiquated theory of revolution, while the rest have embraced the Democratic Party, the Labor Party, or their continental equivalents.

The collapse of traditional socialism has left contemporary theorists of revolution with equally unsatisfactory alternatives. Some cling to the hope that the industrial working class will still become a revolutionary force, once the socialists have rescued it from the toils of bourgeois ideology. In practice this theory usually leads to attempts to impose correct socialist doctrine on the workers and to force the workers' problems into a socialist framework that does nothing to clarify them—a framework, indeed, that often requires socialists to ignore the real problems of the working class (such as the workers' demand for "law and order") on the assumption that the workers themselves, indoctrinated by the capitalist media, incorrectly perceive the true situation. Since they place such high priority on a "correct" interpretation of "objective conditions," theorists of the proletarian revolution spend much of their time in factional disputes among themselves, and the tedium of these doctrinal disputes further alienates the working class from socialism.

Another approach seeks to rescue the idea of revolution from irrelevance by dissociating it from the traditional view that socialism can emerge only from the struggles of the proletariat, and by pointing instead to new classes or groups that allegedly have developed revolutionary potential. This feat is difficult to manage, however, without stretching the term "revolution" out of all resemblance to its original meaning or else exaggerating the revolutionary consequences that are likely to flow from the activities of blacks, students, and intellectuals. Those who seek substitutes for the proletariat argue that while the working class has ceased to play a revolutionary role, new social groups are ready to leap into the breach—in particular, blacks and students. They contend that "the blacks demand revolution," but in fact the black community is far from united in demanding any such thing. Even blacks who regard themselves as revolutionaries do not agree among themselves, let alone with white radicals, about what they mean by revolution.

In addition to the blacks, students and professionals are often described as a revolutionary force. In the case of students, this conclusion rests more on wishful thinking than on careful analysis. A large minority of students, and possibly even a majority on a few campuses, may well sympathize with radical attacks on the university or with aspects of those attacks. The attacks themselves, however, are seldom revolutionary, whatever the accompanying rhetoric. Most student demands can be accommodated without altering the structure or content of higher education. Writers on the student movement are able to make a case for its revolutionary potential only by drawing a labored analogy between the university and the corporation, which enables them to equate the position of students in the university with that of workers in General Motors or International Harvester. But students do not work for the universities in the sense that auto workers work for General Motors; blacks and youth "are useless classes [that is, they are economically superfluous] having little to contribute to economy and society." After their graduation, to be sure, they go to work—not in most cases for the university but, directly or indirectly, for the corporations—as technicians, functionaries, bureaucrats, teachers, and welfare workers, and of course also as professionals. This fact does create the possibility that the university and university politics might come to play an important role in the development of a new kind of "working-class" consciousness; but the student movement, in spite of its revolutionary pretensions, has so far not provided a clear and explicit analysis, or incorporated this analysis into its practice, of the situation created by the unprecedented importance of the "knowledge industry" in advanced industrial society. In the student movement of the sixties, demands for "student power" played a far more prominent part than their intrinsic importance warranted. They were advanced under the double illusion that students constitute a class in their own right and that the demand for student power is therefore similar to the demands of industrial workers for a share in the powers enjoyed by management.

A third group often seen as potentially revolutionary is the professional stratum. In one respect this theory is quite different from the theory that students will provide the backbone of the revolution, since it tries to locate the source of revolutionary energy not in a group's detachment from industrial society but, on the contrary, in discontents that are nourished by unsatisfactory conditions of work. This theory recognizes that professionals forced to put their talents at the service of war, "urban renewal," and other socially destructive programs may lose their self-respect or else begin to question the validity of a system that forces them to use their professional training in this way. The needs of professionals, like the needs of the working class in general, are increasingly ill-served by a system that depends on war and waste for its survival, thereby generating uncontrollable material and spiritual disorder. It does not follow, however, that professionals are becoming revolutionary in the traditional sense; and if we spend our time trying to detect signs of this, we may miss seeing things that are much more important though not necessarily revolutionary, such as the growing dissatisfaction of doctors with the AMA and of lawyers with the existing structures of the legal profession. Here again a revolutionary perspective can blind us to changes that are already in motion or tempt us to force these changes into an analytical mold that obscures their real significance.

3

THE ISSUE OF "LAW AND ORDER" HAS RECENTLY BECOME PROMINENT in national and local elections. Instead of seeking to understand its origin, many radicals—along with most of the liberals— interpret the need for order as incipient fascism. They argue that productive workers are so strongly committed to the existing industrial system that they will gladly opt for fascism to preserve it. Not only does this view confuse a commitment to order and economic security with a commitment to capitalism as such, but it seems to imply, when coupled with an analysis that insists on the revolutionary potential of blacks and students, that economic expendability alone can serve as a basis for revolutionary discontent. From this we can only conclude that any revolution likely to occur in advanced countries will be, by definition, a minority revolution imposed on the rest of society by a self-appointed vanguard whose economic superfluity liberates it from "false consciousness."

In the face of such analysis it is necessary to insist that unless a movement for change enlists the active support of the great majority, it is unlikely to accomplish anything that would be recognizable as democratic socialism. This means, among other things, that the student movement will have to transcend its character as a student movement and forge links with those who work in the main institutions of industrial society. Whether it does this has become one of the most important political questions of our day. If it is to succeed, the movement will not only have to abandon the obsolete Leninism that various factions have embraced for lack of a better theory, it will also have to abandon those attitudes and postures of the new left that betray its upper middle-class origins. I have in mind particularly those attitudes that have led so many radicals to confuse the search for personal "authenticity" with the search for cultural alternatives to capitalism, and to define personal liberation, moreover, as freedom from work-discipline and from authority in general. The trouble with this definition of the "cultural revolution" is that it tends to divert attention from work to leisure, thereby reinforcing one of the strongest and most dangerous tendencies of advanced capitalist society—the attempt to compensate for the meaninglessness of work by holding out the possibility of spiritual fulfillment through consumption. Contrary to a widespread cliché of popular sociology, "the challenge of leisure" is not the most important issue in advanced society. The most important issue remains work—the loss of autonomy on the job, the collapse of high standards of workmanship, the pervasive demoralization that results from the mass production of goods that are widely recognized as intrinsically worthless by those who produce them, and the general crisis of a culture historically oriented around the dignity of labor. As temporary members of a leisure class, students do not experience any of these evils directly; and because students tend to be drawn, moreover, from the more affluent sectors of society, they are likely to be attracted to political and cultural perspectives that define liberation, in effect, as the creative use of leisure or, worse, as the search for ever more sophisticated, shocking, and "radical" styles of consumption in sex, drugs, culture, and politics.

As prospective workers, however, students do experience the many-faceted crisis of work, and it is not only their enforced leisure but also the knowledge that they are being trained for meaningless work that underlies their rebellion. In addition, much of their academic training is itself meaningless, either because it has no recognizable relation to the process of qualification for work or because it makes so few demands on the critical intelligence. Exploration of these issues might serve as the initial steps toward building a genuine student-worker alliance, based on an awareness that intellectual workers, like other workers, are victims of the social processes that have proletarianized workers in general by reducing even intellectual work to a set of disconnected processes that not only offer no satisfaction in themselves but lead to socially disastrous results.

One of the major tasks confronting the left is to show how the urban crisis and the more general "environmental crisis" originate in capitalist production. Agitation around ecological issues, if these issues were properly explained, would help to create a common consciousness of deprivation among students, workers, and members of the "new middle class" by showing that the industrial system victimizes *everybody*—except the very rich, who can provide themselves with means of escape from the environmental devastation their own policies have brought about. Pollution, noise, congestion, violence, crime, the physical and moral destruction of the city in the interests of developers, the ravaging of the landscape, suburban sprawl, and the deterioration of the schools have created widespread fear, resentment, and anger in the working and middle classes; but this anger, instead of venting itself against the corporations, too often finds secondary targets—the blacks, liberals, radical students, "bureaucracy," "government interference." The left then misinterprets the symptoms of popular resentment as incorrigible racism, devotion to the status quo, and proto-fascism, and writes off the working class and new middle class as reactionary. Instead, the left should be trying to demonstrate that the deterioration of the environment and the collapse of public service, which people experience most acutely in their capacity as consumers and citizens, must be attributed not to the blacks or to the state but to the corporations and to a system of production that has outlived its economic and social utility. Deprivations and anxieties experienced as community issues, in other words, or as a generalized misery that seemingly defies class analysis, must be shown to have their origin in the realm of work and in the class relations that arise from the existing system of production.

I think it is misleading to imply, however, that a mass movement for change will not emerge until the kinds of tensions and strains now experienced chiefly by students become generalized throughout the population—that is, until the population as a whole experiences "the irrelevance . . . of ideologies based on scarcity." This assumes that capitalism itself is capable of generalizing affluence. It also assumes that the working and middle class have at present no interest in social change, whereas in fact they suffer from a whole variety of fears and anxieties that might even attract these classes to socialism if they could be convinced that socialism meant something more than a search for "a less repressed, more human, more spontaneous life-style." The so-called cultural revolution identified with one wing of the new left contains many promising possibilities, but in its present form it does not represent an alternative social vision capable of attracting large masses to its support. In saying this, I do not mean to align myself with those who argue that cultural questions are secondary and that the cultural revolution will have to wait for the political revolution. On the contrary, I believe that cultural questions are central to any movement for socialism. But the "counter-culture" of the sixties denies the possibility of satisfaction through work and envisions utopia as generalized leisure, thereby reaffirming, instead of contradicting, the vision of industrial society itself—one that it cannot realize but which it holds up as the highest good, in the face of centuries of experience that have taught us that work is one of the deepest of man's needs. The cultural task confronting the left is not to overthrow the work ethic, which is already under attack from within capitalist society, but to invest it with new meaning. The left has not yet addressed itself to that question.

One of the reasons for this failure is the influence of an obsolete revolutionary tradition on leftist thought and action. The persistence of that tradition either obscures the importance of cultural questions altogether by encouraging the illusion that a revolutionary seizure of power, at some unspecified point in the future, will automatically usher in the golden age; or else it encourages radicals to define the cultural problem in purely negative terms, as an all-out assault on "middle-class" values. The revolutionary tradition effectively conceals the fact that in most modern revolutions, the overthrow of the old regime took place only after alternative patterns of culture had established themselves side by side with the dominant ones. (Where this did not happen, as in Russia, the revolution ended in a cultural disaster.) The new cultures themselves, furthermore, drew heavily on older values which the ruling classes were in the process of gradually discarding. In our own time, the ruling class has broken the last ties to its own cultural traditions and has imposed on society a technological anticulture characterized by its ruthless disregard of the past. The agent of the new anticulture is the bulldozer, which destroys familiar landmarks, liquidates entire communities, and breaks down every form of continuity. Under these conditions the idea of revolution as a sharp, sudden, and total break with the past loses the meaning it had in societies on which, for all their restless movement, the past still lay as a dead weight. "Revolution" today may represent, among other things, the only hope of preserving what is worth preserving from the past, including man's natural habitat itself; but if that is the case, it is time that the nineteenth-century idea of revolution is drastically revised or abandoned altogether.

[IX]

The Professional Revolutionary: Erikson's Gandhi

G andhi's Truth, EVEN MORE BRILLIANTLY THAN ITS PREDE-
cessor, Young Man Luther, shows that psychoanalytic
theory, in the hands of an interpreter both resourceful
and wise, can immeasurably enrich the study of "great lives"
and of much else besides. With these books, Erik H. Erikson has
single-handedly rescued psychoanalytic biography from neglect
and disrepute.

The early practitioners of the method, including Freud himself, used it almost exclusively to debunk and deflate. Erikson
understands that to reduce illustrious men to their symptoms
explains everything except the one thing that most needs to be
explained—their greatness itself. He has made this problem the
central focus of his biographies and thereby produced works as
subtle, delicate, evocative, and allusive as the early models were
clumsy and one-dimensional.

To have restored psychoanalysis to intellectual respectability,
not only among biographers but among social scientists generally, would alone have established Erikson as one of the
outstanding exponents of psychoanalysis now writing. In a series
of other works, meanwhile—on youth, identity, culture, and
many related subjects—Erikson has begun a major reorientation
of psychoanalysis itself. Breaking with the rigid determinism
according to which the personality takes its final shape during

infancy, he has insisted on the importance of later experience and especially of the "identity crisis" so often experienced by people in their late teens or early twenties. His concern with questions of identity has led Erikson in turn to consider the role of culture in shaping identity as well as the role of identity crises in great men as an influence on the history of culture.

Almost from the beginning, psychoanalysis has sought to become a theory of society as well as a therapy for individuals. Most psychoanalytic theorists have been unsuccessful in leaping from the biographical to the historical without sacrificing the precise insights derived from clinical practice in favor of vague and empty speculations about history and pre-history—Freud himself setting a bad example with theories like that of the "primal horde." Erikson's ideas, however, rest on the solid footing of clinical encounters. The concept of the identity crisis, drawn from careful observation and practice, serves as the basis from which Erikson has launched remarkable investigations of the religious temperament, of the problem of generations, and—especially in his recent work—of the need for "a new ethics" as the only alternative to the existing philosophical chaos.

Gandhi's Truth consists of a psychological reconstruction of Gandhi's early years in Kathiawar on the Arabian Sea and his years of exile in London and South Africa, followed by a detailed analysis of the strike of textile workers in Ahmedabad in 1918, in which Gandhi first put into practice his own variety of militant nonviolence or Satyagraha.

With great care Erikson traces the unfolding of a "precocious and relentless conscience," laying special stress on the way in which Gandhi's nursing care of his aging father, a civil servant whose health and career were both declining during his son's youth, not only served to conceal the wish to replace the father but set the pattern "for a style of leadership which can defeat a superior adversary only nonviolently." He examines the effects on Gandhi of his premature and in many ways disastrous marriage, which left him with a horror of sexuality but which also made impossible the monastic retreat to which his developing religiosity might have led. In Gandhi's case the quest for saint-hood therefore had to take political form.

As for "the event" itself—the textile strike over which Gandhi assumed leadership—it serves Erikson as an exploratory and therefore unusually interesting exercise in nonviolence, a "revolutionary kind of human ritualization." The strike ended in an ambiguous and inconclusive victory for the workers but this is perhaps less important than the remarkable discipline and courage they displayed in the course of their struggle—qualities that persuaded Gandhi that "dharma ['wider propriety within one's total fate,' in Erikson's words] had not vanished from India, that people do respond to an appeal to their soul."

On the strength of this material—the richness and almost inexhaustible suggestiveness of which cannot be conveyed in a summary—Erikson proposes a number of conclusions. Space permits us to deal with only one; the assertion that Satyagraha—"truth-force"—represents "a better and more expeditious way of righting wrongs," in Gandhi's words, than other forms of political action. Unlike the others, Satyagraha seeks to cure men of the "righteous and fanatic moralism" that is the major source, in Erikson's view, of irrational violence.

Moreover, it is the only politics that instead of dividing men seeks to reconcile them (while at the same time pursuing revolutionary objectives) and thus contributes to the struggle for "more inclusive identities"—the sense of mankind as a single species instead of a collection of mutually hostile subspecies. It does this by recognizing the humanity of the adversary and by seeking to shame him rather than to exterminate him—for instance, by forcing him to act in ways inconsistent with his own ideals of decency and honor. The objection that nonviolence can only work against adversaries that already possess highly developed standards of decency—that it is useless, for instance, against fascists—misses the point, since according to Satyagraha, decency is latent in all men as part of their very humanity. To decide in advance that certain adversaries are incapable of decency is therefore to accuse them of inhumanity and to fall into precisely that arrogant moralizing from which Satyagraha proposes to deliver us in the first place.

A much more important question is whether nonviolence represents the only political escape from moral arrogance. This question takes on new urgency at a time when the American left has largely abandoned nonviolence for a neo-Leninism that is the quintessence of "righteous and fanatic moralizing." It is fortunate that Erikson has chosen this moment to confront us with so fresh and compelling a restatement of the case for nonviolence. Violence as such, however, may be a false or at least a misleading issue. Gandhi himself wrote, in the aftermath of the Ahmedabad strike, that most of his followers had taken up nonviolence not from a consciousness of their own dignity and strength but "because they were too weak to undertake methods of violence." For a time he decided that "we shall not be fit for swaraj [home rule] till we have acquired the capacity to defend ourselves." "This new aspect of nonviolence," he added, " . . . has enmeshed me in no end of problems."

What these reflections suggest is that the political choice lies not between violence and nonviolence but between the disciplined use of force, free from bloodthirsty moralizing, and irrational riot. Erikson rules out the Western revolutionary tradition as an alternative to nonviolence, partly for the good reason that it has too easily allied itself with cold-blooded violence and terror, but partly because he mistakenly assumes that revolutions are invariably violent. In fact they tend to degenerate into irrational violence only when a self-chosen "vanguard" of professional revolutionaries tries to impose its will on the majority.

This leads us to the most interesting point to emerge from Erikson's book—one that incidentally helps to explain why large-scale outbreaks of violence have so often followed nonviolent campaigns both in India and in the United States. While Gandhi was implacably opposed to Leninism, he was at one with Lenin (without realizing it) in believing that struggles for change have to be led by professional revolutionaries. In Gandhi's case, this belief took the form of the demand that the true

Satyagrahi abstain from sexual relations. "A passive resister," according to the Mahatma, ". . . can have no desire for progeny."

What this means in practice is a leadership that has cut itself off from "generativity" and "householdership," to use Erikson's terms, and from all the daily concerns connected with the maintenance of life. For this reason it is essential, according to Erikson, that nonviolence no longer remain restricted to ascetics and practical saints; "for the danger of a riotous return of violence always remains at least latent if we do not succeed in imbuing essential daily experiences with a Satyagraha-of-everyday-life." It is not likely, however, that a politics in which an exalted ideal of personal heroism plays so large a role can ever become genuinely popular or, indeed, even ought to become popular. "Your duty," Gandhi wrote to an unfaithful follower, "lay in honouring [your commitment to the movement], even if your entire family were to starve in consequence." A movement that finds it necessary to use such language is élitist almost by definition, and even though it may attract a mass following among the weak and oppressed, that following can easily turn to irrational violence if its expectations are too rudely disappointed.

In asking for a Satyagraha-of-everyday-life, Erikson would seem to be demanding a contradiction in terms. Nevertheless his proposal has enormous value, because it exposes the crucial weakness not only of the nonviolent tradition but of the revolutionary tradition as well—their common failure to root revolutionary action in the everyday "maintenance of life." On one level Gandhi dealt wisely with this problem and commands our continuing attention, for as Erikson points out, he was always "cautious in leaving intact ancient fundaments for which he had no immediate revolutionary alternatives." The problem for Western radicals is to combine this wisdom, together with Gandhi's insistence on the humanity of one's adversaries, with a revolutionary practice that does not depend for leadership on "vanguards" of the elect. Otherwise nonviolence itself can become a form of moral arrogance as pernicious as any other.

[X]

After the New Left

AN INTERMINABLE WAR IN INDOCHINA; THE REVOLUTIONARY MOVE-ment elsewhere in disarray; the American left fragmented and driven onto the defensive; Nixon acting belatedly but with apparent success to disarm his opponents; public services in decline; the quality of public discussion lower than ever; demoralization and drift on every side—the political scene has seldom looked more dreary. Only a few years ago the glacial rigidity of American politics appeared to be breaking up. Even habitual pessimists proclaimed a "great thaw." Columbia, Paris, the dumping of Johnson seemed so many proofs that the diverse strands making up the new left had finally coalesced as a movement, a political force.

Now it appears that the new left, even in the moment of its apparent triumphs, had already passed the peak of its influence. The Chicago convention was an end rather than a beginning. The nomination of Humphrey and, even more important, the smooth handing on of the war from a Democratic to a Republican administration showed how limited was the left's capacity to influence national events; while the government emerged from the turmoil of 1968 slightly shaken but capable of carrying on a hateful war, of intimidating or outflanking its critics, and even—as recent events have shown—of acting with decisiveness and imagination.

The collapse of the new left became unmistakable in 1969 with the split in SDS, the emergence of the Weathermen, and the virtual disappearance of the antiwar movement. The Chicago trial, the Spock case, the Berrigan affair, and the harassment of the Panthers forced radicals on the defensive and obliged them to expend their energies on self-preservation. Meanwhile the assassination of Martin Luther King and Robert Kennedy removed the foremost leaders of an aspiring liberal resurgence, while the failure of the McCarthy campaign solidified the defeat of left-leaning liberals.

Throughout the sixties, there had been a reciprocal relation between Kennedy liberalism and the new left, easily overlooked by radicals who insist that the left thrives on repression. If the radical opposition widened the space available to respectable dissent and forced some establishment politicians to the left (the growing radicalism of Robert Kennedy himself being the clearest example), it is also true that the new left was helped into being in the first place by the new sense of expectancy introduced into American politics by John F. Kennedy, whatever his intentions, and kept alive by his brother. The advent of Nixon, Agnew, and Mitchell coincided with the dissipation of the moral energies of the black movement (briefly revived—a last gasp—after the death of King), the collapse of the antiwar movement, the sudden decline of campus militancy after Cambodia, and the spread of a new mood of uncertainty and resignation.

The degree of its dependence on the surrounding political environment reveals the failure of the American left to develop an autonomous life. The new left either refused or was unable to learn much from its predecessors, even from their mistakes, and in the end paid heavily for its indifference to the past. Conceived in many ways as a direct repudiation of the old left, it rejected not only the dogma and sectarian factionalism of the old left but whatever might have been gained from a more sympathetic understanding of its history. Too often the new left confused dogma with ideas and tried to live without them, preferring pure intentions to clear thinking. When it turned out after all that the movement needed an "analysis," many elements of the new left embraced Marxism in its most rigid and sterile forms, or third world revolutionary doctrines quite inapplicable to the United States, and began to engage in sectarian polemics as pointless and trivial as those of the 1930's.

The absence of continuity in American radicalism—in American life generally—made it possible for the radicals of the sixties to discover all over again the existence of oppression and exploitation, the power of the ruling class, and the connection between capitalism and foreign wars. In their excitement, they quickly proceeded from reformist to revolutionary ideas, not only leaving most of their followers behind but glossing over a host of difficulties—both tactical and theoretical—that were inherent in the adoption of revolutionary goals. It should at least have been treated as an open question whether classical conceptions of revolution, deriving from a conjunction of historical circumstances not likely to recur, have any meaning in an advanced industrial society. A major theoretical problem for the new left was precisely to work out a new conception of social reconstruction, in other words to formulate new ideas about revolution itself instead of being content with unanalyzed images from the past. In the absence of any real analysis of the concept or its applicability to contemporary American life, "revolution" quickly became the emptiest of clichés and was used indiscriminately by radicals, liberals, conservatives, advertising men, and the media, usually to describe changes that were nonexistent.

Useless as the word soon became, it had important effects on those who continued to take it seriously. Consider its influence on the antiwar movement. As soon as the leaders of the movement realized that the Indochina war could not be attributed simply to diplomatic bungling but had roots in the social structure of advanced capitalism (roots which have yet, however, to be fully explained), they began to insist that this recognition be immediately embodied in the movement's practice. This at least seemed to be the intention of the much-publicized transition "from dissent to resistance," announced in 1966–67, although it was not always clear whether this slogan implied an escalation of strategy or merely more militant forms of civil disobedience. (Even in the latter case, however, the almost unavoidable tendency was to justify new sacrifices by the announcement of revolutionary objectives.) In any case, "from dissent to resistance" was a misleading slogan for a movement that would continue to depend on "dissenters" for much of its effectiveness. Even as a tactic, "resistance" led the antiwar movement into attacks not only against the war but, increasingly, against the entire apparatus of military-corporate domination both at home and abroad, while at the same time the adoption of an "anti-imperialist" perspective unavoidably narrowed the movement's ideological appeal and its base of support. A dangerous dispersion of energies followed from decisions made by the antiwar movement in 1966 and 1967—decisions that arose not so much from calculation of their political consequences as from the need to make an adequate response to the rising militancy of the young, to the agony of the choices confronting men eligible for the draft, and to the atrocity of the war.

The history of the student movement in many ways paralleled that of the antiwar movement, if indeed their histories can be disentangled. After the student left discovered the university's links to the war machine and the corporations, it needed to develop an analysis of higher education that would simultaneously explain why the university had become the center of opposition to the war. An analysis that treated the university simply as an agency of oppression could not explain why so many students had apparently resisted brainwashing and consistently took positions more critical of American society than those taken by other citizens. The problem confronting the student movement was to expose and attack the university's "complicity" in war and exploitation without forgetting that it was precisely the relative independence of the universities (or, more accurately, of the colleges of arts and science), together with the fact that they were at least formally committed to values directly counter to those of industrial capitalism, that made them a good ground on which to fight.

The adoption of revolutionary points of view did nothing to clarify these issues. It encouraged on the one hand a misplaced class analysis of the university itself, in which student "proletarians" confront a ruling class made up of administrators and faculty, and on the other hand a preoccupation with the "real" problems outside academic life, especially those of the working class, which led student activists to abandon the attempt to reform the university and in many cases to leave academic life altogether. These positions, however much they differed from one another, shared an unwillingness to confront the difficulty of explaining the university's relation to society or the relation of students to the class structure as a whole. Were students to be regarded as future members of an oppressive bourgeoisie, whose defection from this class and rejection of "bourgeois life styles" therefore constituted the first stage of the "cultural revolution" called for by Abbie Hoffman? Or were they apprentices to a new kind of technical intelligentsia, in which case student rebellion might be considered, in Norman Birnbaum's phrase, as an anticipatory strike of the work force? These questions concealed an even more fundamental issue: Had the class structure of industrial society changed in such important ways as to render much of traditional Marxism obsolete? The inability of the "Marxist" left to answer these questions helps to explain the rapid growth of a left based on youth culture, on "liberated life styles," which at least takes a clear position in favor of the first of these hypotheses, and which is prepared to interpret even a change of costume as a "revolutionary act"—thereby reducing the complexities of revolutionary action to an absolute minimum.

"Marxism-Leninism" had something of the same effect on the Black Panthers as it had on SDS. It widened the split between political and cultural radicals. It also widened the split between liberals and the left, although in the case of the black movement this split had already become irreconcilable by 1966 and was precipitated not by the adoption of explicitly revolutionary objectives but by the revival of militant black nationalism.

The advocates of black power did not at first regard themselves as revolutionaries. For some time they remained indifferent to socialism or Marxist ideology. Their criticism of the civil rights movement went deeper than anything that could be summed up in the formula "revolution vs. reform." They attacked the whole idea of integration as a social goal. Arguing that the genuinely distinctive features of the culture of American blacks had been wholly overlooked by the civil rights movement, they held up, by implication, the goal of a culturally pluralistic democracy in place of the homogenenized society toward which civil rights agitation seemed destined to lead. In some ways their conception was similar to the vision of a "transnational America" advanced by Randolph Bourne and other cultural radicals during World War I and later taken up by the Harlem renaissance.

The idea of cultural pluralism was, to be sure, only a single strain in the movement for black power. The movement also split from the civil rights movement over tactical issues: expulsion of whites, willingness to use violence. By insisting on the connection between black politics and black culture, however, the advocates of black power broke decisively with the civil rights movement and the liberalism of the early sixties (which regarded culture as a matter of private choice, hence as something falling outside the domain of politics), while at the same time anticipating many of the themes of the later new left. Unfortunately, the black power movement did not succeed in working out a political program that incorporated its insights into black culture. Self-determination for the ghetto was all too clearly exposed to the criticism that it would perpetuate poverty under a more dignified name. Without an adequate politics, cultural nationalism tended to lapse back into political quiescence and into the religious fantasies from which, among other sources, it had originally sprung.

The political activists, on the other hand, in the process of distinguishing themselves from "reactionary" cultural nationalists like Ron Karenga, tended to lose sight of cultural issues altogether. The Panthers' "revolutionary nationalism" provided a purely verbal resolution of the difficulty. Even the political ideas of the Panthers, which at first promised to unite elements of the Marxist tradition with a recognition of the need for decentralization and "community control," degenerated into a vague summons, reminiscent of the late thirties and early forties, for a "united front against war and fascism," as the exigencies of self-defense forced the Panthers into an alliance with elements of the old left.

"Left politics," Michael Miles writes in his interesting book, *The Radical Probe,* "abhors an ideological vacuum." When the makeshift radicalism of the early sixties proved incapable of giving strategic direction to the movement, it gave way to "Marxism-Leninism," the most easily available leftist ideology. Old leftists emerged from their obscurity and offered ideological advice. It did not matter that they themselves were rudely repudiated; the prestige of their ideological tradition overcame generational barriers. By the late sixties, two varieties of Leninism had emerged—an old-fashioned economic determinism mindful of "objective conditions" and stressing the need (as Progressive Labor contended) for the left to place itself under the guidance of the proletariat, and an extreme voluntarism that treated revolution as a pure act of will and never tired of intoning the meaningless slogan of Che: "The duty of the revolutionary is to make the revolution." The adherents of the two positions, equally addicted to a belief in the decisive role of political vanguards, contended for mastery of what remained of the left. Bored or repelled by their polemics, the new left constituency broke into fragments—"new politics" people, peaceniks, Catholic anarchists, feminists, Trotskyists, cultural radicals of one sort or another. The revolutionary fervor of the later sixties had raised the usual euphoric expectations which, subsiding, left a familiar residue of disenchantment. Cultural and political radicalism, briefly joined in a period of rising political hopes, split apart, the political radicals increasingly absorbed in their ideological pronouncements, the cultural radicals denouncing all politics as a snare and a delusion.

Deprived of its political basis, the youth "culture"—the vaguely defined revolt against affluence still led, insofar as it is led at all, by Jerry Rubin and Abbie Hoffman—has turned sour and ugly, even as it spreads downward through the generations. Very young adolescents—precocious fugitives from respectability, prematurely hardened tramps and migrants—are now appropriating the forms of cultural revolt, but with little understanding of the political content which formerly gave to the rebellion of youth such moral power as it had. Long hair, ragged clothing, rock, drugs, a contempt for the authority of the past—these persist as the outward trappings of alienation but are emptied of their political core. The claim of alienated youth to represent society's embattled conscience is correspondingly diminished. Formerly the uneasiness and disgust with which the liberal middle class confronted the youth culture was tempered not only by a wish to believe, as good Americans, that idealism and moral purity are always on the side of youth, but by the undeniable seriousness underlying the movement, which manifested itself as political courage. To many young people today, however, the risks once associated with radical action seem to have gone for nothing; even the very recent past appears remote and "irrelevant." The political struggle appears lost—has already, in fact, become incomprehensible—and in its place appears a new cynicism and toughness, a suspiciousness extending even to brothers, and a casual acceptance of crime and violence —feebly justified as "ripping off the system"—as a means of survival. These tendencies are naturally strengthened by the willingness even of many middle-class liberals to countenance severe repression, as the moral claims of the youth culture grow more and more attenuated. Desperate and bitter, brutalized by drugs and police, the youth culture sinks into the underworld and becomes increasingly indistinguishable from the lumpenproletariat.

There are signs, however, that many of those who were demoralized and disoriented by the collapse of the political left and the degeneration of the cultural revolt—including some of the cultural radicals themselves—are once again finding their way back to political action. Some of the academic dropouts have returned to school, with the hope of changing the professions from within. Having tried to survive as independent activists or intellectuals, they are rediscovering the importance of institutional ties. Professional work and organizations turn out to be not purely imprisoning; they also provide some minimal support for the creative use of one's talents, together with the necessary fellowship of one's peers. Nor are the professions completely closed to innovation, as many radicals had supposed. The old guards are still entrenched, but the number of dissidents is growing.

All the professions, even medicine, are in ferment. Ralph Nader has uncovered among young lawyers an unexpected devotion to public concerns. Young architects are challenging urban renewal, young teachers the stultified schools. Biologists and physicists are debating whether they have an ethical obligation to concern themselves with the uses to which scientific discoveries are put. So far little has come of all this; two or three years ago, indeed, it would have been dismissed as well-meaning reformism. Revolutionary rhetoric, however, though it still thrills the media, no longer commands the terrified respect of the left, the revolutionaries having all too obviously failed to revolutionize even their own lives. Besides, many of the present-day reformers are themselves former revolutionaries, graduates of SDS, and cannot be intimidated or impressed by the ostentatious display of revolutionary manhood. They have no illusions about reform, but neither are they without hope. Is it possible that these stirrings in the professions foreshadow a more general movement of people at their work, trying to turn their work into something at once more satisfying and less deleterious in its social effects—a new kind of labor movement?

2

WHETHER THE PRESENT COLLAPSE OF THE LEFT SIGNIFIES THE BEGINning of another long interlude of political stagnation—an interlude American society can scarcely afford—or whether it proves to be only a temporary setback depends in part on whether we can assimilate the experience of the sixties and profit from it. We need sober historical guidance to these events. In place of that, publishers offer a flood of books on student rebellion, the "counter-culture," "the black revolution," and woman's liberation —books more or less indistinguishable from one another in the haste with which they are thrown together, in the shrillness with which they compete for attention, and in their inability to say anything that is not already worn from overuse.

In the midst of this inconsequential outpouring, a handful of books—Michael Miles's *The Radical Probe,* Michael Walzer's *Political Action,* Saul Alinsky's *Rules for Radicals,* Robert A. Dahl's *After the Revolution?*—distinguish themselves from the others by their modesty and by a quiet assumption that the age of radical politics is not over—and that therefore there is still much to be learned from the recent past. Except for Miles's *The Radical Probe,* these books do not directly address themselves to the radicalism of the sixties, but every one of them has been deeply affected by it. Because their authors, with varying degrees of deliberation, have tried to absorb the events of the past decade, these books implicitly raise questions of historical interpretation and force an attentive reader to make his own assessment of the period. Yet they do not cater to the fashionable interest in radicalism; nor do they strike radical poses.

Miles's book is by far the best account of student radicalism to have appeared. The author, a young Berkeley-trained historian, not only provides a convincing explanation of the roots and development of the student movement (including some neglected aspects of the black student movement), he discusses and rejects official interpretations of its origin, dissects the official liberalism on which these interpretations are based, and places the conflict between student radicalism and official liberalism within the larger antagonisms in industrial society.

The student movement, Miles argues, is neither a generational revolt, an expression of youthful alienation, nor the product of permissive child rearing. Radical students often share their families' values; "alienated youth and radical youth are distinct, not identical groups." The former are more likely to be drawn to cultural rebellion, which Miles regards as a species of pseudo-radicalism living vicariously off the achievements of technology and echoing "the dominant order's confidence in 'automation' and 'technology,' even as it disassociates itself from them in rural communes."

Still less can the new left be understood as a movement of technologically obsolescent intellectuals. Zbigniew Brzezinski's theory that intellectuals are "historical irrelevants" who "will have no role to play in the new technetronic society" is shown by Miles to rest on a vulgar technological determinism and on "the unstated assumption . . . that in the 'technetronic age,' technicians are the men of power." On the contrary, he argues, it is still generalists, not specialists, who wield power. "Managers, not technicians, dispose of technical resources; while politicians, not their advisors, make political decisions." As for the intellectuals, expansion of higher education and the growth of an educated mass constituency, which is at least potentially amenable to their influence, assures them, in Miles's judgment, of a larger role than ever before.

Behind the assumption that student intellectuals belong to a displaced class Miles detects a larger assumption, namely, that the United States has become what is variously described as a post-industrial, post-scarcity, cybernetic, or technetronic society. It is essential to his argument that the fraudulence of such theories be exposed. Miles accomplishes this not only by showing that power has by no means shifted from the owners and managers of property to the technicians, but by challenging the belief—shared by the technocrats and the cultural radicals alike—that automation has eliminated the need for work. The current rate of increase in productivity per man hour "is not higher than the rates of other periods of industrialization. Automation does not represent a rise in the rate of technological change so much as an increase of productivity in new fields outside heavy industry." The service sector of the economy, in particular, has been growing far more rapidly than the agricultural and manufacturing sectors—especially government, which increasingly supplies not only welfare but "the infrastructure of capitalist development," and education, which now accounts for 6 per cent of the gross national product. The "knowledge industry" as a whole—the part of the economy that, "broadly defined, has to do with the production and distribution of information and knowledge," including data processing and "research and development" as well as education—accounts for 30 per cent.

Here lie the origins of student rebellion, according to Miles. "The student movement is a product of the industrialization, under capitalist forms of organization, of new areas of human enterprise: education, knowledge, and culture among them." The need of government and the corporations for research and development—especially in military technology and counter-insurgency—and for large numbers of trained technicians and professionals has led to an unprecedented expansion of higher education. It does not matter that much of the training offered by the university is demonstrably irrelevant to the jobs for which students are being trained. The university retains a monopoly of certification, and increasing numbers of people are therefore obliged to pass through it in order to qualify for work.

In the course of its expansion, the university has come more and more to be operated on industrial lines. Its service functions take precedence over teaching and scholarship. Financing is assumed by the state. "As less faculty time has been available for teaching and the quality of the effort has declined, [the universities] have employed industrial solutions: high inputs of educational technology and the sweat labor of graduate teaching assistants." The student body becomes increasingly heterogeneous, and the sense of a university community gives way to "an educational 'city' with more subcultures, ferment, and personal options but also with more impersonality and less loyalty to the central administration." The administration itself grows into a many-headed monster, effectively controlling the new "conglomerate university" through the budget while encouraging faculty illusions of autonomy. (Miles thinks that latent opposition between faculty and administration, hitherto softened by growth, will become manifest in the academic depression of the seventies, which will cruelly expose the faculty's lack of power.)

The enormous growth of the university and of the knowledge industry transforms old institutions and creates the possibility of new political alignments, but it does not therefore signify the transition to a new form of social organization. "This is not post-industrial society; it is super-industrial society." Miles argues that the student movement must be understood as a protest against the industrialization of higher education—more specifi-cally as a protest against deteriorating conditions of work in the "knowledge factory." This last interpretation requires us to con-sider students as apprentices for technical and professional work. Miles is not altogether consistent on this point; at times he regards them as consumers—a highly misleading analogy, I think.

The student movement has so far, in Miles's view, been led by "a critical, left-oriented intelligentsia," and has taken the form of an ideological war between intellectuals and mandarins—"the scholarly and technocratic professionals." Professional and even technical students have occasionally been drawn into the move-ment, however, especially when it has raised the issue, however tentatively, of whether intellectual workers are to control the conditions of their work and the uses to which it is put. Archi-tecture students occupied Avery Hall during the Columbia uprising; at MIT, scientists and science students organized the research stoppage of March 4, 1969. The professional and techni-cal students—a new middle class in "embryo"—are the natural constituency of the student movement, according to Miles. The movement has a "symbiotic" relation to this new stratum. Al-though neither student radicals nor their families are rooted in it, many radical students are bound for careers in teaching or some other sector of the knowledge industry, and the underly-ing issue raised by the student rebellion—control of that indus-try—is of special concern to technicians and professionals.

"The most profound question concerning the future of the student movement is whether it portends the emergence of a radical movement in other sectors of the population." Miles understands that this depends on how deeply radicalism penetrates into the new middle class and whether that class is able to make effective alliances with "the new working class, the oppressed minorities, and such progressive elements of the blue-collar working class as may appear." He does not underestimate the obstacles to radicalism among professionals and technicians, of which the most important is the habit of specialization and the bureaucratic outlook usually associated with it. On the other hand, the industrial system's need for the carefully controlled production of knowledge means that increasing numbers of intellectual workers will face declining autonomy, regimentation, and loss of status. A diminishing proportion of them will reach the higher levels of the technical élite. Many will sink to the level of the intellectual proletariat, swelling the already growing numbers of teachers, low level civil servants, public employees, and clerical workers, among whom there have already been signs of labor unrest, as in the stirrings among young schoolteachers against city bureaucracies and their own unions. Their common subordination to bureaucratic control may overcome the many barriers between the professional and technical strata and the new working class, bringing into being a new labor movement.

Miles does not stress the point, and I am here extrapolating from his argument, but it is important to recognize that such a labor movement would bear little resemblance to traditional unionism. It would not demand the improvement of working conditions in the narrow sense; it would demand control of the intellectual "product" by the producers themselves.

Whether the student movement becomes the basis of a new labor movement depends in considerable part, according to Miles, on whether student radicalism overcomes the influences that have recently crippled it—dogmatic Marxism, infatuation with the traditional working class, terrorism, chic cultural protest. Deploring dogmatism and posturing, Miles nevertheless insists on the "ideological dimension" of student protest—an aspect of the movement that many of its friends have tried to minimize. One of the signs of current political exhaustion is a renewed distrust of ideology. As we shall see, this distrust runs through all the other books under consideration. Many observers would regard the ideological element in student protest as regrettable and unnecessary; Miles regards it as central. In his judgment, the underlying seriousness of the student rebellion reveals itself nowhere more clearly than in the conflict between a technocratic and managerial ideology on the one hand and the ideology of the radical intelligentsia on the other—mutually exclusive views of the world which, indeed, postulate the historical extinction of the adversary. Just as Brzezinski regards the intellectuals as "historical irrelevants," so the left-wing intellectuals hope to eliminate the technocrats as a class. It is just because it has an ideological dimension, in Miles's view, that student rebellion may portend a larger movement, "since there is not the slightest possibility of the left organizing these social forces [the new middle class, new working class, etc.] without a systematic alternative vision which first identifies these progressive social forces in its analysis and then appeals to them in its social content." An ideology in this sense is inseparable from the search for a constituency and serves not to encourage but to check the left's propensity for fantasy.

Miles's analysis of the student movement raises a number of general questions that will be discussed in the course of this essay. In summarizing the arguments advanced in *The Radical Probe,* I have unavoidably presented a somewhat schematic picture of the book, particularly of Miles's use of concepts like the new middle class and new working class—the limitations of which he himself seems to be fully aware of. These concepts have been taken over by the more intelligent wing of the American left from C. Wright Mills and from radical French theorists like Serge Mallet, André Gorz, and Alain Touraine. When these social groupings are treated at a high level of abstraction and assimilated to established categories like "middle class" and "working class"—categories that have fairly definite empirical content—an impression of concreteness and precision can be produced that belies the highly amorphous quality of these new "classes." At the present stage of empirical knowledge about advanced industrial society, the use of such terms represents a drastic simplification of reality. The superficiality of theories of "post-industrial society" ought to warn us of the dangers of the sort of instant social analysis that is becoming more and more prevalent on the left as well as among technocrats. At the same time, the complexity of the existing class structure should not become an excuse for rejecting theoretical speculation of any kind.

3

MICHAEL WALZER'S BOOK, CAREFULLY AND DELIBERATELY CONFINED to a discussion of tactics, reflects the current disenchantment with ideology and diminished expectations of what political action can accomplish. In spite of his caution, however, Walzer has written a useful essay. Even though it concerns tactics rather than substantive issues facing the left, in its own way it is another attempt, by one who took part in the civil rights and antiwar movements, to understand the meaning of the recent past and to draw practical conclusions from it.

Walzer's milieu is the world of "citizen politics"—of meetings in living rooms and church basements, of petitions, canvassing, and marching, into which normally quiet men and women, temporarily forsaking their well-ordered private lives, are drawn by indignation and "concern." Walzer believes that amateur politics is the only way to save the country from the disasters wrought by professionals, but he recognizes its principal limitation: this kind of politics is ephemeral and lacks deep roots in the life of the community. Because people pursue "citizen politics" only at their leisure, influence and leadership tend to gravitate to those who have plenty of free time, together with the patience to endure interminable meetings—that is, to "people who are marginal to any particular local community."

Citizen politics stands in marked contrast to "established political parties and labor unions which are essentially associations of adult males rooted in their communities." Nor does the disproportionate role played by women—who do have strong community ties—compensate for this tendency, since the women too often play subordinate roles, as in everything else. Marginal types, particularly upper-class college students, wield an influence out of proportion to their numbers or to the soundness of their political ideas, overawing and intimidating the others by their radicalism or driving them away in desperate boredom.

Moreover, it is an unfortunate characteristic of amateur movements that the people likely to be attracted to them, finding themselves for the first time plunged into political action and newly conscious both of injustice and of the strength of the forces apparently attempting to perpetuate it, fall easy victim to sweeping ideologies.

> Once a man has taken a stand on a particular issue, he is tempted to take a stand on every issue. One thing leads to another; everything interconnects. He is pressed toward a total ideological position; he yearns for intellectual coherence, unity, completion . . . a total view of political life [which] . . . can be expressed, politically, at meetings, marches, and demonstrations, in those stark slogans whose loud reiteration is a hallmark of sectarian militancy and a hostile act against the unbelieving world.

This passage indirectly but accurately describes the experience of a considerable segment of the antiwar movement.

In order to counter the exaggerated influence of militancy, Walzer advocates "plain speech" and the semi-professionalization of amateur politics. If movement workers were paid for their time, ordinary citizens could take a more active part, and discipline would improve. The movement should try to earn money rather than beg for it. Fund raising "enables large numbers of people to express their support for the movement in ways that also utilize their everyday competence"—thus "a successful auction, book fair, or bake sale is a (minor) triumph for peace, integration, women's rights, socialism, or whatever: so many people are doing something and not merely waiting for the Revolution." This passage illustrates the strength of *Political*

Action—its understanding of the need for radicals to respect the plain facts of everyday life—but also shows the limits of Walzer's political imagination. Leaving aside the demotion of socialism, itself an all-encompassing theory unavoidably productive of "ideological" disputes, to the level of another political cause, one can surely draw on people's "everyday competence" in more interesting and important ways than by involving them in bake sales. Walzer's eminently sensible and sometimes acute perceptions of tactical problems are tied to an extremely narrow conception of political strategy, all too evidently derived from the early phases of the peace and civil rights movements and from "reform" Democratic politics. Walzer seems to be asking us to return to these modes, characteristic of the fifties and early sixties, without asking himself the question that will surely be asked by historians of the period: If this kind of politics held out any promise, why was it supplanted by the more militant radicalism of the mid-sixties? Walzer's impatience with the histrionic and suicidal tendencies of the new left prevents him from seeing that the movement was a response, after all, to a genuine historical need, the demonstrated failure of polite reformism: the failure of the peace movement to end the cold war or to prevent Vietnam, the failure of the civil rights movement to achieve racial justice, the failure of reform Democrats to reform the Democratic Party.

To be sure, we must not belittle the real though minor achievements of these movements; we should not expect change to be sudden and total; above all, we should not leap from their failures to the conclusion that it is "no longer possible to work within the system." But an awareness of these dangers does not justify an attempt to return to the politics of the early sixties as if nothing had happened in the meantime. To treat the radicalism of the later sixties as simply a prolonged mistake, from which only negative lessons can be drawn, is to miss what now emerges as its most interesting feature—the new left's groping toward a new political strategy in which reformist tactics are used to promote objectives that go beyond conventional reformism and are informed by a vision (unfortunately not yet a very coherent one) of alternatives to the existing structures within which, nevertheless, political action has to take place.

Walzer dismisses hope of revolution as a delusion—rightly, I think, if revolution means a traditional seizure of state power. But he assumes that this leaves us with only electoral and pressure group politics: "I am inclined to think that there are no other kinds." He does not consider the possibility that the student movement may point to a third type of politics—a politics that aims to change the structures of powerful institutions by challenging prevailing modes of work. His conception of "citizen politics" achieves a necessary realism and modesty by excluding in advance questions that are likely to give rise to "ideological" disputes, but nevertheless have to be confronted by any movement hoping to bring about real changes. His argument needs to be taken further than he is willing to take it. If the object is to bring movement politics closer to everyday life, doesn't this suggest that the movement needs to identify itself more closely with people's work? The dangers of marginality and super-militancy seem to be attributable in large part to the fact that people engage in citizen politics only in their spare time. Amateur politics, therefore, becomes preoccupied with the ways in which industrial society impinges on people in their capacity as householders, members of neighborhoods, parents, and consumers. The job stands off to one side (as it does in our social life itself); amateur politics appeals to "citizens," not workers.

By no means do I intend to suggest that the alternative lies in a revival of trade union strategies, such as is currently being advocated by certain doctrinaire Marxists under the guise of spreading "revolutionary consciousness" to the working class. Trade union politics excludes almost everything of importance, demanding higher wages and better working conditions for auto workers, for example, without asking about the social consequences of the unlimited production of automobiles. Wage demands reinforce the capitalist premise that everything has its price and help to sustain the illusion that the deterioration of the public environment is somehow unrelated to the policies of "private" corporations. The flight of industry to the suburbs leaves urban neighborhoods impoverished and contributes to the so-called crisis of the cities, but the working class, so long as it views that crisis from traditional trade union perspectives, has no way of explaining it except to blame everything on the government, the blacks, outside agitators, or the general decline of morals.

"Citizen politics" avoids these pitfalls by concentrating on issues that affect the community as a whole. But it is no better able than trade unionism to show the *connection* between conditions at work and deteriorating neighborhoods, schools, and public services. Neither amateur activists nor old-time trade unionists challenge the fatal split between home and work—the system under which people are in effect compensated for loss of dignity and autonomy at work by increased leisure and higher wages to spend on consumer goods and leisure-time activities. It is because work is seen merely as a means to something else, instead of an intrinsically satisfying and necessary activity, that people no longer concern themselves with its social consequences. The auto worker who drives long distances to work along choked highways, under polluted skies, suffers directly from the social consequences of the automobile. But his union does not concern itself with those consequences or with the corporate policies that help to bring them about; nor does the worker dream that he himself might have something to say about what use is made of the cars he produces or about better ways to produce less harmful cars. To him the production of cars is his means of support, nothing more. The civic-minded conservationist and amateur reformer, on the other hand, tend to forget that the production of cars is, among other things, people's means of support; they think solely of the car's effect on the "environment."

What seems to be needed, then, is a fusion of community politics and trade union politics—two dissident traditions that have increasingly grown apart. The product of this fusion would not be simply a new unionism or a new kind of community organizing but a new form of politics altogether, centered on the factory—and on the research and development laboratory, the intellectual assembly line, the professions, the media—but always heedful of work in its larger social implications. As we have already seen, it is precisely because the "working conditions" in the modern university in some ways approximate those of the more highly developed sectors of modern industry, and because the underlying issue raised by student politics within the university—the social uses of knowledge—mirrors the overriding issue for society as a whole, that the student movement of the sixties can be regarded as anticipating, perhaps even as a preparation for, whatever the new politics will be in the seventies and eighties.

4

IF WE THINK OF THE PROBLEM OF RADICAL POLITICS AS THAT OF combining styles of action inherited from the labor movement with a determination to see work in its relation to all phases of community life, we ought to be able to learn something from the career of Saul Alinsky. When he turned to community organizing in the late thirties, Alinsky consciously borrowed techniques he had learned in the labor movement. A new political type emerged—the professional organizer, whose constituents are not workers but citizens.

After reading Walzer's plea for a partial professionalization of citizen politics, one immediately recognizes in the organizer the professional calm and skepticism by means of which Walzer hopes to counter the disproportionate influence of fanatical militants. In a long career beginning in the "back-of-the-yards" section of Chicago and including work with Canadian Indians, the organization of FIGHT in the Rochester ghetto, and the building of the Woodlawn Organization in Chicago, Alinsky had to rely on the fact that he was a professional with marketable talents and a demonstrated record of competence. He describes the organizer's work with a candor verging on cynicism, stressing the need for the organizer to keep himself discreetly in the background. "Much of the time . . . the organizer will have a pretty good idea of what the community should be doing," but if he tries to prevail through the force of his own arguments the community will reject him as an outside agitator. Instead, he uses "guided questioning" and learns to rely on "skillful and sensitive role-playing." Alinsky anticipates and disarms the objection: "Is this manipulation? Certainly, just as a teacher manipulates, and no less, even a Socrates. As time goes on and education proceeds, the leadership becomes increasingly sophisticated. . . ." The organizer's job "becomes one of weaning the group away from dependency upon him. Then his job is done." To those who would argue that Alinsky proposes merely to give his clients the illusion of deciding for themselves he can reply that it is only by means of this illusion, artfully encouraged in the initial stages of organization, that exploited people overcome the habit of deference and feelings of helplessness engendered by the vastness and impenetrability of modern society.

It may be further objected that the poor ought to furnish their own leadership from the beginning. Why should they rely on outside organizers at all? Shouldn't they oppose to their oppressors not the slick expertise of the organizer but the strength and dignity of their own ways? These objections, in Alinsky's view, betray the middle-class reformer's inclination to romanticize the poor, although he realizes that poor people themselves may seize on these ideas in order to explain their own inaction. He sees the poor—like all people—as normally lazy and uncurious even about their own oppression, preferring the safety of known misery to the uncertainty of action. At the same time they are embarrassed by their failure to act, especially in the presence of an organizer, and appeal to middle-class rhetoric about "cultural identity" in order to excuse it. A conversation between Alinsky and a group of Canadian Indians shows how this self-deception works.

INDIANS: Well, we can't organize.
[ALINSKY:] Why not?

INDIANS: Because that's a white man's way of doing things. . . . You see, if we organize, that means getting out and fighting the way you are telling us to do and that would mean that we would be corrupted by the white man's culture and lose our own values.

Alinsky comments:

It was quite obvious what was happening since I could see from the way the Indians were looking at each other they were thinking: "So we invite this white organizer from south of the border to come up here and he tells us to get organized. . . . What must be going through his mind is: 'What's wrong with you Indians that you have been sitting around here for a couple of hundred years now and you haven't organized to do these things?'"

Because the new left so often ignores such self-deception or unwittingly encourages it, Alinsky impatiently condemns much of the radicalism of the sixties. The new left, he says, valued the purity of its principles more than practical results. Instead of taking the poor as they are, it romanticized and at the same time patronized them. It spoke in abstractions about the class struggle, instead of confronting the immediate issues that matter to the poor: jobs, inflation, discrimination, violence in the streets. "If the real radical finds that having long hair sets up psychological barriers to communication and organization, he cuts his hair."

These criticisms accurately expose many of the weaknesses of the new left, but they do not necessarily leave us with a workable alternative. For one thing, Alinsky exaggerates the effectiveness of his own methods. He speaks of "bringing to heel" one of the Chicago department stores and of engineering the "downfall" of Eastman Kodak, when all he means is that these companies made certain concessions to organized pressure from blacks. Alinsky's habit of setting himself limited objectives causes him to overestimate the importance of their achievement. No doubt it is tactically necessary for the organizer "to convert the plight into a problem," but the problem should not be allowed to obscure the underlying plight. To personalize the adversary, as Alinsky urges again and again, is, moreover, to regress to a more primitive level of political awareness. It is important to insist on the concrete as against empty slogans and abstractions, but this does not mean that every general question can be dissolved in a discussion of tactics.

Although Alinsky's organization often concerned itself indirectly with job discrimination and other matters pertaining to people's work, it was mainly concerned with citizens and consumers. At the end of his career Alinsky turned to organizing middle-class stockholders to use their proxies against corporate policies that led to pollution and despoliation of the environment. In Rochester, Alinsky persuaded Kodak stockholders to assign their proxies to FIGHT or to come to stockholders' meetings and vote against Eastman's discriminatory hiring policies. In *Rules for Radicals* he argues that this tactic should be used on a wider scale. "The way of proxy participation could mean the democratization of corporate America"—nothing short of a "revolution." A more "revolutionary" strategy, however, would attempt to put the corporations under the control not of the stockholders, but of those who work in them. The community organizer thinks of his constituents almost automatically as consumers. This is at once his strength and his weakness.

In *Reveille for Radicals,* written in 1946, Alinsky attacked the labor unions for dealing with the worker only as a worker, instead of keeping "clearly in mind the obvious and true picture of the worker who votes, rents, consumes, breeds and participates in every avenue of what we call life." Whatever was fruitful in Alinsky's subsequent career sprang from this initial insight. At the same time, the shift from union politics to community organizing precluded the possibility of describing industrial society in class terms. Alinsky had to reject a socialist orientation in favor of neo-populism—the "people" against the "tycoons." Like many radicals of the late thirties and early forties, Alinsky rejected the stupidities of American socialism, by that time almost exclusively identified with the Communist

Party, only to fall into a Deweyite celebration of democracy as process. "The objective is never an end in itself," he wrote in *Reveille*. What mattered was "the passionate desire of all human beings to feel that they have personally contributed to the creation and the securing of any objective they desire." Having divested his movement of any suspicion of "ideology," having substituted "citizens" for "workers" and interests for classes, and having exalted process over objectives, Alinsky was free to define "participation" itself as the objective of community organization—of politics in general.

Alinsky's attack on the new left overlooked the degree to which this exaltation of participation, which his own career did so much to identify with American radicalism, not only was a major influence on the early new left ideas of "participatory democracy" and "community organizing" but helped to mislead young radicals and to prepare the way for subsequent disappointments. Instead of providing a historical explanation for those features of the new left that he disliked—its cult of revolutionary purity, its infatuation with failure, its dogmatism—Alinsky psychologized about them, characteristically attributing these failings to bourgeois affluence and generational revolt. But the sectarianism of the later new left, as I have already suggested, might better be seen as a consequence of the poverty of its early ideas—and notably of its own obsession with participation as an end in its own right. For the idea of "participatory democracy," while it may have served initially as a necessary corrective to the bureaucratic centralism so long associated with parties of the left, rapidly degenerated into political primitivism, the old dream of a primary democracy without factions or parties—in other words, of a political community without politics.

As Robert A. Dahl observes, the notion that primary democracy is the only pure and acceptable form of democratic authority rests on a pair of fallacies—the belief that small communities can achieve complete independence from the surrounding society, and the belief that they can avoid the development of factions. Since parties and factions make their appearance anyway, the advocates of primary democracy "seem either naïve or Machiavellian: naïve when they speak of the people as if the people were a single, well-defined, harmonious unit, Machiavellian when they use the rhetoric of power to the people to conceal their attempts to gain power for their own faction." This observation, though stated in the form of an abstract principle, provides us with another clue to the degeneration of new left organizations. The early advocates of participatory democracy believed that it was possible to submerge ideological differences in appeals to love and brotherhood. This delusion exposed them to the manipulation of well-disciplined factions such as those which eventually gained control of SDS and destroyed the organization in the course of trying to destroy one another. The experience of the new left shows that a mystique of participation is no substitute for well-defined political ideas and a political program.

For all his tactical realism, Alinsky shared with the early new left a disposition to dismiss ideas and programs as "ideological." Again and again he argued that ideas are merely a cloak for self-interest, that action takes precedence over understanding, and that the objective of political action is "never an end in itself" but a means of rousing people "to a higher degree of participation." No one can deny that the size and complexity of modern societies have given rise to feelings of powerlessness or that apathy has become a political issue in its own right. It is dangerous, however, to equate democracy with participation and to encourage the belief that it is possible for people to take part directly in every decision that "affects their lives." Efforts to implement these beliefs end by integrating people more securely than ever into structures in which, whether they are controlled by the existing powers or by demagogues of the left, popular control is strictly an illusion.

The mystique of participation has had a profoundly misleading influence on recent American radicalism. It is a symptom of the general malaise of modern culture that watching a play, reading a poem, or getting an education are defined as passive and spectatorial, inherently inferior in the quality of their emotional satisfaction to acting in a play, writing a poem, or simply "living." The notion that education and "life," art and "reality," understanding and action are radically opposed derives ultimately from the opaqueness of the structures in which we live and from a despair of understanding them. Official propaganda encourages this belief as assiduously as the so-called counterculture, which in this respect (as in many others) merely reflects prevailing values—or, more accurately, takes them more literally than they are taken by the ruling class. Thus, although the cult of participation encourages among other things a distrust of professionalism, the institutions of American society continue to be operated by professionals. It is only the left which, both in its politics and in its culture, clings to the illusion that competence is equally distributed among people of good intentions and regards any attempt to uphold professional standards as a betrayal of democracy.

Clearly this criticism does not apply to Saul Alinsky, who was nothing if not a professional; indeed, his professionalism accurately defined the limits of his belief in participation as an end in itself. For the left as a whole, however, belief in the intrinsic value of participation has no such limits. Its distrust of professionalism does not rest merely on a healthy disrespect for "experts" or on an awareness of the ways in which the concept of professionalism has been progressively debased (not least in the academic professions, where it has become synonymous with timid pedantry and a pose of "scientific objectivity"). It reflects an intellectual orientation which, pushed to its furthest extreme, scorns not only professionalism but the "work ethic" itself, on the grounds that spontaneous and sensuous enjoyment of life is the only genuine form of participation in its pleasures, while submission to a discipline is inherently "alienating."

5

APPLIED TO POLITICS, THE CULT OF PARTICIPATION RESULTS IN AN unworkable definition of democracy as the direct involvement of all the people in every political decision, no matter how minute. The chief value of Dahl's *After the Revolution?* lies in its sustained attack on the folklore of primary democracy. It is useful to be reminded, however elementary the point may seem, that "participatory democracy" in the strict sense works, if it works at all, only in very small communities; and that because the complexity of industrial society makes it impossible for such communities to achieve complete autonomy, those who advocate direct democracy as a general program are advocating, in effect, a return to a simpler stage of social and economic organization. One might add that decentralization, a measure of which is undoubtedly desirable, does not automatically lead to democratic results. Unless it is accompanied by a shift in political power, the decentralization of certain administrative functions may serve merely to reduce friction and to placate dissatisfaction with existing practices. ("The organizing principle of the new model [corporate or academic] institution," writes Michael Miles, "will be centralized control through decentralized structures.")

In the manner of one starting from the first principles of political theory, Dahl argues that democracy depends not on the direct participation of every individual but on the ability of the people to organize collectively, to make themselves heard as a body, to choose responsible representatives, to recall them at their pleasure, and in short to determine the main lines of public policy. (Clearly, these things depend on the distribution of economic and educational resources.)

It is obvious that all institutions in American life are not equally democratic. "Private" corporations, academic or industrial, are not even formally democratic in their organization, unlike the state. Before arguing that they should be, according to Dahl, one must consult the "principle of competence," according to which authority should be exercised by those who are best qualified to exercise it and who understand the consequences of their decisions. To insist on democracy in the operating room or on the bridge of an ocean liner would be madness for patients and passengers. The argument for democracy in the state therefore depends on the proposition that "the ordinary man is more competent than anyone else to decide when and how much he shall intervene on decisions he feels are important to him." In order for this argument to apply also to the university or the private corporation, it must be shown that these institutions, although in most cases nominally private, actually embody political power, are intertwined with the state, and are public in everything but name.

Dahl rather uneasily skirts the issue of the university. If we were to apply his categories to this particular case, we should have to distinguish at the outset between democratizing the corporate structure of the university, so as to give the entire university community access to its corporate decisions (for example, whether or not to engage in military research, to expand into the ghetto, to add new departments and programs, or to make major changes in the curriculum), and democratizing the classroom itself, as many cultural radicals are demanding. In the former case, the principle of competence would favor the institution of democratic procedures; in the latter, their adoption would quickly complete the wreckage of an already debased higher education. It is also important that we distinguish among various kinds of democratic procedures. Those that would assure students a corporate voice in university policy are clearly to be preferred to selective student representation on university committees, a form of co-option admirably designed to diminish what little influence students now enjoy.

The industrial corporation no doubt presents an even clearer case for democratization, and Dahl's discussion of this institution makes Alinsky's talk of "proxy participation" seem shallow by comparison. There can be no question of the political character of the national and international corporation, Dahl argues: "The appropriation of public authority by private rulers . . . is the essence of the giant firm." Only a "purely ideological bias" prevents us from thinking of "all economic enterprise as a public service," in which employees and consumers, and in many cases the public in general, have as much interest as the stockholders.

How can this interest best be served? Nationalization—which Dahl identifies, perhaps too simply, as the "socialist" remedy—by no means guarantees that the public most affected by corporate decisions will be adequately protected. Workers, moreover, may lose their right to strike. A more plausible solution, but one that Dahl believes is no more satisfactory, is the gradual incorporation of consumer representatives on corporate boards. This is the strategy advocated by Ralph Nader and others—a variant of Alinsky's "proxy participation." Dahl thinks that consumer representation, even if it were effective, would simply convert the corporation into "a system of rather remote delegated authority." It would be difficult to agree on what interests should be represented or on how they were to control their own representatives. Nevertheless this innovation, which corporations might accept in preference to more radical arrangements, "would probably be enough to deflate weak pressures for further change."

Since the alternatives seem equally unsatisfactory, Dahl has come to prefer the syndicalist solution (although he fails to acknowledge it as such): control of the corporation by its own employees. "Self-management" would "transform employees from corporate subjects to citizens of the enterprise." He recognizes the objection that the American working class may be incapable of self-management. Even more than the capitalist class, it is imbued with archaic ideas about property, which confuse property with ownership instead of defining it simply as a bundle of rights. Dahl concedes, moreover, that the American worker regards his job "as an activity not intrinsically gratifying or worthwhile but rather as an instrument for gaining money which the worker and his family can spend on articles of consumption. In this respect, the modern worker has become what classical economists said he was: an economic man compelled to perform intrinsically unrewarding, unpleasant, and even hateful labor in order to gain money to live on." The transformation of the work place into a "small society" would require a transformation of the worker's attitude toward work.

Dahl thinks that these attitudes, however, might change once self-management was actually in operation. "If a significant number of employees . . . were to discover that participation in the affairs of the enterprise . . . contributed to their own sense of competence and helped them to control an important part of their daily lives, then lassitude and indifference toward participation might change into interest and concern." Dahl believes that worker control is especially likely to be sought by workers who still view their work as a profession—that is, by the technical and professional strata themselves. At this point he abruptly drops the argument and turns to a discussion of decentralization.

His failure to press it leaves several difficulties unresolved. In the first place, he relies on "external controls, both governmental and economic," to protect the interests of consumers and the community in general, whereas one of the best arguments for worker control is that corporate employees, because they are also citizens of society as a whole, are competent not only to manage the corporation's internal affairs, with the help of professional managers, but to protect the interests of society. This suggestion appears utopian only if one refuses to imagine the impact that a takeover of corporate power by workers might have on the economy.

Dahl argues that it would be "unworldly" to suppose that once the workers control an enterprise they will spontaneously act "in the interests of all." The trouble with this argument is that it pays too little attention to the political battles through which self-management will have to be achieved and to the possibility that these battles will serve as a political education for those who initiate them. Indeed it is precisely the antisocial consequences of private production that are likely to generate a movement for worker control. To Dahl's objection—"if self-management were introduced today, tomorrow's citizens in the enterprise would be yesterday's employees"—one can only reply that self-management is hardly likely to be introduced from above. It will have to be "introduced" by the workers themselves, not "today," but after long struggles in the course of which the workers' outlook could be expected to undergo changes that seem almost inconceivable at the present time.

By ignoring the political movements that would be necessary to make self-management a reality, Dahl exposes his argument to another objection, namely, that his case for worker control is curiously abstracted from current political life. If his argument for "self-management" were to carry more than the force of a political scientist's recommendation, it would have to be shown that political forces already in motion make it a real and not merely a hypothetical alternative. It would have to be shown, in other words, that worker control of production is a concrete historical possibility not only in Yugoslavia, where he shows that it works fairly well, but in the United States. Dahl's reluctance to embark on a discussion of this question suggests a lingering belief in the separability of academic disciplines—history, presumably, can safely be left to historians, while political scientists concern themselves with an abstract model of the political process. He prefers to regard the structure of the corporation as a question "more technical than ideological," a matter "less of principle than of practical judgment." This is reminiscent of Alinsky's attempt to turn the "plight" into a "problem." The reason these formulations are evasive is that changes in the social structure will come about only when they are incorporated into the program of a political movement. Mass politics, moreover—the only agency of democratic change—contains an unavoidable admixture of ideology. Questions of principle cannot be indefinitely postponed.

Whatever the weaknesses of his argument, however, Dahl has identified the central issue of contemporary domestic politics, control of the corporation. Even if the student movement foreshadowed a new "labor movement," the results would be inconsequential unless the new labor movement confronted this question. The student movement itself has raised it only by implicit analogy with the struggle against the university. For that matter, the student movement has paid very little attention to the possibility of transforming itself into a movement of professional and technical employees. Instead it has cultivated a militantly anti-professional ideology. The emergence of a movement for "self-management" of the corporation therefore presupposes a transformation of student politics itself. The mere existence of a student movement and of young graduates who are carrying its attitudes into corporations, professions, and bureaucracies, however, is one reason to think that the private corporation may yet find itself confronted with a powerful challenge to its very existence.

Another reason, already noted, is the probability that the working conditions of technical and professional employees will further deteriorate. If this happens, they may make common cause with schoolteachers, public servants, and petty civil servants, who already face countless hardships.

6

STILL ANOTHER DEVELOPMENT THAT MAY HAVE WIDE-RANGING political implications is the revival of the "woman question." Worker control of the corporation would require a change not only in attitudes toward work but in attitudes toward leisure, consumption, and domestic life. It is now generally recognized that the privatized, mother-centered family is one of the bastions of the consumer economy. No institution more clearly embodies the separation between work and the rest of life, and no institution, not even the corporation itself, illustrates so specifically the bad effects of this separation.

The precarious political and economic stability that was reestablished after the Great Depression rested as heavily on a rehabilitation of domesticity, mildly challenged during the twenties and thirties by the new sexual freedom and the appearance of a new type of "career woman," as it did on military spending. The arrangement whereby private consumption compensates for loss of autonomy at work, and for the absence of a vigorous public and communal life, depended on a new sentimentalization of the family, in which the nineteenth-century cult of domesticity was refurbished with images of the suburb as a refuge from the city.

An attack on suburbia—as banal at times as the reality it sought to describe—characterized the new left from the beginning. Recently there has been added to it a more pointed and specific attack on the family. At its worst, this new feminism merely makes explicit one of the tendencies that was implicit in the old—repudiation of men, a heightening of the sex war. At its best, it provides the clearest perspective from which to view the degradation of work into a meaningless routine and the hollowness of the pleasures that are offered in its place. Domestic life, far from having been enriched by its isolation from work, has been steadily impoverished. It is more and more difficult to recognize in the contemporary family—although of course everyone knows exceptions to the general pattern—the description of bourgeois domesticity provided by Max Horkheimer in 1941 as the last defense of a rich and autonomous inner life against the encroachments of the mass society.

> The middle class family, though it has frequently been an agency of obsolescent social patterns, has made the individual aware of other potentialities than his labor or vocation opened to him. As a child, and later as a lover, he saw reality not in the hard light of its practical biddings but in a distant perspective which lessened the force of its commandments. This realm of freedom, which originated outside the workshop, was adulterated with the dregs of all past cultures, yet it was man's private preserve in the sense that he could there transcend the function society imposed upon him by way of its division of labor.

Today family life increasingly exists in a vacuum and has become vacuous. This fact in many ways sums up the contemporary plight.

What will emerge from the new criticism of the family is not yet clear. Whether the latest wave of feminism leaves a more lasting mark than earlier waves depends on its ability to associate criticism of the family with a criticism of other institutions, particularly those governing work. If the attack on the family results merely in the founding of rural communes, it will offer no alternative either to the isolated family or to the factory, since in many ways the rural commune simply caricatures the new domesticity, re-enacting the flight to nature and the search for an isolated and emotionally self-sufficient domestic life. To be sure, it reunites the family with work, but with a kind of primitive agricultural labor which is itself marginal. The "urban commune," in which the members work outside, avoids these difficulties, but it is not clear that it is more than a dormitory—in particular, it is not clear whether it can successfully raise children.

Lately there has been a tendency for the attack on the family, like so many other fragments of the new left, to degenerate into a purely cultural movement, one aimed not so much at institutional change as at abolishing "male chauvinism." I have already criticized the illusion that a "cultural revolution," a change of heart, can serve as a substitute for politics. Here it is necessary only to add that the criticism applies with special force to feminism, since the peculiar strength of this movement is precisely its ability to dramatize specific connections between culture and politics—between the realm of production on the one hand and education, child rearing, and sexual relations on the other. It ought to be recognized, for example, that large numbers of women will not be able to enter the work force, except by slavishly imitating the careers of men, unless the nature of work undergoes a radical change. The entire conflict between "home and career" derives from the subordination of work to the relentless demands of industrial productivity. The system that forces women (and men also) to choose between home and work is the same system that demands early specialization and prolonged schooling, imposes military-like discipline in all areas of work, and forces not only factory workers but intellectual workers into a ruthless competition for meager rewards. At bottom, the "woman question" is indistinguishable from what used to be known as the social question.

It would be foolishly optimistic to conclude from the existence of the woman's movement, the student movement, and the black movement, and from growing signs of uneasiness among professional and technical workers in various strata of the population, that the basis for a "new politics" already exists. These movements are no more than portents; they exist, moreover, in isolation from each other. If we have learned anything from the sixties, it is that the "system" is much less vulnerable than many radicals had supposed. The realization of its strength can become an occasion for premature despair or for renewed attempts to create a radical coalition. Those who despair of politics will find it hard to understand why I have devoted so much attention to a few books that deal for the most part with tactical issues and that eschew the claim to sweeping historical synthesis and blinding socio-cultural insight that we have come to expect of political statements emanating from the left. But it is precisely tactical realism, a respect for the commonplace, and renewed attention to the way in which the crisis of modern society is rooted in the deteriorating conditions of everyday life that the left most urgently needs to acquire.

[XI]

Populism, Socialism, and McGovernism

I

THE FAMILIAR MATERIALS OF POPULAR DISCONTENT, QUIETLY PER-
sisting through three decades of "affluence," seem once again to
be rising to the surface of American political life. Distrust of
officials and official pronouncements; cynicism about the good
faith of those in positions of great power; resentment of the
rich; a conviction that most things in life are "fixed"—these attitudes were there all along, of course, forming part of the folk
wisdom of the American working class, but they attracted little
attention so long as it was possible to believe that the worker
had become middle-class in his tastes and outlook. Now that they
seem to be taking political form, the illusion is harder to
maintain.

A grass-roots rebellion against the Democratic Party establishment gives rise to the McGovern and Wallace candidacies,
antagonistic movements that nevertheless have in common that
both are hated and feared by the official leaders of the party and
flourish in the face of official attempts to suppress them. In Illinois the Daley machine suffers a sharp setback. In Lordstown,
Ohio, GM workers are raising not the traditional issues of bread-
and-butter unionism but a more disturbing question: Why does
work have to be organized in such a way as to make it boring
and meaningless? Studies show—what we hardly needed studies
to find out—that most Americans are bored with their jobs. A

Harris poll reveals the equally unsurprising information that our political institutions are distrusted by a majority of the people.

Distrust and boredom are two sides of the same mood; both flow from the experience of being without power. Having no control over his work, over governmental policy, over the press and television, or over the education of his children, the citizen feels himself manipulated to suit the interests of the rich and powerful. Busing—its unreality decried by established political spokesmen—has become an important issue in American politics because it represents for many people the most palpable form of outside interference with their lives: the sacrifice of defenseless children to a bureaucratic design imposed from above. (That the children themselves seem not to mind is perhaps beside the point.)

In the new political climate—the existence of which the Democratic primaries, more than anything else, have made known—people are rediscovering "populism." In the fifties scholars ridiculed populism as a backward-looking agrarian fantasy. Some saw in the populism of the 1890's the seeds of American "fascism." Others interpreted it as "paranoid," anti-intellectual, and obsessed with issues of merely symbolic importance—the progenitor of McCarthyism and other right-wing movements "against modernity." In the late fifties and early sixties a number of historians began to challenge these interpretations, arguing that the populists were neither nativist nor anti-Semitic, reminding us that populism was a genuinely radical movement with a radical program. In some cases they asserted an identity—spurious, in my view—of populism with socialism.

This new scholarship has had the effect of making populism intellectually respectable again. Joseph Kraft, in a review of the *Populist Manifesto* recently published by Jack Newfield and Jeff Greenfield, expresses the older view of populism when he worries that a revolt against economic injustice, of the kind Newfield and Greenfield are trying to encourage, would degenerate into a demagogic crusade in which "the malign side of populism" would once again assert itself—"the side that in the past has fostered isolationism, anti-intellectualism, hostility to Jews and Catholics, and what Richard Hofstadter called the 'paranoid style' of American politics." But it is precisely the association of isolationism, anti-intellectualism, anti-Semitism, and political paranoia with populism that can no longer be taken for granted. The revival of populism as a subject of general concern, while it derives in the first place from recent political events, also derives from—or at least was facilitated by—the scholarly rehabilitation of populism. According to the interpretation that prevailed in the fifties, populism was a rear-guard movement, rooted in the status anxieties of a declining class, the petty bourgeoisie; and although it would doubtless continue to manifest itself in such reactionary forms as Goldwaterism and the John Birch Society, it could hardly be regarded as the wave of the future. The recent reinterpretation of populism, by stressing its radicalism, has made it contemporary again—for many people, indeed, has made it a more appropriate answer to the crisis in American society than the radicalism of the sixties.

A new populism might be expected to appeal not only to those directly victimized by economic injustice but to students and intellectuals who are tired of the ideological wrangles of the left and seek relief in a broadly based reform coalition in which theoretical niceties are subordinated to practical results. The populist revival reflects more than the growing impatience of the "average American"; it also reflects the disillusionment of many leftists and ex-leftists. Clearly the new populism is one of several candidates hoping to inherit what remains of the new left, others being woman's liberation, the "counter-culture," and some form of socialism.

It may be suggestive of a new mood on the left that Newfield and Greenfield barely mention the new left; they simply by-pass it. In their eagerness "to return to American politics the economic passions jettisoned a generation ago," they seem to assume that nothing at all can be learned from the radicalism of the sixties. They pass over that complex experience with a brief criticism of the youth culture (actually of Charles Reich), a few snide references to "middle-class radicals," and the observation—which hardly disposes of the subject—that "the New Left in its Weatherman, Panther, and Yippie incarnations has become anti-democratic, terroristic, dogmatic, stoned on rhetoric, and badly disconnected from everyday reality."

They say nothing about the civil rights movement, the anti-war movement, or the new left attack on the multiversity. By their own admission their program does not address itself to "the legitimate grievances of blacks, or the women's movement," or to "civil liberties, disarmament, and ecology." Their populism speaks to "concrete economic interests." In appealing frankly to "self-interest" as the motive force of politics, it is unashamedly liberal, while at the same time seeking to dissociate itself from the "elitist" and manipulative liberalism of Adlai Stevenson, Eugene McCarthy, and the Ivy League technocrats in the Defense Department. The populist program is "designed to move us closer toward justice, not Shangri-La."

Newfield and Greenfield propose a variety of economic reforms. They would attack the concentration of wealth and economic power by means of antitrust suits, federal regulation of corporations, and tax reform. (In tax reform, their suggestions resemble the unamended McGovern proposals, combining higher rates for the rich with exemption for the poor and closing various loopholes.) Newfield and Greenfield would bring banking and insurance companies under control by means of public representation on boards of directors. Similarly they see union participation in management as a means of bringing corporations to public accountability. (This of course is not the same thing as worker control.) They demand public ownership of utilities (so did the populists in 1892), land reform designed to break up concentrations of land ownership and to thwart real estate developers, and reform of communications to prevent monopoly and encourage diversity.

Rightly convinced that "law and order" is a real issue for working people and not simply a slogan of right-wing demagogues, they advocate gun control, an end to police corruption and bureaucracy, penal reform that would emphasize rehabilitation instead of custody (another good nineteenth-century proposal), and, somewhat ominously, an end to "police practices that hinder the work of deterrence"—measures, it must be said, that hardly go to the heart of the problem. They propose a program of national health insurance, closer supervision of the drug industry, and a restructuring of the medical profession to allow "paraprofessionals" to play a larger role (but without noting the implications of this last suggestion for professional training in general). In short, they favor an "attack on economic privilege" all along the line.

The first thing to be said about this program is that it is too modest even within its own limits. There is no reason for populists to ignore such important issues as housing, transportation, and education, as Newfield and Greenfield do, or to pass so lightly over questions of foreign policy. Instead of examining the connection between American foreign policy and the concentration of wealth, Newfield and Greenfield subscribe to the questionable thesis that what is wrong with foreign policy can be attributed to the influence of intellectuals committed to "the mode of technocratic thinking and operating." They treat racism purely as an economic matter: the concentration of economic power "leaves whites and blacks competing over too scarce public resources." They by-pass the complicated issue of school desegregation, probably because it does not readily yield to an economic interpretation.

Again and again the authors try to avoid the troubling questions of the fifties and sixties by reviving issues that were central to American politics before these new issues arose; yet in many cases the roots of these issues must be traced directly to the "populist" administrations of Roosevelt and Truman. Newfield and Greenfield hark back nostalgically to Harry Truman's "give-'em-hell" campaign of 1948—"one of the last examples of a successful populist coalition"—but forget that it was Truman who formulated the containment policy and made the first American commitments to Vietnam.

Some of the omissions and evasions of the *Populist Manifesto* are peculiar to the Newfield-Greenfield version of populism, and it is accordingly possible to imagine a slightly more rigorous statement of the case; but most of these evasions are intrinsic to populism itself. Certainly populism has never been "anti-imperialist in foreign policy," as Newfield and Greenfield claim. In *The Roots of the Modern American Empire*, William Appleman Williams showed that American farmers saw an expansionist foreign policy as enlarging their markets; nor did the populist leaders quarrel with this assessment. There is admittedly a tradition in populism that sees war as a conspiracy of international bankers and munitions-makers, but this tradition is compatible with nationalist and even jingoist views and hardly provides a solid basis on which to oppose American expansionism—though it might be of some use at the moment in extricating ourselves from Vietnam. Nor is populism reliably antitechnocratic, as Newfield and Greenfield also maintain. In its more sophisticated forms—as in the sociology of Lester Frank Ward and Thorstein Veblen—it advanced a technological interpretation of social "evolution" according to which the new technological and scientific élites were functionally indispensable to advanced industrial society, and thus assured of a commanding position in it.

Finally, populism, because it treats politics as a reflection of economic self-interest, has always found it difficult to explain the connections between politics and culture. Newfield and Greenfield with good reason believe that culture should not be confused with or substituted for politics (as in the theories of the counter-culturists); but this does not mean that the connections between them can be safely ignored. To make these connections, however, requires a theory of class and an understanding of the way in which class interests, seldom presenting themselves directly in economic form, are mediated by culture, which in turn acquires a life independent of its social origin. Racism, for example, though it once furnished a rationale for slavery and other forms of exploitation, no longer has a clear basis in economic self-interest; nevertheless it survives as a powerful force in American society and cannot be eliminated simply by a more equitable distribution of goods.

Eliminating racism demands, at the very least, an equalization of educational opportunity; but here again a merely quantitative approach to the problem—more spending on schools, an attack on "privilege"—cannot deal adequately even with its economic complexities (such as the relation between school taxes, segregated suburbs, and disintegrating cities), let alone with the cultural questions to which discussions of education are likely to lead: Is compulsory schooling inherently biased in favor of existing class structures? Is there some relation between the schools' monopoly of education and the declining educational content of work—and for that matter of leisure?

2

THE NARROWNESS OF POPULISM APPEARS IMMEDIATELY IF WE TURN from the *Populist Manifesto* to Michael Harrington's elaborate restatement of the socialist position in his *Socialism*. Since socialism is simultaneously a theory, a body of practice with a long and complex history, and an ideal, Harrington has to deal with a vast range of material, including much that cannot even be touched on here. Essential to his undertaking are a reinterpretation of Marx; a historical analysis of "socialism" in practice in the U.S.S.R., China, and the "Third World"; an analysis of the social democratic tradition in western Europe; and an account of "the American exception." These will be considered here in that order, although the book weaves them together in a manner sometimes illuminating and sometimes confusing.

Harrington's version of Marxian theory owes much to the recent work of George Lichtheim, Shlomo Avineri, and David McClellan. It restores Marx's early writings to a position of central importance while denying a radical break between the young and the mature Marx. It stresses the philosophical origins of Marx's thought and insists that Marxism forms a unified whole that cannot be broken down into Marxian economics, Marxian sociology, and other fragments. It treats as crucial to the meaning of Marxism Marx's controversies with Jacobinism on the one hand and with Lassalle's state socialism on the other. What caused Marx to reject both these positions, according to Harrington, is that both ignored the social, economic, and cultural preconditions that Marx regarded as absolutely indispensable for the creation of a socialist order. The Jacobin tradition, surviving in the conspiratorial movements led by Blanqui and Bakunin, hoped to realize socialism through an act of revolutionary will and the heroic sacrifices of a revolutionary élite basing itself on the outcasts and dregs of society—Bakunin's "proletariat in rags." Lassalle, on the other hand, wanted to ally the emerging industrial proletariat in Germany with the reactionary anticapitalism of the landed nobility. His tactics helped to prepare the way for Bismarck's revolution from above.

Marx, however, insisted that socialism had to rest on economic abundance, on modern technology and modern culture generally, and on relations of production already "socialized" by capitalism. He argued that by demanding cooperative labor on an unprecedented scale capitalism had brought the workers out of their isolation and thus created conditions in which for the first time it was possible for them to think of themselves, in Harrington's words, as "cooperators in the gigantic enterprise of satisfying human needs." The "socialization" of labor made possible productivity on an unheard-of scale; but bourgeois society, according to Marx, by imprisoning this technology in a system of private commodity production, prepared the way for its own destruction and its succession either by a new form of barbarism or by socialism. This "contradiction" is Marx's central theme, Harrington properly insists; and it "is more relevant today than when he wrote *Das Kapital.*"

If this makes Marx sound a little like a Menshevik, insisting that it is impossible to skip historical stages on the way to socialism, the confusion may lie in the very notion of "stages." Drawing again on Lichtheim—and also perhaps, though without acknowledgment, on Eric Hobsbawm's introduction to Marx's

Pre-Capitalist Economic Formations, where this question is discussed—Harrington makes it clear that Marx, after flirting with a crude theory of historical stages in the *Communist Manifesto,* treated the development of capitalism out of feudalism in Europe as a unique and unprecedented event, not likely to recur elsewhere in the world. He saw no inevitable progression from slavery to feudalism to capitalism. Those who proceeded to read this meaning into Marx's analysis of primitive accumulation in the West transformed, according to Marx himself, a specific historical discussion into a "historico-philosophic theory of the general path every people is fated to tread, whatever the historic circumstances in which it finds itself."

The rise of a socialist movement in Russia, near the end of Marx's life, raised this issue in a way that showed the intersection of practice with theory. Far from arguing, as the Mensheviks were later to argue, that Russia's backwardness condemned her to repeat the "stages" of historical development in the West, passing first through a bourgeois revolution and thence to socialism, Marx and Engels came to believe, as they put it in 1882, that a revolution in Russia might "give the signal to a proletarian revolution in the West"—just as Lenin believed it would in 1917.

This does not mean that they endorsed the theories of Bakunin, Herzen, and the Russian populists that peasant communes in Russia could in themselves form the basis of a socialist society. Indeed the more closely they considered the "Asiatic mode of production," the more they came to identify the lack of private ownership in land with the rural stagnation prevailing in large parts of the globe. Bakunin's ideas, according to Marx, were "schoolboy's asininity! A radical social revolution is bound up with historic conditions; the latter are its preconditions. It is thus only possible where there is capitalist production and the proletariat has at least an important role."

There remained the possibility, however, that a socialist revolution in Europe, whether touched off by a Russian revolution or by some other crisis, would itself contribute materially and culturally to Russia's economic development. Rather than positing a naïve theory of historical "evolution," Marx recognized that events in one part of the world influence events in other parts, and that the outcome of developments in a country like Russia (and to an even greater degree in countries under Western colonialism) to a considerable extent depended on development in the more advanced countries. Not that the Russians lacked the moral autonomy or the capacity to make a revolution; but if it was true that socialism demanded certain preconditions to be found only in the West, the form that a Russian revolution would take depended on European events.

It is well known that Lenin, whatever his other departures from Marxism, also believed that the success of the Bolshevik revolution depended on a socialist revolution in Europe. When this revolution failed to take place—or rather, when the social democrats joined with the bourgeoisie in putting it down, at least in Germany—Lenin was faced with the difficult task of explaining how the Bolsheviks could claim to be leading the socialist reconstruction of a country still on the verge of capitalism. In particular he had to justify the Bolshevik Party dictatorship in the face of the condemnation by Marx and Engels of élitist and conspiratorial tactics. "In the process," Harrington observes, "he laid the ideological basis for a totalitarian regime which, I suspect, he would have abominated."

Confessing that "in effect we took over the old machinery of state from the Tsar and the bourgeoisie," and that the Russian workers "have not yet developed the culture required" to build a more democratic political structure, Lenin nevertheless tried to convince himself that educational work among the peasants—a "cultural revolution," in his phrase—"would now suffice to make our country a completely socialist country." In an even greater departure from Marxism, he also insisted that the problems of Russian backwardness could somehow be solved by joining Russia to countries even more backward, since "in the last analysis, the outcome of the struggle will be determined by the fact that Russia, India, China, etc., account for the overwhelming majority of the population of the globe."

Whatever ideological gloss Lenin might choose to put on the situation, the fact remained that in the absence of a European revolution, the "socialist" state in Russia would have to perform the role of the bourgeoisie, and moreover that it would have to carry out the work of primitive accumulation under extraordinarily unfavorable conditions, in a world still dominated by Western imperialism. Under these circumstances, as Marx had foreseen, socialism amounted to no more than the collectivization of poverty.

More recent experiments with "socialism" in countries even more backward than Russia in 1917, according to Harrington, have only confirmed the wisdom of Marx's original insight. The attempt to impose socialism on such countries as China, Cuba, and North Vietnam has led to one or another variety of "bureaucratic collectivism" (a concept Harrington derives from Max Schachtman), or else, in countries like Egypt, to a "socialism of the barracks" in which the military regimentation of an agricultural population is justified in the name of an ideal with which it has nothing in common.

Harrington's argument, it will be seen, hardly commends itself to Western radicals who look for deliverance to an uprising of the Third World; nor will it commend itself to latter-day Leninists or followers of Mao, Che, and Frantz Fanon. Nevertheless a great many Americans who call themselves socialists will find little to disagree with in the argument up to this point. More dubious is Harrington's analysis of developments in the advanced countries. A detached view of the matter would seem to require recognition that social democracy in Europe has become as much a dead end as Leninism and its offshoots in Russia and the non-Western world. Not that a "balanced view" demands that both branches of the socialist tradition receive equal criticism. But if we exaggerate the accomplishments of European social democracy, we shall find it difficult to explain the persistence of capitalism and imperialism. At the very least it would seem important not to begin with a prejudice in favor of social democracy. To say, for example, that the failure of the proletarian revolution in Europe—the same event that had such disastrous consequences in Russia and other undeveloped countries—left the Western socialists in a cruel dilemma, cast both as "doctors" and as prospective "heirs" of an ailing system, is true but inadequate. In order to complete the observation, we need to note the socialists' own contribution to the failure of that revolution. Harrington sees that World War I was a turning point for European socialism, but it seems to me that he minimizes the lasting damage it inflicted on the movement.

In an early chapter he makes the important point that "the very growth of the socialist movement [in prewar western Europe] was, in some measure, a result of working class optimism in a society in which the masses were making some real gains." Responsible to a growing constituency, organized increasingly along the lines of the bourgeois parties, and increasingly enmeshed in bourgeois political institutions, the social democratic parties were "utterly unprepared to take to the streets" when "World War I broke out and revolutionary tactics against the government itself were required if the antiwar promises were to be redeemed." But it is necessary at once to add that the socialist movement never recovered from this debacle. Without invoking as an explanation of its behavior the theory that its constituency, the working class of western Europe, is in reality a privileged sector of the world proletariat—a theory Harrington rightly rejects on the grounds that it stretches the term "proletariat" beyond recognition and ignores important differences within the Third World "proletariat" itself—we should still have to admit that the social democratic movement has pretty consistently supported imperialist wars ever since 1914. In particular it has enthusiastically endorsed, at least until recently, the international crusade against communism. It is this dismal record that makes it doubtful whether social democracy any longer represents the hope of those who long for fundamental changes in our social and political life, and for whom the most important evidence of the need for change lies in the reckless, destructive, militaristic, and inhuman policies of the Western powers, especially the United States.

Social democracy has a bad record in domestic affairs as well—and this part of its history is clearly understood by Harrington, though he seems reluctant to draw the proper conclusions. Because they clung doggedly to an outmoded program of nationalizing industries, European social democrats, whenever they were in power, much too readily accepted responsibility for taking over decrepit industries, while the healthy ones remained in private hands. Thus in western Europe nationalization had served to "socialize the losses of capitalist incompetence," in Harrington's excellent phrase, while at the same time acting "as a subsidy to the private sector." Harrington shows that the social democratic parties have adopted as their own the cult of economic growth; he shows that they are increasingly attracted to managerial and technocratic solutions; in short, he shows that they have gradually become exponents of a kind of "socialist capitalism." Yet his only criticism of the 1959 Godesberg program of the German Social Democratic Party, which marked the complete triumph of these tendencies in European social democracy, is that its revisions of the orthodox program, while "overdue," "went too far."

Among other things, the Godesberg program announced that "the Social Democratic Party has ceased to be a party of the working class and has become a party of the people." This was one of the changes, according to Harrington, that was "overdue," since Marx himself, "once he got over the simplifications of the Communist Manifesto . . . never believed that society was polarizing into two, and only two, classes, and every serious socialist tactician who came after him was aware of the need to reach out beyond the proletariat." Harrington's argument is disingenuous. The question is not whether it is necessary to "reach out beyond the proletariat"—something nobody in his right mind would deny—but whether history (or at any rate modern history) is conceived as a struggle between classes or merely between "the people" and their oppressors. If the latter, then populism is fully as appropriate a position as socialism; surely Americans do not need Marx to instruct them in the rights of "the people."

It is not easy to see in what sense a party identifying itself as the "party of the people" can be said to be a Marxist party at all. Harrington concedes that the Godesberg program—which also abandoned public ownership as a panacea, not in favor of something more radical, however, but in favor of various welfare programs—does "not go beyond American liberalism." But here again his chief criticism—that the German Social Democrats were "much too optimistic about capitalism"—seems to miss the point, namely, that they had nothing to put in its place. They were too optimistic, Harrington goes on to explain, because they ignored the persistence of poverty; but poverty too is something we did not need Marxism to discover or to account for. The authors of the *Populist Manifesto* comment again and again on the persistence of poverty, citing Harrington's own book, *The Other America,* as an authority; but they certainly do not draw the conclusion that poverty is a function of bourgeois class rule or that socialism is the only possible solution.

Reading Harrington's account of European social democracy leaves one in some confusion. On the one hand, it appears that the social democrats have failed as an opposition and have in fact become indistinguishable from welfare liberals. On the other hand, it is not clear what Harrington thinks they should have been doing instead. It is certainly not my own view that they should have been engaging in revolutionary terrorism. A popular movement has a responsibility to its constituency (although one of these responsibilities is to educate it, instead of merely reflecting its narrowest prejudices) and cannot afford the luxury of intransigent noncooperation in the everyday affairs of the state. The price of having a constituency at all is that one has to look out for its immediate interests. But it does not necessarily follow that a socialist party should content itself, in the words of the Godesberg platform, with "a step by step change in social structure." Such a policy goes beyond recognizing the need for immediate reforms; it implies a piecemeal theory of social change, according to which socialism will somehow emerge as the sum total of liberal reforms.

Not all European socialists, of course, have subscribed to this theory. Some of them in fact have tried to work out a version of socialism that avoids the dangers of Leninism and social democracy alike; and one of the puzzling things about Harrington's book is that these socialists—the most interesting in Europe since World War I—are completely ignored. Why does his book contain only isolated references to Rosa Luxemburg and Gramsci, and no reference at all to that important movement in European Marxism led by Lukács, Korsch, and the Frankfurt school? Why, for that matter, is there no discussion of the philosophical crisis of Marxism—the growing tendency toward positivism in *both* Leninism and social democracy—from which these theorists were trying to rescue Marxian thought? Harrington's account of Marxism is itself indebted to this theoretical movement, which was responsible for rediscovering the early Marx and for reemphasizing his Hegelian origins. Nevertheless, Harrington's long and seemingly exhaustive study of socialism ignores it, perhaps because this particular reinterpretation of Marx was aimed as much against social democracy as against "bureaucratic collectivism." But precisely because it tried to restore to European socialism a revolutionary perspective, the absence of which Harrington occasionally seems to deplore, it would seem to deserve some consideration, if only in order to help us to understand why it failed to have any practical consequences.

3

IF HARRINGTON'S ANALYSIS OF SOCIALISM IN WESTERN EUROPE IS unsatisfactory, his treatment of the United States is even worse. It requires us to believe that the United States has for years harbored a vital and growing social democratic tradition, an "invisible mass movement," and that we have been unable to recognize it, not because it doesn't exist, but because our eyes are blinded by European models and precedents. This "invisible mass movement" is, of course, the American labor movement, which has built a "political apparatus" that constitutes "a party in all but name."

Whereas the usual interpretation of American labor history sees the defeat of socialism in the AFL in the 1890's as a decisive event marking the complete capitulation of the AFL to a policy of business unionism, Harrington argues that this defeat was only temporary and that in effect "the AFL reversed its 1894 decision over the next thirty years." Without admitting as much, the AFL abandoned its opposition to political action when it joined the Conference on Progressive Political Action in 1922 and backed LaFollette in 1924. The organization of the CIO in the thirties, together with the formation of Labor's Non-Partisan League, Harrington believes, completed the reorientation of the American labor movement and gave to the New Deal, in which the unions allegedly played an important role, a "social democratic tinge," in words Harrington quotes from Richard Hofstadter. Recent leftist historians, according to Harrington, ignore the underlying radicalism of the New Deal only because they are blinded by the rabid antiliberalism of the sixties. (How then do we account for the fact that Hofstadter himself came to a similar conclusion about the New Deal in 1948? He found it essentially opportunistic, patching up the structure here and there while leaving the underlying problems unsolved.)

That the labor movement could have transformed itself into a social democratic movement without adopting a socialist ideology does not greatly trouble Harrington; for it had long since been apparent to Marx himself, as he wrote in 1846, that "communist tendencies in America" might originally take "seemingly anti-communist, agrarian form." Admitting that Marx and Engels "clearly expected that in the not-too-long run the exigencies of capitalist production would bring forth a socialist movement in the United States just as in Europe," Harrington nevertheless leaps from Marx's comments on American agrarianism to the much more general and dubious conclusion that socialism first appeared in America "in a capitalist guise" and that, indeed, this "dialectical irony" (!) is "still in force over a hundred years later."

One can only wish that the "guise" were not so impenetrable. Is it merely a willful blindness that prevents us from seeing a socialist in George Meany, whose vaporings about securing "for the great mass of the people . . . a better share of whatever wealth the economy produces" are quoted by Harrington to show that his "definition of socialism . . . more or less coincides with that of the revisionist social democrats" in Europe? Not only is Meany a socialist in disguise, according to Harrington, but the heavy union support for Humphrey in 1968 shows that "labor had clearly made an ongoing, class-based political commitment and constituted a tendency—a labor party of sorts —within the Democratic Party." It is with an effort that we remember that the unions, during all this time, were among the staunchest supporters of American foreign policy. Harrington passes over the cold war in silence and refers to Vietnam only to suggest that this unfortunate incident provoked an "estrangement" between the labor movement and middle-class radicals and prevented "academics and journalists" from seeing "the profound change in labor's social programs and political organization"—a "change," it appears, that was demonstrated by its ardent support of Humphrey in 1968!

My skepticism about Harrington's "invisible social democracy" does not rest on the belief that the American working class is hopelessly reactionary and has to be written off as a force for change. Nor do I deny that a radical tradition runs through the history of the working-class movement, a tradition that has been ignored by historians who identify radicalism too narrowly with the formation of socialist and labor parties, and conclude that the American working class has therefore been bourgeois from the beginning. Stripped of the conclusions to which Harrington pushes it, much is valuable in his interpretation of working-class history. For example, he comes down heavily on the cliché that a relatively high standard of living has made the American worker conservative. On the contrary, Harrington argues, "The egalitarian ideology and the lack of clearly defined limits to social mobility made for greater individual discontent among the workers."

Nevertheless, when we consider the collapse of working-class radicalism after World War II, the purge of Communists from the CIO, the unions' unremitting anticommunism and support of the cold war, their support for defense spending, and their indifference to ecological issues or questions of worker control, we must wonder what has become of earlier traditions of labor radicalism. Would it be too much to say that their revival depends, among other things, on the overthrow of the present leadership of the labor movement? Harrington refuses to consider this possibility. He has convinced himself that the union movement in its present form already amounts to a secret social democracy. Is this why it supports Humphrey against McGovern? I disagree with Harrington's belief that the most effective way for American socialists to act is by affiliating themselves with the left wing of the Democratic Party; but even if this were an effective strategy, we would still have to know where it leaves the labor unions, which are in the *center* of the Democratic Party, and on some issues on its right.

Harrington's impressive scholarship, his exposition of Marx, his lucid discussion of Leninism and the false socialism of the Third World, his astute observations about the failure of social democracy in western Europe are enlisted in support of a program for the United States that in many ways resembles the populism advocated by Newfield and Greenfield. To be sure, Harrington understands the difference—in theory—between socialist planning and neo-capitalist planning. He recognizes the limits of liberalism; he sees the broader implications of such issues as housing and transportation (as Newfield and Greenfield do not). In the end, however, he advises us to work through the unions and the Democratic Party—and this at a time when large numbers of people are finally beginning to question the historic inevitability of those institutions.

In one respect the Newfield-Greenfield variety of populism actually seems preferable to Harrington's socialism, since it is conceived explicitly as *"a movement,"* not as "a faction yoked to one political party or one charismatic personality." It has the additional advantage of being unencumbered with an ideology most Americans associate with despotism. If "socialism" is to issue merely in liberal reforms, why should their success be jeopardized by associating them with socialism?

Once again I hope it is clear that I do not see the alternative as a policy of ultra-leftism. Like Harrington, I believe that revolution is unlikely and that the left should abandon its revolutionary pretensions and follow a policy of "strategic reforms." But Harrington denatures this concept—which he borrows from André Gorz—by identifying it with traditional social democratic tactics, whereas structural reform is "by definition," according to Gorz, "a reform implemented or controlled by those who demand it" and is intended as an alternative not only to Leninism but to social democracy as well. Structural reform is incompatible with the present policies of the trade union movement. It is also incompatible with the kind of planning that seeks merely to "reorder priorities." To say with Harrington that "the people rather than the corporations with Government subsidies should decide priorities" is too abstract; what this means concretely, as Gorz points out, is that the struggle to reduce military budgets— to take an example made timely by the McGovern campaign— "will remain mere agitation and abstract propaganda so long as the labor movement has not worked out, factory by factory, industry by industry, and on the level of national planning, a program of reconversion and reorientation of the armament industries." Lacking such a program the left, even if it finds itself in power, will be "torn between the political desire to abandon the program [of military spending] and the pressure from the unions at the factory level for whom the existing program has come to mean the defense of their employment."

The 1972 primary campaign in California provides a vivid illustration of this conflict, in which Humphrey was able to identify himself precisely with the unions' defense of their jobs.

What is heartening about the California election and about the primaries in general is that these tactics did not prevent Mc-Govern from attracting working-class support (though not, it would seem, the support of workers directly dependent on military spending, like the aerospace workers of California). McGovern's success may mean that many workers no longer regard the labor leadership as altogether representative of their political interests. Instead of trying to persuade themselves that the union bosses are socialist in all but name, socialists should welcome this disaffection and do everything possible to encourage it.

4

LEST THE ASTONISHING RISE OF GEORGE MCGOVERN BE TAKEN AS A demonstration of the wisdom of social democratic strategies and of the possibility that socialists might be able to constitute themselves as the left wing of the Democratic Party, it is necessary to remind ourselves that McGovern's election would hardly mark the beginning of a peaceful transition to democratic collectivism. The importance of McGovern lies in the fact that he won the Democratic nomination, in spite of the combined opposition of the party chiefs and the labor bureaucrats, by appealing directly to the belief of many people that their officially constituted representatives are no longer responsive to their needs. More than the issue of tax reform, more even than his unyielding opposition to the war, the issue of "credibility" worked in McGovern's favor.

Having won the nomination, his only hope of election was to continue to exploit this issue and to identify himself with a growing revolt against the political establishment. He could not have hoped to win either the nomination or the election in the ordinary way. Events after California made this doubly clear. After McGovern's victory there, normal political decencies demanded that Muskie endorse McGovern and that the party close ranks behind the front-runner, who had far outdistanced the competition. Their refusal to do so, even in the face of the virtual certainty of McGovern's nomination, shows that the party leaders are unreconciled to their defeat and that they may prefer the entire party's defeat to the election of a candidate who wrested the nomination without their approval. McGovern's attempts to reassure the party bosses were for the most part rudely rebuffed; in their eyes he was another Goldwater, an "extremist" with no chance of election.

The irony was that the Democrats' only chance of returning to power was precisely to identify themselves with the disaffection abroad in the country. In a conventional campaign—the only kind the Democratic leadership knows how to organize—Nixon held all the cards. Running as a great international statesman and peacemaker, Nixon could win on the strength of his ceremonial diplomacy, while confining his campaign to equally empty and ceremonial appearances. Faced, however, with an opponent who was determined to make an issue of the war, the economy, and governmental "credibility" in general, Nixon might have reverted to his former style, thereby confirming the long-standing popular suspicion that tricky Dick is not a man you can trust. To put the matter more broadly, the Democrats in 1972 could nullify the advantages inherent in controlling the presidency only by appealing directly to popular discontent.

But since this also meant reorganizing the party itself, the Democratic leaders could hardly be expected to participate enthusiastically in such a campaign. McGovern would have had to win the presidency the same way he won his party's nomination—on his own, with his own organization, and with only perfunctory support from the unions and the party hierarchy.

A McGovern victory on these terms—here we come to the nub of the matter—would have created a significant opening in American politics. It would have set in motion popular forces which could not be appeased by his own programs (and whose active support and pressure on Congress and the bureaucracy he would need even to make a beginning in re-allocating wealth and dismantling the military-industrial apparatus). Those programs are "extreme" only in the context of the total vacuity of other candidates' programs. While their implementation would have had consequences far from negligible for American society, they by no means embody the kind of comprehensive attack on the problems of neo-capitalism that is required. They would probably create as much dissatisfaction as they would allay. Moreover, even their enactment was unlikely without various kinds of compromises.

Political conditions following the inauguration of McGovern might have been somewhat reminiscent of conditions in 1933–34, when the New Deal acted as a stimulus to popular movements that sought to go beyond the New Deal and threatened for a time to overthrow it. The "revolution" that many observers predicted in 1934 never materialized, partly because the Roosevelt administration made concessions to popular demands for such reforms as a graduated income tax and social security, partly because one of its leading spokesmen (Huey Long) was assassinated, and partly because the strongest and most effective wing of the left—the Communist Party—decided that communism was "twentieth-century Americanism" and gave uncritical support to the New Deal as the opening wedge of the socialist revolution; the very strategy Harrington urges today. It is in keeping with his general outlook that Harrington regards the disaster of the popular front as a piece of consummate political realism. The popular front strategy, he says, "worked better in the United States," even though it was dictated by Moscow, than the sectarianism of the socialists.

Even if we set aside the socialists, who had their own problems, this judgment leaves us with the difficulty of explaining the collapse of the Communist movement after the war and the ease with which it was expelled from the CIO. A better interpretation would be that the militant industrial unionism promoted by the Communist Party in the late thirties, unaccompanied by a militant politics or a critical view of American culture, left the party ideologically indistinguishable from American liberalism and to a considerable extent dependent on its fortunes. When liberals found themselves on the defensive after the war, they readily sacrificed their own left wing to the popular outcry against subversion, while the party's subservience to Moscow made it possible for it to be depicted as a foreign menace. As the left wing of the New Deal coalition, the Communists were more vulnerable than they would have been as an independent political movement.

Whether a somewhat similar political situation in the 1970's would have a different outcome depends, in part, on whether the left is better prepared to deal with the new populism than the left of the thirties was prepared to cope with the New Deal. The Communists' pratfalls in the thirties, particularly their ungainly leap from the super-revolutionism of the "third period" (1929–34) to the ultra-reformism of the Popular Front, are an object lesson in what to avoid. Merely negative lessons, however—even if these were clearly understood—would take the left only a certain distance toward the wisdom it needs. More than ever, radicals need to ponder their history.

In doing so, they will find in Michael Harrington's book many of the insights they need to absorb. That Harrington's book is not likely to provide reliable guidelines to current political practice does not invalidate its other virtues. Wisdom is not the monopoly of any particular political position. For that matter there is also much to be learned from the new populism, if only because it is closer to the country's mood than the new left ever was. If radicals and intellectuals adopt toward this movement an attitude of superior disdain, they will show that they have not only learned nothing from their recent experiences but are probably determined to remain ignorant.

[XII]

The "Counter-Culture"

1. Reich's Revolution in Manners

THAT A WOULD-BE DISTURBER OF THE POLITICAL PEACE SHOULD
reach hundreds of thousands of readers ought to be a matter for
rejoicing. Unfortunately Charles Reich's criticism of American
life, for all his obviously good-hearted intentions, does not cut
very deep. It can be accepted without any profound unsettling
of existing habits of thought. In many ways the book reinforces
those habits and thereby deepens our confusion instead of helping to dispel it.

Reich has said that he wished to explain the young to their
troubled parents, and it is clear that it is parents, not the young,
who are buying and reading *The Greening of America* and
finding in it not so much a clear explanation of the youth revolt—which in its rejection of traditional individualism Reich
does not even understand—as a reassurance that things are
working themselves out in the best possible way. It seems that
the "kids," for all their bluntness and unpredictability, have
caught a vision of a brighter future. After all they are only trying
to put into practice their parents' ideals. They "accept" those
ideals; what they object to is merely "their parents' failure to live
these same ideals." By taking seriously the old American dream,
the younger generation has initiated a bloodless revolution. "It
will not be like revolutions of the past"—those decadent Old
World revolutions in which men fought passionately over politics, used swords and guns against each other, and shook the
social order to its foundations, incidentally causing bitterness

and suffering. Our revolution "will not require violence to succeed, and it cannot be successfully resisted by violence." Already it is "spreading with amazing rapidity, and already our laws, institutions and social structure are changing in consequence." The change goes deeper than merely political change. Compared with the youth upheaval, "a mere revolution, such as the French or the Russian, seems inconsequential—a shift in the base of power." Those who look to politics for change, Reich believes, do not understand "the crucial importance of *choosing a new life-style.*"

There is something incorrigibly American about the illusion that great changes can take place without a great price having to be paid for them. In belittling the revolutions of the past, Reich tries to wave away the pain and suffering that necessarily accompany a genuine social transformation. Because he chooses to remain ignorant of history—substituting for historical analysis a diagrammatic sketch of the development of three stages of "consciousness"—he blinds himself to a fact that no one interested in changing American society can afford to ignore: precisely because change is painful, people have to be desperate in order to risk it. Bad as things are, the prospect of chaos is usually worse. That is one reason advocates of change have to offer programs of their own, and not merely programs but a coherent social vision, a new culture. Even then, masses of people will not risk the uncertainties of revolutionary change unless they have come to the point of having nothing left to lose.

For Reich, however, it is enough for people simply to choose new "life-styles." Reich sees revolution as something that begins with individuals; this too is very American. The sense of history as a collective undertaking is entirely foreign to American individualism. For this reason Americans are uneasy with politics, a collective expression. "Politics" signifies corruption, compromise, deals; true statemanship is "above" politics, or entirely outside it. Reich shares this ingrained American suspicion of politics. He dismisses the belief that change comes through changing institutions as an attribute of an outmoded "consciousness"—"Consciousness II" (as distinguished from "Consciousness I"—*laissez-faire* liberalism—and "Consciousness III"—the youth revolt). Both socialists and liberals suffer from the disease of Consciousness II. They still believe in politics.

Consciousness III, on the other hand, knows that politics is a snare and a delusion. It understands that "the controlling factor" in history "is consciousness." It knows that "we can make a new choice whenever we are ready to do so. We can end or modify the age of science and we can abandon the Protestant ethic." We can begin the revolution right now by growing our hair. "Can anyone doubt that [long hair] will reach all the men in our society within a few years?" It is in comparison with such momentous transformations that "mere revolution" seems "inconsequential."

Reich belongs to a long evangelistic tradition in the United States, a tradition that regards social life—insofar as it regards social life at all—as the product of innumerable "choices" made by individuals. Brother, repent! "[T]he central fact about Consciousness III [is] its assertion of the power to *choose* a way of life." Marx, we are told, made the mistake of thinking that "consciousness is determined by material interests." What Marx actually said was that "social existence" determines consciousness—that "legal relations," for example, "could neither be understood by themselves, nor explained by the so-called general progress of the human mind," but "are rooted in the material conditions of life." Thought does not exist in a vacuum. Men make their own history, since society itself, while rooted in biological necessity, is largely the creation of human culture; but men make history within limits set by the history they have already made. Marx knew that without a demonstration that the material basis of socialism had been created by the conditions of bourgeois society itself, his criticism of capitalism would remain disembodied and would carry no more weight than any other kind of moral exhortation.

Not so with Reich. He interprets the revolt of the affluent young, and the fact that it is opposed by the working class, to mean that consciousness is a matter of personal assertion, particularly in a stage of social development at which "the economic ceases to be of primary concern in men's lives." Only in America could this kind of statement pass for social criticism. Never mind the distortion of Marx. One does not have to be a Marxist to see that the collective provision for man's material needs—food, shelter, reproduction of the species—is the basis of social life, or that a rising standard of living (greatly exaggerated by Reich in any case) does not suddenly make those questions irrelevant or even of less than "primary concern." Of course men also need culture—a rich structure of meanings that makes sense of experience. But culture cannot be regarded as a matter of individual "life-styles." It is a collective creation, itself deeply influenced by the ways in which society organizes the production of material needs. A society that leaves production to "private enterprise" will get a culture to match, one characteristic of which is precisely the tendency to see culture as the product of private choice. In this respect Reich is truly a man of his times.

Advocates of change, one would suppose, would find it necessary to understand the distribution of power in the United States. Has the basis of power changed? Has the possession of property lost its political importance? Has a managerial class replaced the capitalists? These are questions of great complexity and importance, with which serious students of American society have been engaged for some time. Instead of wrestling with them, Reich accepts the clichés of pop sociology and draws from them the comforting picture of a society that can be altered through acts of individual will. Since "there is no class struggle; today there is only one class" and since "there is no longer any ruling class except the machine itself," we are all free, even millionaires (especially millionaires?), to choose "liberation instead of the plastic world of material wealth" and to exchange "wealth, status and power for love, creativity, and liberation."

Reich's diagnosis of what is wrong with American society, like his conception of the way in which everything that is wrong will be righted, consistently overestimates the importance of "individual freedom." Reich is quite correct in asserting that what is wrong cannot be understood merely as economic deprivation. "The real question for the worker just as for the black man, is 'who am I? what sort of culture should I have . . . ?'" This statement contains an important insight, but it should not obscure the fact that economic deprivation still exists; nor should it be taken to mean that cultural questions are not class questions at the same time. The issue for workers, and for Americans in general, is: What kind of culture should *we* have? Even here, Reich's formulation of the issue still suffers from the assumption that culture is a matter of private choice. His principal indictment of American society is not that it tolerates alarming levels of poverty or destroys the environment or makes interminable war against other peoples, still less that it fails to project a coherent world view, but that it interferes with personal freedom. The "system," with its "false consciousness" (another empty phrase, much employed by Reich), denies extended vacations to the office worker, free speech to the G.I., long hair to the high school student. It inhibits the "search for self." Advertising creates a demand for leisure, for tropical vacations, and "sensuality," which it cannot satisfy—and this disparity between expectations and reality in turn engenders revolt. Without pausing to consider which social groups have an interest in preserving the present arrangements—he prefers to talk vaguely of "forces"—Reich expounds at great length on the decline of personal "satisfaction": "adventure," "travel," "sex," "nature," "growth, learning, change," "responding to own needs" ("staying in bed when the need is felt, drinking a milk shake on a hot afternoon, or stopping everything to watch a rainstorm"), "wholeness," "sensuality," "new feelings," "expanded consciousness," "affection," "community," "brotherhood," "liberation."

Three points need to be made about this catalogue. In the first place, an efficiently organized industrial system can tolerate a wide range of private satisfactions, providing they remain private. Hence a demand for more "satisfactions" is hardly a revolutionary program. In the second place, the demand itself reflects a pinched and meager conception of the good life, one that owes much to advertising and travel brochures—embodiments of the very culture Reich professes to deplore. Finally, as we have already had occasion to note, Reich has no conception of social life or culture that goes beyond the individual. He observes that the industrial system—since it often gives the impression of running out of human control—denies us the satisfaction of "creating an environment," but he defines this purely in personal terms: "Taking whatever elements are given, natural, human, and social, and making a unique pattern out of them as one's own creation." Once again we see how the progressive educator's ideal of individual "creativity" blunts the edge of any radical critique of American culture, which would have to begin with a recognition that "creating an environment" is a collective undertaking, and that it is precisely the collective decision to create a more humane environment—as opposed to personal hedonism—that the industrial system as presently constituted cannot tolerate.

One more example will suffice to show how Reich personalizes and therefore trivializes every issue that he takes up. At one point he deplores the university's obsession with scholarly "productivity." A more serious critic would proceed to an analysis of the body of scholarship produced by current conditions. He might try to show that the flood of scholarly monographs in no way enriches our understanding and in fact impedes the necessary work of theory and synthesis. He might also try to show that much of this work is ideological in content, serving to legitimate existing social relations. Instead, Reich objects that writing scholarly books is rarely a "creative" experience for the individuals engaged in it. This completely misses the point: it is precisely because the activity does offer genuine pleasure that there is so little disposition to criticize the institution that makes it possible, the modern university. As long as the university allows us to "do our own work," we ask no questions of it. The real problem of academic life is not how to find private satisfactions but how to create a *community* of scholars. More teaching and less research—Reich's solution—is a trite and hollow formulation that obscures the underlying question of *what* we are to teach.

The prevailing social and cultural conditions in the United States are far too grim to allow us to be diverted by instant radicals, with-it professors, and Pollyannas of whatever ideological persuasion. A threadbare garment of individualism, optimism, and evangelical enthusiasm cannot take on new splendor by being decked out with love beads.

2. Change Without Politics

PHILIP SLATER'S BOOK The Pursuit of Loneliness CONTAINS MANY sharp observations about American suburbs, the suburban family, the divorce between home and work, the bad consequences of the segregation of sexes and age groups, and about what might be called the psychopathology of possessive individualism. The Pursuit of Loneliness examines with a certain refinement many of the themes that were crudely presented in Charles Reich's Greening of America. Whereas Reich sentimentalized the "counter-culture" and exaggerated its revolutionary potential, Slater realizes that cultural changes will have little effect unless accompanied by "other changes." He sees that as long as the "new culture" remains merely a youth culture it will make "few inroads into the structure of post-college life" and will serve, in fact, merely to strengthen the consumer economy by creating a market for youth-oriented products.

Unfortunately, Slater is very vague about the "other changes" that will have to accompany cultural change. His analysis of American culture needs to be supplemented by social and political analysis; but Slater is clearly uncomfortable in this realm and never succeeds in breaking out of psychological categories, drawn from Freudian anthropology and neo-Freudian cultural criticism (Marcuse, Fromm, Keniston), which are helpful up to a point but finally become constricting unless informed by a sense of political reality.

The tendency to reduce every political phenomenon to a psychological origin often means that obvious explanations are ignored in favor of extremely tortuous ones, as when Slater attributes resentment against hippies not even in part to political hatred but to the secret envy of adults "discontent[ed] with their own lives"—an interpretation, incidentally, that greatly exaggerates the attractions of the hippie "culture" and the degree to which it is in fact "more loving, expressive, creative, cooperative, honest," and so on. As in many descriptions of hippiedom by well-meaning admirers, it is hard to recognize here its increasingly desperate and ugly alienation.

Because Slater claims too much for psychological explanations, his work lacks a political-historical dimension; but even as a cultural analysis, it is grotesquely oversimplified and shows no understanding of the process of cultural change. In order to persuade us that the "counter-culture" represents a genuine alternative to the "old culture" of scarcity and predatory competition, Slater would have to show that it has absorbed many elements of the existing culture while infusing them with new meaning. Instead, he presents the "new culture" simply as the antithesis of the old, a procedure that quickly degenerates to the level of a parlor game. "The old culture . . . tends to give preference to property rights over personal rights, technological requirements over human needs, competition over cooperation, violence over sexuality . . . Oedipal love over communal love, and so on. The new counterculture tends to reverse all of these priorities." How delightfully simple! Does Slater think that early bourgeois culture simply "reversed the priorities" of feudalism?

In social theory it is sometimes useful to abstract from a complicated empirical context "ideal types," which illustrate aspects of historical development with particular clarity. Max Weber's concept of the Protestant ethic helped to clarify the relations between religion and economics by isolating aspects of the capitalist character. Weber did not propose, however, that this device could substitute for historical analysis, with its complexity and ambiguity. He was careful to point out that a clear-cut opposition between the "spirit of capitalism" and earlier modes of life existed in the realm of theory alone.

Slater knows no such reservations; indeed he does not seem to be conscious of the methodological problem. His concepts of "old" and "new" cultures do not function as ideal types but merely as stereotypes, derived from popular wisdom, from the distorted representation both of middle-class life and of the youth culture provided by the media, and from the denigration of suburbia fashionable in the 1950's—which provided the radicalism of the sixties with so many of its themes. The deficiencies of Slater's book far outweigh its merits. Written at the end of the sixties, when the "counter-culture" still retained a faint aura of innocence, in a harder time *The Pursuit of Loneliness* seems already dated.

3. Some Cultural and Political Implications of Ethnic Particularism

IN THE NINETEENTH AND EARLY TWENTIETH CENTURIES IT WAS widely believed that modern civilization eradicated the pre-industrial cultures with which, in its relentless expansion, it came into contact. Marxists, for example, were convinced that the "universalizing" tendency of capitalism would inevitably destroy all vestiges of regional and tribal particularism, break down local and parochial attachments, and lay the groundwork for a truly international culture. Their belief in the disintegrating impact of industrial civilization on earlier cultural forms was inseparable from their conception of cultural emancipation as the progress from a comfortable but stagnant rural domesticity to a cosmopolitanism transcending local and even national loyalties.

It was not only the Marxists who viewed the march of civilization in these terms. The dominant school of sociology in the United States, the structural functionalism associated with Ward and Veblen and later with the Chicago school, saw "traditional" cultures as being overwhelmed by contact with modernism. The Chicago school regarded the American city as a laboratory in which this process could be studied in detail, as the immigrant cultures, and later the culture of Southern Negroes, visibly dis-integrated in the acid of city life. The urban sociology of Park, Burgess, and Frazier represented in some ways the scientific version of a national myth, the myth of the melting pot—and also, it might be noted, an urban equivalent of the Turner thesis, according to which the frontier was the solvent in which European cultures dissolved into Americanism.

Recent work in history, sociology, and anthropology has made it clear that so-called traditional cultures are more resistant to modern civilization than had been supposed. Historians of working-class culture in England and the United States are beginning to show that pre-industrial attitudes—in particular, pre-industrial concepts of community—survived industrialism and were, in fact, absorbed into the labor movement; furnished the basis, in other words, of much of the resistance to industrial capitalism. Students of black culture in the United States are coming to somewhat similar conclusions. In the Third World, revolutionary movements in the twentieth century have often allied themselves—incongruously from the point of view of orthodox Marxism—with movements of national independence and with the defense of national cultures not only against Western imperialism but against the globalizing tendencies of socialism itself, as embodied in the foreign policy of the Soviet Union. The experience of pre-industrial peoples brought forcibly into contact with modern technological society has been highly ambiguous. On the one hand, industrial technology and mass communications have had an undeniably disruptive effect on many patterns of pre-industrial culture; but on the other hand, they have often strengthened the determination to preserve older ways, precisely as a defense against disorganization and loss of identity. Whether we look at the struggle against imperialism in the non-Western world or at separatist and particularist movements within the advanced countries themselves, recent history presents a curious spectacle. In the face of powerful influences tending to level regional and ethnic differences and to promote uniformity and standardization—influences which, it once ap-

peared, were inexorably bringing into being a global technological and rationalized society and were thereby laying the basis for
what Gramsci called the cultural unification of mankind—there
has been a surprising resurgence of ethnic and regional particularism, not only in the undeveloped countries but in French
Canada, in Northern Ireland, and among American blacks.

In the United States, and probably in other advanced countries
as well, the revival of ethnic particularism has coincided with a
new wave of enthusiasm for popular culture on the part of intellectuals and educated people generally—an enthusiasm verging
on sentimentalism. Support for black culture is at least as great
among educated whites as it is among blacks themselves; and
whites are much more likely to romanticize it, since they do not
experience at first hand the poverty that is also an element of
black culture, along with its positive features. It has always been
tempting for intellectuals and other privileged persons to seek in
vicarious identification with oppressed and outcast groups a
release from the complexity of modern society and from "bourgeois hang-ups." To the jaded bourgeois intellectual, lower-class
culture presents itself as spontaneity, an uninhibited sexuality, a
certain loose-jointedness—an alternative, as Mabel Dodge Luhan
once put it, to "a dismal accretion of cars, stoves, sinks, *et al.*"
Among the poor themselves, a healthy realism sets limits to
fantasies about the moral superiority of poverty.

The identification of reason with technological rationalization
has given rise to a revolt against reason itself, one aspect of
which is a revival of cultural primitivism among the educated.
Intellectual and literary culture has come to be widely regarded
as an instrument of exploitation and domination; thus we have
the demand, advanced by some black nationalists and supported
by many white radicals, that "black culture" replace "white culture" in the schools; that English be taught as a foreign language; and that in the universities, black studies be defined as a
completely autonomous branch of learning. To what extent is
the scholarly interest in black culture itself tinged with these
attitudes?

In a recent essay on black culture—an essay devoted to the rehabilitation of Melville J. Herskovits and an attack on the concept of the "culture of poverty"—John Szwed suggests in passing that the expulsion of whites from the civil rights movement was prompted not only by the blacks' desire to assert political control but by a rejection of "unreasonable and irrelevant white cultural models of change." This assertion seems to me to reflect a fairly widespread tendency to furnish cultural explanations for clearly political events, a tendency that can easily end in the complete rejection of politics as itself another "white cultural mode of change"—for it has been argued that organization, agitation, the formulation of programs, and the attempt to influence opinion and win power are "white men's ways" that can be adopted by blacks and other minorities only by sacrificing their indigenous values.

The assertion that black radicalism rejects "white cultural models of change" also helps to point up the importance of the way culture is defined. The anthropological concept of culture as a people's total way of life, which has given rise to what Szwed calls the "cultural approach" to the study of society, is often confused with culture in the narrower sense of accumulated ideas and techniques, transmitted for the most part in writing. That this confusion has become pervasive is suggested by the popular use of the term "life-style" to include everything from novels to the length of people's hair. One of its consequences is a growing disposition to regard culture in the more restricted sense—literary culture or "high culture"—not as potentially the common property of all men, but as something peculiarly bourgeois, white, or male, depending on the polemical frame of reference. The revolt against capitalism, racism, and the oppression of women becomes identified with a revolt against culture; or worse, the revolt against culture becomes a substitute for the revolt against capitalism, racism, and sexual exploitation.

Until recently, high culture was regarded, even by radicals—one is tempted to say, especially by radicals—not as the monopoly of any particular class or race but as mankind's inheritance. Gramsci once wrote:

> In the accumulation of ideas transmitted to us by a millennium of work and thought there are elements which have an eternal value, which cannot and must not perish. The loss of consciousness of these values is one of the most serious signs of degradation brought about by the bourgeois regime; to whom everything becomes an object of trade and a weapon of war. The proletariat will have to take on the work of reconquest, to restore in full for itself and all humanity the devastated realm of the spirit.

Partly because the proletarian movement never successfully addressed itself to this task, we now find ourselves confronted with demands for cultural autonomy that confuse intellectual culture with bourgeois "life-styles" and reject the former along with the latter. The discovery that ethnic cultures (in the broad sense of the term "culture") have been unexpectedly resistant to homogenization coincides with, and to some extent may be informed by, a misguided and regressive rebellion against literary culture that seeks in a sentimental myth of the folk an antidote to bourgeois decadence. Were the political movements to which the scholarly rediscovery of ethnicity corresponds—movements for ethnic equality and self-determination—to adopt this primitivism as their own, they would then be adopting "irrelevant white cultural models" with a vengeance.

There is nothing about black culture, no matter how we define it, that makes it undesirable or unnecessary for blacks to acquire the ideas and techniques that men have accumulated in the course of trying to understand nature and society and to use nature for their own purposes. To argue otherwise is to argue for permanent cultural inferiority and political subordination; and this is the case no matter what value one sets on black culture in the larger sense. Strictly speaking, the issues are quite separate, and the two meanings of the term "culture" must be kept distinct. Nevertheless, as I have already indicated, the tendency to equate high culture with bourgeois domination is closely related to a tendency to romanticize black culture and to exaggerate its distinctiveness. The issue is not whether black people have a culture. In the essay already alluded to, the writer sets up a straw man, the contention that Afro-Americans have been "stripped" of their culture, and then proceeds to demolish it—incidentally with many asides to the effect that anyone who questions his own interpretation of the distinctiveness of black culture must be politically on the side of integration. But surely the question is no longer whether blacks have been "stripped" of their culture but whether the culture they do have is primarily African in origin or whether it has been formed in response to oppression in America, as the theorists of the "culture of poverty" have tried to show.

The history of Harlem helps to clarify this issue. As late as the twenties, even after the mass migration from the South had begun to be felt, Harlem retained a vigorous community life. It was at once more prosperous and more self-sustaining than it has since become. The collapse of the Negro artisan class, the Great Depression, the economic deterioration of New York City in general, and perhaps also the ideology of integration, combined to render Harlem vulnerable not only to economic but to cultural penetration from outside. It became an after-hours playground for whites looking for forbidden pleasures and hungry for soul. Black music, black sex, black pleasure of all kinds became highly marketable commodities. Harlem took on the trappings of a "hustling society," in the words of Malcolm X, adopting as its "first rule" the hustler's principle "that you never trusted anyone outside of your own close-mouthed circle."

Those who deny the pathological elements in the culture of poverty would do well to ponder Malcolm's account of his own degradation, in a world where high status meant a light skin, straight hair, the company of white women, and flashy clothes (manufactured by white merchants especially for the ghetto and sold at inflated prices). Relations between blacks and whites—sexual relations in particular—came to be founded on a pattern of mutual fascination, exploitation, and degradation. The revival of black nationalism in the fifties and sixties, with its Puritanical morality and its reassertion of the work ethic, was directed precisely against this kind of cultural "integration." It reflected an awareness that the two races had too long, and at too close range, witnessed each other's shame.

Unfortunately, this same nationalism proved unable to formulate an adequate politics. Like other black nationalist movements in the past, it advocated physical separation. At the same time it put forward a mythical view of the Negro past, which encouraged an escapist preoccupation with Africa. Neither at the political nor at the cultural level did it succeed in expressing the two-sidedness of the life of American blacks. For a time, it appeared that the black power movement of the mid-sixties would achieve a real unity, combining an emphasis on the distinctive elements in black culture with a struggle for power in American society as a whole. But this movement quickly split in two. The political wing propounds a new integrationism in the name of "Marxism-Leninism," while the cultural nationalists ignore politics altogether. Meanwhile a new generation of academics had rediscovered popular culture as a field for scholarly research—and also, perhaps, as a way of resolving nagging doubts about their own relevance. The question, as I have already suggested, is whether this new scholarship will encourage a better understanding of the relations between modern technological society and the pre-industrial cultures it has partially absorbed, or whether it will merely surround poverty with the romantic glow of the intellectuals' own alienation. An appreciation of the resilience of pre-industrial culture could contribute, however indirectly, to the growth of a genuinely antitechnological politics. Romanticizing poverty, on the other hand, would merely prolong the present political stalemate and at the same time encourage a process of cultural "Balkanization"—a regression to a state of generalized ignorance disguised as ethnic pluralism and having as its political counterpart a system of repressive decentralization, combining "community control" of culture with centralized control of production, and a colorful proliferation of "life-styles" with the underlying reality of class domination.

4. The Cultural Crisis: A Manifesto

RECENT CONFLICTS IN ACADEMIC LIFE HAVE PITTED A BANKRUPT liberalism against an equally bankrupt radical opposition. The liberal values of pluralism and free inquiry have come to be embodied—or caricatured—in the multiversity, an institution that in effect sells its services to the highest bidder behind a facade of scholarly detachment and objectivity. The degradation of the universities and the learned societies invites the radical demand for "relevance" and for academic institutions that will "serve the people." Such reforms, in which the liberal establishment often finds it expedient to acquiesce, merely complete the politicization of academic life. Culture ceases to be regarded as among other things the expression of standards and principles that transcend the social order and are therefore inherently critical of it, and instead becomes identified either with the defense of the status quo or with revolutionary movements to the needs of which culture, we are told, must be strictly subordinated. Those who reject both these conceptions of knowledge nevertheless find themselves torn, in the absence of a clearly articulated alternative, between a sterile academic quietism and a sterile activism. Many today appear apologetic about having chosen a scholarly career, demoralized by the conflicts raging in the university, and all too often reduced to silence.

The crisis of academic culture, which is both a cause and effect of this demoralization, reflects a more general crisis of culture. With the dissolution of the tradition of critical rationalism, modern culture tends to split into the extremes of technological or bureaucratic rationalization and irrationalist revolt. The crimes and disasters that have marked the history of advanced countries in the twentieth century have undermined confidence in rationality, particularly when rationality is so often identified with bureaucratic regimentation and manipulation, with an amoral technology that produces immoral social conditions, and with ideological defenses of Western imperialism.

The disastrous split between fact and value has given rise to a concept of scientific objectivity that has banished from the natural and social sciences, and even from history and philosophy, the ethical and political questions with which learning ought to be centrally engaged: questions of how society can best be organized so as to promote justice, peace, and the fullest realization of human creativity. Those disciplines which consider themselves scientific have retreated to a narrow scientism—a pretended neutrality that usually serves to legitimize the existing social order and to discourage criticism of it. The assertion of values is left to the humanities; but these—no longer regarded, even by themselves, as capable of making verifiable statements about objective reality—have sunk to a degraded and essentially ornamental status. The humanities, therefore, even when they seek to be genuinely critical, can be safely ignored. Deprived of a rational basis, criticism of the industrial order tends more and more to take the form of subjectivism—of an assertion of "artistic truth" against "scientific truth," of the elaboration of private visions of the world, of the cult of myth, or of the celebration of madness itself as a high form of reason.

The political left, which because of its commitment to change might have been expected to offer a way out of the cultural crisis of industrial society, has come instead to embody that crisis. It veers between an identification with scientism and uncontrolled technology on the one hand and, on the other, a cult of action for action's sake and of "radical will." The left's failure to transcend the cultural crisis and to reassert the rational traditions from which it sprang helps to explain its ineffectiveness as a political force. While we do not urge intellectuals to renounce political commitments and activity, we do insist that their principal responsibility lies in the field of culture and that their most important political contribution can only be made through the pursuit of their respective intellectual callings. The overwhelming urgency of the political crisis must no longer be allowed to divert intellectuals from their own special work of interpreting the world and thereby developing a sound understanding of the possibilities and limitations of political action. Instead of subordinating their work to directly political causes of one kind or another, intellectuals must concern themselves with attempting to produce a critical analysis of all phases of advanced industrial society and to communicate this body of knowledge to nonspecialists—that is, to train an educated public.

We must begin with the state of our own disciplines and with the general state of the academic profession. It is now generally admitted that the profession needs to be reformed. The appearance of radical caucuses in the various disciplines, the formation of committees of "concerned scholars," the intense debates about the scholar's responsibility that regularly erupt in professional meetings, all attest to a sense of acute crisis. Scientists are debating whether they have an ethical obligation to concern themselves with the uses to which scientific discoveries are put. Anthropologists question whether it is proper to work on projects that support programs of counterinsurgency. All of the professional organizations have been confronted with demands to identify themselves with opposition to the war, with attacks on racism, and with the fight against poverty.

As striking as the sense of crisis is the confusion of the discussions to which it has given rise. Those who oppose the radical demands vacillate between intransigence and capitulation, between a pretense not to know what the discussion is about and a sentimental celebration of the young. Radical demands are themselves confused and often conflicting. Sometimes they seek to disengage the university from its social commitments by attacking military research, at other times they seem designed to redress the balance by adding a whole set of new commitments to social reform. Radical demands, moreover, are open to the objection that they show little attention to the maintenance of academic standards or the responsibility of teachers to provide intellectual leadership, not merely to echo the preoccupations and prejudices of their students. Radicals in the professions have begun to raise questions about scholarly responsibility and the ends scholarship is to serve, but they have provided few coherent ideas about the nature of their own disciplines.

The situation in history provides a case in point. The steady deterioration of historical scholarship and its transformation into either technical or trivial pursuits can no longer be denied. The existing professional organizations probably cannot and certainly will not arrest this decline. But the radical opposition has done little to clarify the issues. Its conception of "radical history" too often boils down to a reversal of the ideological distortions of the establishment and to a contemptuous dismissal of all "bourgeois" historiography. In refusing to build on the work of their predecessors, the "radical" historians merely perpetuate a tendency that has plagued American historiography for years—the tendency to assume that every problem, no matter how minute, must constantly be examined afresh; that the work of earlier historians is necessarily unreliable; that only the "original sources" can be trusted; that monographs are therefore superior to syntheses; and that general ideas represent so much ideological baggage that has to be swept away by each succeeding generation. The failure to achieve a balance between theory and empirical work is a general failure of American historiography that cannot be remedied by setting "radical history" in the place of "liberal history." For that matter, the very notion of "radical history" betrays a mechanistic view of the relation between politics and culture, in which liberal historiography is seen, not as a complex body of work that must be criticized on its merits before it can be transcended, but as an automatic reflex to the needs of the capitalist order that can be countered by a radical historiography based on some vaguely defined sense of sympathy with the underprivileged.

If a genuine reconstruction of higher learning is to take place, it will have to be carried out by the students of today and especially by the graduate students—the prospective inheritors of the university. These students desperately need intellectual guidance, as they themselves are the first to recognize. The university has largely failed to provide it. The overriding problem confronting scholars for some time to come will be how to bring into being an intellectual community that ought to exist but does not exist in the universities—a community of intellectuals devoted to a searching examination of technological society and culture and of the place of knowledge in a social order to which knowledge seems at once indispensable and superfluous.

Our general perspective is socialist. We fully recognize, however, that socialism, as it has so far appeared in practice, has not offered to the world the regime of individual liberty to which we are wholly committed. We also recognize that Marxian theory at best represents only the initial premises of a critical theory of advanced society, not a fully developed body of unimpeachable truth. Recent historical scholarship makes it clear that Marx's own thought has been subjected to a variety of misinterpretations by those who regard themselves as Marxists. The nature of "Marxism" has never been more problematical than at the present time. Nor has Marxism had much to say about a problem which, in a period of drastic cultural discontinuity, increasingly emerges as central—the need to distinguish between "culture" and "ideology," to erect safeguards against a complete assimilation of the two concepts, and to understand the way in which culture not only is shaped by class conflicts but is in important respects independent of them. The lack of any sustained and systematic analysis of the relation between society and culture is one of the most outstanding weaknesses of classical Marxism. In seeking to overcome it, we shall have to confront not only the full complexity of the historical record itself but a long tradition of conservative criticism of modern culture that has too often been ignored by the left. In identifying ourselves with socialism, therefore, we do not claim ideological purity through identification with Marxism—we leave that to earnest sectarians—but signify our belief that any rounded critique of modern society still has to begin with, or at the very least to take account of, Marx.

THE SO-CALLED
POST-INDUSTRIAL
SOCIETY

[XIII]

"Realism" as a Critique
of American Diplomacy

IN THE EARLY 1950's ANYONE SEEKING TO UNDERSTAND AMERICAN diplomacy, to understand his own mounting uneasiness about the course of events since World War II, turned with relief and gratitude to the writings of the new "realists." He turned, that is, to the writings of George F. Kennan; only later did he begin to understand that there were others like Kennan, that he was the founder of a school. Later still came the realization that others had anticipated Kennan in some of his criticisms of American foreign policy, and that his underlying premises themselves were not perhaps so new as they had appeared at the time. But the question of Kennan's intellectual antecedents was beside the point. What mattered was that at a time when the serious discussion of foreign affairs had almost ceased, when isolationism was dead and internationalism tainted on the one hand by the Wallace crusade and on the other by the excesses of those who were already talking about "winning" the cold war, Kennan revived the discussion and invested it with a new interest.

Kennan demonstrated that it was possible to criticize people like Woodrow Wilson and Franklin Roosevelt without falling into the heresy of isolationism. For a generation of disturbed and somewhat disillusioned liberals, that was a revelation of inestimable importance. By the 1950's, a good many liberals had begun to suspect that something had gone wrong with American foreign policy. They had begun to suspect, moreover, that whatever it was that had gone wrong could no longer be blamed on Henry Cabot Lodge or Senator Borah or Senator Nye or Charles Lindbergh or any of the other traditional villains of American liberalism. That there was something wrong with liberalism itself, however, was a proposition which it seemed impossible to entertain without at the same time putting oneself in the camp of the enemies of liberalism. In these circumstances the bafflement of the conscientious liberal was extreme; it threatened to immobilize him completely.

American Diplomacy, Kennan's first and still his most valuable book, pointed a way out of the difficulty. From the perspective he established in those lectures, the whole dispute between isolationists and internationalists faded into the background. What was historically wrong with American foreign policy was its rigidity, its misguided idealism, its rather simple-minded belief in the efficacy of legal and moral principles—habits of mind that were characteristic of isolationists and internationalists alike.

The "legalistic-moralistic" tradition, as Kennan called it, ran "like a red skein" through American foreign policy. The belief in the universal applicability of our own standards of international justice and in the desirability of getting other nations to subscribe to them had blinded us again and again to the realities of world politics. Our naïve notion of "aggression" as an outright abridgment of the right of self-determination had blinded us to subtler forms of aggression. It blinded us, also, to the difficulties of punishing aggression by collective action—the law-abiding nations against the outlaws. Worst of all, it confused pragmatic questions with ethical questions, questions of right with questions of power. "Whoever says there is a law must of course be indignant against the lawbreaker and feel a moral superiority to him. And when such indignation spills over into military contest, it knows no bounds short of the reduction of the lawbreaker to the point of complete submissiveness—namely, unconditional surrender." Thus the legalistic approach to world affairs, beginning with a desire to do away with violence, ended by making violence "more enduring, more terrible, and more destructive to political stability than did the older motives of national interest."

For Kennan, the alternative to legalism and moralism lay in a return to "the forgotten art of diplomacy." That meant a revival of balance-of-power politics and what seemed to Kennan the "modest" recognition that "our own national interest is all that we are really capable of knowing and understanding." Provided that our purposes were pure, "unsullied by arrogance or hostility," he did not see how the pursuit of our national interest could fail "to be conducive to a better world."

The impact of *American Diplomacy* was immediate. Overnight, liberals embraced the concept of the "national interest" and found themselves speaking in the accents of *Realpolitik*. Nobody seemed disturbed by this ideological incongruity. American liberals had always been noted for their pragmatism—a word which on innumerable occasions in the past had served to excuse taking opposed positions at the same time. The liberals' adoption of the tenets of the new realism was pragmatic in this sense.

Kennan's own ideological affinity was not very clear. The language of realism was undeniably conservative, although American "conservatives" in the 1950's disowned Kennan at once. But many of Kennan's observations—his rejection of total war, for instance—seemed radical; at least they put him in the company of radicals. Much of what he said about World War I echoed the complaints of radicals at the time. He would certainly have agreed that the war, as one editor of *The Nation* wrote to another in 1922, had been continued "beyond its natural economic limit" and that the character of the world was thereby decisively altered.

On the other hand, there was Kennan's call for a return to "old-fashioned diplomacy." Traditionally it was conservatives who defended balance-of-power politics and derided the dream of an international order run according to legal principles. It was conservatives who were skeptical about causes and crusades, distrustful of "enthusiasm" in any form. Kennan shared this distrust. Not only that, he expressed certain reservations about democracy itself, reminiscent of Tocqueville. "People are not always more reasonable than governments. . . . Public opinion . . . is not invariably a moderating force in the jungle of politics." Just the reverse, in fact; in the case of World War I, public opinion had exerted a decidedly bad effect. It was the mutual hatreds of peoples, inflamed by ideology, that had made it so difficult for governments to make peace. Walter Lippmann, another spokesman for a realistic view of foreign policy, went even further along these lines. It was when the existing governments had to turn to the people for help in carrying on the war, Lippmann wrote in *The Public Philosophy,* that they lost the last opportunity to make peace and to save what was left of the old order. The consequences of this surrender to public opinion had been "disastrous."

All this was clear enough; yet one still puzzled over the general bent of the new realism. Did it imply a radical critique of present as well as past policy? And if it did, how useful would it prove to be as an instrument of such criticism, when it reflected a point of view which seemed in so many respects to blend in with the prevailing conservatism?

The passage of time did not immediately clear up the mystery. In politics, Kennan seemed to be moving steadily toward the position advocated by the left—by the Labour Party in Britain, by socialists and radicals in America. He abandoned containment, which he had helped to formulate, and advocated "disengagement" in Europe. After his Reith Lectures in 1957, Dean Acheson attacked him as an isolationist. That in itself would have endeared him to the left.

Yet the two volumes of his *Soviet-American Relations,* which he published in the late fifties, pleaded more openly than ever for a revival of the techniques of traditional diplomacy. The second volume was dedicated, in fact, to the memory of DeWitt Clinton Poole and Maddin Summers (consuls at Moscow during World War I), "of whose faithful and distinguished efforts in Russia on their country's behalf this volume gives only an incomplete account." That Wilson would have fared better if he had relied on the judgment of professional diplomats was the burden of Kennan's narrative. The professionals understood power; the amateurs could not see beyond their own principles. Unfortunately it was the amateurs in whom Wilson, himself an amateur, in the last analysis rested his confidence: the senile Ambassador Francis, a political appointee of the most incompetent sort; the addle-headed Edgar Sisson, a Hearst reporter in search of sensational copy; above all the brilliant, impetuous and utterly unreliable Raymond Robins, with his unjustified optimism about Russia and his unwarranted confidence in the eternal verity of his liberal clichés. *American Diplomacy* condemned moralism and legalism in general terms; *Soviet-American Relations* tried to show, by a detailed examination of the day-by-day evolution of policy, that moralism and legalism were inevitable attributes of policy when policy was made by people not trained for the job.

These volumes brought to the surface in Kennan's thought what had not at first been apparent, the professional diplomat's pride of profession. The shift in focus, from the broad perspective of the earlier book to the narrower one of the latter, may have encouraged this tendency, for it led the scholar to immerse himself in the techniques by which diplomatic decisions were arrived at, as opposed to the content of the decisions themselves. An article published in the *American Scholar,* which presumably foreshadowed the third volume of *Soviet-American Relations,* work on which was interrupted by Kennan's return to the foreign service in 1961, carried the tendency further still. Here Kennan abandoned content almost entirely in favor of an examination of technique: ". . . this question of 'how' as distinct from the 'what' of diplomacy is . . . of tremendous importance." Still aware (as most scholars have yet to become aware) that the outcome of the peace conference was largely predetermined by the Allies' crushing defeat of Germany—that is, by the decision made in 1917 to prosecute the war to "victory"—and that the peace conference itself, therefore, was an episode of secondary importance, Kennan nevertheless made the history of the conference the text for what had become a favorite sermon: the futility of coalition diplomacy and of summit conferences in particular. He tried to show that Wilson's failure to come to grips with the Russian problem could be attributed in part to the simple fact that there were too many other demands on his time, too many other problems waiting to be solved. Not even the best of statesmanship, in other words, could have succeeded in the atmosphere of Versailles, or of any other meetings of heads of state.

Kennan's opposition to summitry was a thing of long standing. But the extent to which he had become preoccupied with the subject—to the exclusion, it seemed at times, of everything else— had only recently become clear. It was with the U-2 crisis of May 1960 that one finally began to understand the general direction of Kennan's thinking and of the new realism in general. And what the occasion revealed about the new realism was enough to call into serious question its ability to offer a perspective from which to criticize American policy, past or present.

The U-2 affair abounded in revelations. It not only demonstrated once and for all the incompetence of the Eisenhower administration; it also provided a touchstone by which to gauge the motives of the administration's critics. For while the critics agreed that the administration had blundered, they by no means agreed just wherein its worst blunder lay—whether in admitting to espionage or in engaging in it in the first place. Those who objected merely to our having allowed ourselves to be caught, and to our having compounded the damage by admitting what we had been doing, revealed themselves—for the first time in some cases—as committed, at heart, to the policies of the cold war. It was deeply significant, for instance, that this was the line taken by Walter Lippmann. "My criticism is that we have made these overflights an avowed policy." The avowal, not the flights themselves, was the administration's mistake. "As long as the world is as warlike as it has been in all recorded history, there is no way of doing without spying." Such realism as this was enough, for some of us, to call into question the whole realist critique of American diplomacy.

For to some of us the point of the U-2 affair was a good deal simpler, and it concerned not the methods of American diplomacy but its objectives. That "overflights" (which, it should be noted, were quite different from conventional espionage) had been taking place for years, and that they should have continued to take place up to the very eve of the Paris conference, when the prospects of a Berlin settlement looked better than they had looked since the end of the war, seemed to mean only one thing: that the government of the United States preferred a showdown to a settlement, that it was essentially indifferent to the possibility of negotiations with the Soviet Union, that it had embraced the cold war as a way of life. The possibility that Khrushchev himself may have wanted a way out of the conference, at the last minute—a possibility resting on no very impressive evidence, but which enjoyed great popularity as an explanation for the collapse of the conference—was really irrelevant. What mattered was our own indifference. If the other side was indifferent too, so much the worse; but their indifference, even assuming it to have been a fact, hardly excused our own.

At a time when even Adlai Stevenson was urging people to get behind the President, it was perhaps unreasonable to expect anything better from Mr. Kennan. All the same, Kennan's behavior was disappointing. He drew from these events, so endlessly suggestive in their ramifications, only the familiar lesson about the futility of summit diplomacy. "We should look very, very carefully before we submit the prestige of the President of the United States again to what has just happened in Paris." Called upon by a congressional committee to suggest what might be done to improve American diplomacy, he confined himself to a list of strictly procedural reforms: creation of an office of Secretary for Foreign Affairs who would represent the country at conferences, revival of the policy-planning staff, and so forth. Nothing could have seemed more irrelevant, at such a time, than this dry recital. Perhaps the newspapers misrepresented what Kennan said (his testimony was in secret session);

yet what he was reported to have said seemed consistent with the drift of his thinking. He may have made other criticisms as well; but if he did he never saw fit to publish them. Perhaps the whole business had rendered him speechless—a perfectly understandable reaction. But speechlessness was not much help to a country which needed the kind of thoroughgoing criticism toward which Kennan had made a beginning in his Reith Lectures. Kennan had nothing to add to what he had already said. The crisis made it clear for the first time that what he had already said was not enough.

What accounted for the failure of the new realism, at this most critical moment, to offer anything but platitudes—or worse, Lippmann's dissertations on the inevitability of espionage? In the re-examination of the realistic canon, to which these reflections led, a number of weaknesses in the argument now came to light. There was, for one thing, the overemphasis on technique, which merely touched the surface of the subject. For another thing there was the assumption that professional diplomats were free from the ideological illusions which afflicted amateurs. One trained as a historian willingly followed Kennan back to World War I in search of a guide to the present—with the help of Mr. Kennan himself, whose generosity to young scholars had already become proverbial. But what one found when one got there did not bear out the master's faith in professional diplomacy. The diplomats, it turned out, had been as blind as everyone else to the dangers of prolonging the war. Like everyone else, they had allowed the delusion of victory to interfere with their understanding of the Russian Revolution—by which Kennan rightly set such store. If anything could have saved Russia in 1917, it was peace; Kennan himself made the point again and again. Yet when the Provisional Government appealed to the Allies, not for peace (which it did not have the temerity to mention by name), but for a reconsideration of war aims which might serve as the first step toward peace, the diplomatic corps was unanimous in advising the unconditional rejection of the appeal. Kennan's own distinguished ancestor, George Kennan—not a professional diplomat, to be sure, but nevertheless a conservative who talked the language of power politics, hence presumably a realist—even this first George Kennan had bluntly advised the Secretary of State to "give no encouragement whatever . . . to the coalition ministry if it stands for 'peace without annexations or indemnities.'" For such men, peace, in the summer of 1917, was a German plot. This was the view which prevailed in the State Department and, as far as one could see, throughout the foreign service.

Finally, the history of World War I did not seem to sustain the distinction between "ideals" and "self-interest." The whole realist thesis rested on the distinction; historians had tried to trace the conflict through all of recent American diplomacy. Read in the light of what one had come to know about World War I, the case seemed to fall to the ground; the distinction seemed arbitrary and unreal. If the history of the war taught any lessons at all, it was that American policy had failed, not because Americans had made moral judgments, but because the moral judgments they made were so shallow. The trouble with Woodrow Wilson was that his ideals were so superficial, so crude, so circumscribed by his complacent assumption that his kind of democracy—the democracy of Walter Bagehot—represented the pinnacle of political virtue. The trouble with Wilson was not that he went off crusading for high ideals and ignored American self-interest. The trouble was that, like most statesmen, he found it so easy unconsciously to translate the self-interest of his own community into the language of high idealism. The most striking fact about the twentieth-century dream of world peace and order, of which Wilson was to become the prophet, was not that it was utopian but that it was a one-sided Utopia, a world made safe not for democracy but for ourselves.

From the point of view of three-fourths of the world, Wilson's famous quarrel with Clemenceau, which appeared so momentous to the new realists (as to all Western scholars), was less important than their shared determination to keep that same three-fourths in its place. From this broader perspective, liberal internationalism was itself a kind of imperialism, almost indistinguishable from the old. And it was the liberal Lloyd George, joining Wilson in refusing to support the counterrevolution in Russia, who assured the French, at the same time, that he did not propose to negotiate with the Bolsheviks. What he proposed, he explained to the Council of Ten—and his words speak volumes about the real nature of the old liberalism—was to give each of the contending factions in Russia a hearing, "to summon these people to Paris to appear before those present, somewhat in the way the Roman Empire summoned chiefs of outlying tributary states to render an account of their actions." The difference between the old imperialism and the new diplomacy was not, after all, so very great. The difference was simply that Wilson and Lloyd George substituted the semblance of international cooperation for the cruder instruments of coercion; bribery and manipulation for naked force. In a world in which the West's power to impose its will by force was already dwindling, Wilson's was bound to be the wave of the future.

Did the Wilsonian policy run counter to American national interests? On the contrary, the national interest demanded it. Farsighted men could argue that his policy, since perpetuated by Roosevelt, by Truman, by Eisenhower, by Kennedy, was suicidal in the long run. But the people who are responsible for defining what the national interest means at a given moment do not think in terms of the long run. What the pursuit of the national interest means, if history is any indication, is the pursuit of a nation's interests in their most immediate, crude, and palpable form. Thus the pursuit of the national interest implies the repression of other people's equally crude and palpable national interests. Against the history of the twentieth century, the new realists' vision of a world in which the mutual pursuit of national interests makes for peace and harmony begins to look like a reversion to the nineteenth-century theory of "harmony of interests," which lay at the heart of the very Wilsonian liberalism against which the realists endlessly inveigh. One would have thought that the idea of an international harmony of interests would have been tenable only as long as the oppressed had no voice in world affairs and could not testify to the contrary. The illusion persists, however, because we persist in ignoring the testimony which they now give in such abundance.

One comes back, finally, to that sentence in *American Diplomacy:* "If our own purposes and undertakings here at home are decent ones, unsullied by arrogance or hostility toward other people or delusions of superiority, then the pursuit of our national interest can never fail to be conducive to a better world." The question is, can the national interest be disentangled from the arrogance and hostility and delusions of superiority that seem to have characterized the behavior of nations at all times? Perhaps it could be, if nations came truly to understand their long-range interests. But that possibility may not be the best premise on which to base a philosophy of international relations that aspires to realism.

[XIV]

Sources of the Cold War: A Historical Controversy

S EVERAL YEARS HAVE PASSED SINCE ARTHUR SCHLESINGER, JR., announced that the time had come "to blow the whistle before the current outburst of revisionism regarding the origins of the cold war goes much further." Yet the outburst of revisionism shows no signs of subsiding. On the contrary, a growing number of historians and political critics, judging from such recent books as Ronald Steel's *Pax Americana* and Carl Oglesby's and Richard Schaull's *Containment and Change,* are challenging the view, once so widely accepted, that the cold war was an American response to Soviet expansionism, a distasteful burden reluctantly shouldered in the face of a ruthless enemy bent on our destruction, and that Russia, not the United States, must therefore bear the blame for shattering the world's hope that two world wars in the twentieth century would finally give way to an era of peace.

"Revisionist" historians are arguing instead that the United States did as much as the Soviet Union to bring about the collapse of the wartime coalition. Without attempting to shift the blame exclusively to the United States, they are trying to show, as Gar Alperovitz puts it, that "the cold war cannot be understood simply as an American response to a Soviet challenge, but rather as the insidious interaction of mutual suspicions, blame for which must be shared by all."

Not only have historians continued to re-examine the immediate origins of the cold war—in spite of attempts to "blow the whistle" on their efforts—but the scope of revisionism has been steadily widening. Some scholars are beginning to argue that the whole course of American diplomacy since 1898 shows that the United States has become a counterrevolutionary power committed to the defense of a global status quo. Arno Mayer's monumental study of the Conference of Versailles, *Politics and Diplomacy of Peacemaking,* which promises to become the definitive work on the subject, announces in its subtitle what a growing number of historians have come to see as the main theme of American diplomacy: *Containment and Counterrevolution.*

Even Schlesinger has now admitted, in a recent article in *Foreign Affairs,* that he was "somewhat intemperate," a year ago, in deploring the rise of cold war revisionism. Even though revisionist interpretations of earlier wars "have failed to stick," he says, "revisionism is an essential part of the process by which history . . . enlarges its perspectives and enriches its insights." Since he goes on to argue that "postwar collaboration between Russia and America [was] . . . inherently impossible" and that "the most rational of American policies could hardly have averted the cold war," it is not clear what Schlesinger thinks revisionism has done to enlarge our perspective and enrich our insights; but it is good to know, nevertheless, that revisionists may now presumably continue their work (inconsequential as it may eventually prove to be) without fear of being whistled to a stop by the referee.

The orthodox interpretation of the cold war, as it has come to be regarded, grew up in the late forties and early fifties—years of acute international tension, during which the rivalry between the United States and the Soviet Union repeatedly threatened to erupt in a renewal of global war. Soviet-American relations had deteriorated with alarming speed following the defeat of Hitler. At Yalta, in February 1945, Winston Churchill had expressed the hope that world peace was nearer the grasp of the assembled statesmen of the great powers "than at any time in history." It would be a great tragedy," he said, "if they, through inertia or carelessness, let it slip from their grasp. History would never forgive them if they did."

Yet the Yalta agreements themselves, which seemed at the time to lay the basis of postwar cooperation, shortly provided the focus of bitter dissension, in which each side accused the other of having broken its solemn promises. In Western eyes, Yalta meant free elections and parliamentary democracies in eastern Europe, while the Russians construed the agreements as recognition of their demand for governments friendly to the Soviet Union. The resulting dispute led to mutual mistrust and to a hardening of positions on both sides. By the spring of 1946 Churchill himself, declaring that "an iron curtain has descended" across Europe, admitted, in effect, that the "tragedy" he had feared had come to pass. Europe split into hostile fragments, the eastern half dominated by the Soviet Union, the western part sheltering nervously under the protection of American arms. NATO, founded in 1949 and countered by the Russian-sponsored Warsaw Pact, merely ratified the existing division of Europe. From 1946 on, every threat to the stability of this uneasy balance produced an immediate political crisis— Greece in 1947, Czechoslovakia and the Berlin blockade in 1948—each of which, added to existing tensions, deepened hostility on both sides and increased the chance of war. When Bernard Baruch announced in April 1947 that "we are in the midst of a cold war," no one felt inclined to contradict him. The phrase stuck, as an accurate description of postwar political realities.

Many Americans concluded, moreover, that the United States was losing the cold war. Two events in particular contributed to this sense of alarm—the collapse of Nationalist China in 1949, followed by Chiang Kai-shek's flight to Taiwan, and the explosion of an atomic bomb by the Russians in the same year. These events led to the charge that American leaders had deliberately or unwittingly betrayed the country's interests. The Alger Hiss case was taken by some people as proof that the Roosevelt administration had been riddled by subversion. Looking back to the wartime alliance with the Soviet Union, the American right began to argue that Roosevelt, by trusting the Russians, had sold out the cause of freedom. Thus Nixon and McCarthy, aided by historians like Stefan J. Possony, C. C. Tansill, and others, accused Roosevelt of handing eastern Europe to the Russians and of giving them a preponderant interest in China which later enabled the Communists to absorb the entire country.

The liberal interpretation of the cold war—what I have called the "orthodox interpretation"—developed partly as a response to these charges. In liberal eyes, the right-wingers made the crucial mistake of assuming that American actions had been decisive in shaping the postwar world. Attempting to rebut this devil theory of postwar politics, liberals relied heavily on the argument that the shape of postwar politics had already been dictated by the war itself, in which the Western democracies had been obliged to call on Soviet help in defeating Hitler. These events, they maintained, had left the Soviet Union militarily dominant in eastern Europe and generally occupying a position of much greater power, relative to the West, than the position she had enjoyed before the war. In the face of these facts, the United States had very little leeway to influence events in what were destined to become Soviet spheres of influence, particularly since Stalin was apparently determined to expand even if it meant ruthlessly breaking his agreements—and after all it was Stalin, the liberals emphasized, and not Roosevelt or Truman, who broke the Yalta agreement on Poland, thereby precipitating the cold war.

These were the arguments presented with enormous charm, wit, logic, and power in George F. Kennan's *American Diplomacy,* which more than any other book set the tone of cold war historiography. For innumerable historians, but especially for those who were beginning their studies in the fifties, Kennan served as the model of what a scholar should be—committed yet detached—and it was through the perspective of his works that a whole generation of scholars came to see not only the origins of the cold war, but the entire history of twentieth-century diplomacy. It is important to recognize that Kennan's was by no means an uncritical perspective—indeed, for those unacquainted with Marxism, it seemed the only critical perspective that was available in the fifties. While Kennan insisted that the Russians were primarily to blame for the cold war, he seldom missed an opportunity to criticize the excessive moralism, the messianic vision of a world made safe for democracy, which he argued ran through all of American diplomacy. As late as 1960, a radical like Staughton Lynd could still accept the general framework of Kennan's critique of American idealism while noting merely that Kennan had failed to apply it to the specific events of the cold war and to the policy of containment which he had helped to articulate. "Whereas in general he counseled America to 'admit the validity and legitimacy of power realities and aspirations . . . and to seek their point of maximum equilibrium rather than their reform or their repression'—'reform or repression' of the Soviet system were the very goals which Kennan's influential writings of those years urged."

Even in 1960, however, a few writers had begun to attack not the specific applications of the principles of *Realpolitik* but the principles themselves, on the grounds that on many occasions they serve simply as rationalizations for American (not Soviet) expansionism. And whereas Lynd in 1960 could still write that the American demand for freedom in eastern Europe, however misguided, "expressed a sincere and idealistic concern," some historians had already begun to take a decidedly more sinister view of the matter—asking, for instance, whether a country which demanded concessions in eastern Europe that it was not prepared to grant to the Russians in western Europe could really be accused, as the "realist" writers had maintained, of an excess of good-natured but occasionally incompetent altruism.

Meanwhile the "realist" interpretation of the cold war inspired a whole series of books—mostly notably, Herbert Feis's series *Churchill-Roosevelt-Stalin, Between War and Peace, The Atomic Bomb and the End of World War II;* William McNeill's *America, Britain and Russia: Their Cooperation and Conflict;* Norman Graebner's *Cold War Diplomacy;* Louis J.

Halle's *Dream and Reality* and *The Cold War as History;* and
M. F. Herz's *Beginnings of the Cold War*. Like Kennan, all of
these writers saw containment as a necessary response to Soviet
expansionism and to the deterioration of Western power in
eastern Europe. At the same time, they were critical, in varying
degrees, of the legalistic-moralistic tradition which kept American statesmen from looking at foreign relations in the light of
balance-of-power considerations. Some of them tended to play
off Churchillian realism against the idealism of Roosevelt and
Cordell Hull, arguing, for instance, that the Americans should
have accepted the bargain made between Churchill and Stalin in
1944, whereby Greece was assigned to the Western sphere of
influence and Rumania, Bulgaria, and Hungary to the Soviet
sphere, with both liberal and Communist parties sharing in the
control of Yugoslavia. These criticisms of American policy,
however, did not challenge the basic premise of American
policy, that the Soviet Union was a ruthlessly aggressive power
bent on world domination. They assumed, moreover, that the
Russians were in a position to realize large parts of this program,
and that only counter-pressure exerted by the West, in the form
of containment and the Marshall Plan, prevented the Communists from absorbing all of Europe and much of the rest of the
world as well.

It is their criticism of these assumptions that defines the revisionist historians and distinguishes them from the "realists."
What impresses revisionists is not Russia's strength but her
military weakness following the devastating war with Hitler, in
which the Russians suffered much heavier losses than any other
member of the alliance. Beginning with Carl Marzani's *We Can
Be Friends: Origins of the Cold War,* revisionists have argued
that Russia's weakness dictated, for the moment at least, a policy
of postwar cooperation with the West. Western leaders' implac-
able hostility to communism, they contend, prevented them
from seeing this fact, a proper understanding of which might
have prevented the cold war.

This argument is spelled out in D. F. Fleming's two-volume study, *The Cold War and Its Origins;* in David Horowitz's *The Free World Colossus,* which summarizes and synthesizes a great deal of revisionist writing; in Gar Alperovitz's *Atomic Diplomacy: Hiroshima and Potsdam;* and in the previously mentioned *Containment and Change.*

But the historian who has done most to promote a revisionist interpretation of the cold war, and of American diplomacy in general, is William Appleman Williams, to whom all of the writers just mentioned (except Marzani, whose work antedated Williams's) owe a considerable debt. Williams's works, particularly *The Tragedy of American Diplomacy,* not only challenge the orthodox interpretation of the cold war; they set against it an elaborate counter-interpretation which, if valid, forces one to see American policy in the early years of the cold war as part of a larger pattern of American globalism reaching as far back as 1898.

According to Williams, American diplomacy has consistently adhered to the policy of the "open door"—to a policy of commercial, political, and cultural expansion which seeks to extend American influence into every corner of the earth. This policy was consciously and deliberately embarked upon, Williams argues, because American statesmen believed that American capitalism needed ever-expanding foreign markets in order to survive, the closing of the frontier having put an end to its expansion on the continent of North America. Throughout the twentieth century, the makers of American foreign policy, he says, have interpreted the national interest in this light. The cold war, in Williams's view, therefore has to be seen as the latest phase of a continuing effort to make the world safe for democracy—read liberal capitalism, American-style—in which the United States finds itself increasingly cast as the leader of a world-wide counterrevolution.

After World War II, Williams maintains, the United States had "a vast proportion of actual as well as potential power vis-à-vis the Soviet Union." The United States "cannot with any real warrant or meaning claim that it has been *forced* to follow a

certain approach or policy." (Compare this with a statement by
Arthur Schlesinger: "The cold war could have been avoided
only if the Soviet Union had not been possessed by convictions
both of the infallibility of the Communist word and the inevitability of a Communist world.") The Russians, by contrast,
"viewed their position in the 1940's as one of weakness, not
offensive strength." One measure of Stalin's sense of weakness,
as he faced the enormous task of rebuilding the shattered Soviet
economy, was his eagerness to get a large loan from the United
States. Failing to get such a loan—instead, the United States
drastically cut back lend-lease payments to Russia in May 1945—
Stalin was faced with three choices, according to Williams. He
could give way and accept the American peace program at every
point—which meant, among other things, accepting governments in eastern Europe hostile to the Soviet Union. He could
follow the advice of the doctrinaire revolutionaries in his own
country who argued that Russia's best hope lay in fomenting
world-wide revolution. Or he could exact large-scale economic
reparations from Germany while attempting to reach an understanding with Churchill and Roosevelt on the need for governments in eastern Europe not necessarily Communist but friendly
to the Soviet Union.

His negotiations with Churchill in 1944, according to Williams, showed that Stalin had already committed himself, by the
end of the war, to the third of these policies—a policy, incidentally, that required him to withdraw support from Communist
revolutions in Greece and in other countries which under the
terms of the Churchill-Stalin agreement had been conceded to
the Western sphere of influence.

But American statesmen, the argument continues, unlike the
British, were in no mood to compromise. They were confident
of America's strength and Russia's weakness (although later they
and their apologists found it convenient to argue that the contrary had been the case). Furthermore, they believed that "we
cannot have full employment and prosperity in the United States
without the foreign markets," as Dean Acheson told a special
congressional committee on postwar economic policy and plan-

ning in November 1944. These considerations led to the conclusion, as President Truman put it in April 1945, that the United
States should "take the lead in running the world in the way
that the world ought to be run"; or more specifically, in the
words of Foreign Economic Administrator Leo Crowley, that
"if you create good governments in foreign countries, automatically you will have better markets for yourselves." Accordingly,
the United States pressed for the "open door" in eastern Europe
and elsewhere.

In addition to these considerations, there was the further
matter of the atomic bomb, which first became a calculation in
American diplomacy in July 1945. The successful explosion of
an atomic bomb in the New Mexican desert, Williams argues,
added to the American sense of omnipotence and led the United
States "to overplay its hand"—for in spite of American efforts to
keep the Russians out of eastern Europe, the Russians refused to
back down. Nor did American pressure have the effect, as
George Kennan hoped, of promoting tendencies in the Soviet
Union "which must eventually find their outlet in either the
break-up or the gradual mellowing of Soviet power." Far from
causing Soviet policy to mellow, American actions, according to
Williams, stiffened the Russians in their resistance to Western
pressure and strengthened the hand of those groups in the Soviet
Union which had been arguing all along that capitalist powers
could not be trusted.

Not only did the Russians successfully resist American demands in eastern Europe, they launched a vigorous counter-
attack in the form of the Czechoslovakian coup of 1948 and the
Berlin blockade. Both East and West thus found themselves
committed to the policy of cold war, and for the next fifteen
years, until the Cuban missile crisis led to a partial détente,
Soviet-American hostility was the determining fact of international politics.

Next to Williams's *The Tragedy of American Diplomacy,* the
most important attack on the orthodox interpretation of the cold

war is Alperovitz's *Atomic Diplomacy,* which reconstructs the evolution of American policy during the six-month period from March to August 1945. Alperovitz shows that as early as April 1945, American officials from President Truman on down had decided to force a "symbolic showdown" with the Soviet Union over the future of eastern Europe. Truman believed that a unified Europe was the key to European recovery and economic stability, since the agricultural southeast and the industrial northwest depended on each other. Soviet designs on eastern Europe, Truman reasoned, threatened to disrupt the economic unity of Europe and therefore had to be resisted. The only question was whether the showdown should take place immediately or whether it should be delayed until the bargaining position of the United States had improved.

At first it appeared to practically everybody that delay would only weaken the position of the United States. Both of its major bargaining counters, its armies in Europe and its lend-lease credits to Russia, could be more effectively employed at once, it seemed, than at any future time. Accordingly, Truman tried to "lay it on the line" with the Russians. He demanded that they "carry out their [Yalta] agreements" by giving the pro-Western elements in Poland an equal voice in the Polish government (although Roosevelt, who made the Yalta agreements, believed that "we placed, as clearly shown in the agreement, somewhat more emphasis" on the Warsaw [pro-Communist] government than on the pro-Western leaders). When Stalin objected that Poland was "a country in which the U.S.S.R. is interested first of all and most of all," the United States tried to force him to give in by cutting back lend-lease payments to Russia.

At this point, however—in May 1945—Secretary of War Henry L. Stimson convinced Truman that "we shall probably hold more cards in our hands later than now." He referred to the atomic bomb, and if Truman decided to postpone the showdown with Russia, it was because Stimson and other advisers persuaded him that the new weapon would "put us in a position," as Secretary of State James F. Byrnes argued, "to dictate our own terms at the end of the war."

To the amazement of those not privy to the secret, Truman proceeded to take a more conciliatory attitude toward Russia, an attitude symbolized by Harry Hopkins's mission to Moscow in June 1945. Meanwhile, Truman twice postponed the meeting with Churchill and Stalin at Potsdam. Churchill complained, "Anyone can see that in a very short space of time our armed power on the Continent will have vanished." But when Truman told Churchill that an atomic bomb had been successfully exploded at Alamogordo, exceeding all expectations, Churchill immediately understood and endorsed the strategy of delay. "We were in the presence of a new factor in human affairs," he said, "and possessed of powers which were irresistible." Not only Germany, but even the Balkans, which Churchill and Roosevelt had formerly conceded to the Russian sphere, now seemed amenable to Western influence. That assumption, of course, had guided American policy (though not British policy) since April, but it could not be acted upon until the bombing of Japan provided the world with an unmistakable demonstration of American military supremacy.

Early in September, the foreign ministers of the Big Three met in London. Byrnes—armed, as Stimson noted, with "the presence of the bomb in his pocket, so to speak, as a great weapon to get through" the conference—tried to press the American advantage. He demanded that the governments of Bulgaria and Rumania reorganize themselves along lines favorable to the West. In Bulgaria, firmness won a few concessions; in Rumania, the Russians stood firm. The American strategy had achieved no noteworthy success. Instead—as Stimson, one of the architects of that strategy, rather belatedly observed—it had "irretrievably embittered" Soviet-American relations.

The revisionist view of the origins of the cold war, as it emerges from the works of Williams, Alperovitz, Marzani, Fleming, Horowitz, and others, can be summarized as follows. The object of American policy at the end of World War II was not to defend western or even central Europe but to force the Soviet Union out of eastern Europe. The Soviet menace to the "free world," so often cited as the justification of the containment policy, simply did not exist in the minds of American planners. They believed themselves to be negotiating not from weakness but from almost unassailable superiority. Nor can it be said that the cold war began because the Russians "broke their agreements." The general sense of the Yalta agreements—which were in any case very vague—was to assign to the Soviet Union a controlling influence in eastern Europe. Armed with the atomic bomb, American diplomats tried to take back what they had implicitly conceded at Yalta.

The assumption of American moral superiority, in short, does not stand up under analysis.

The opponents of this view have yet to make a very convincing reply. Schlesinger's article in *Foreign Affairs,* referred to at the outset of this essay, can serve as an example of the kind of arguments that historians are likely to develop in opposition to the revisionist interpretation. Schlesinger argues that the cold war came about through a combination of Soviet intransigence and misunderstanding. There were certain "problems of communication" with the Soviet Union, as a result of which "the Russians might conceivably have misread our signals." Thus the American demand for self-determination in Poland and other eastern European countries "very probably" appeared to the Russians "as a systematic and deliberate pressure on Russia's western frontiers." Similarly the Russians "could well have interpreted" the American refusal of a loan to the Soviet Union, combined with cancellation of lend-lease, "as deliberate sabotage" of Russia's postwar reconstruction or as "blackmail." In both cases, of course, there would have been no basis for these suspicions; but "we have thought a great deal more in recent years," Schlesinger says, ". . . about the problems of communication in diplomacy," and we know how easy it is for one side to misinterpret what the other is saying.

This argument about difficulties of "communications" at no point engages the evidence uncovered by Alperovitz and others —evidence which seems to show that Soviet officials had good reason to interpret American actions exactly as they did: as attempts to dictate American terms. In reply to the assertion that the refusal of a reconstruction loan was part of such an attempt, Schlesinger can only argue weakly that the Soviet request for a loan was "inexplicably mislaid" by Washington during the transfer of records from the Foreign Economic Administration to the State Department! "Of course," he adds, "this was impossible for the Russians to believe." It is impossible for some Americans to believe. As William Appleman Williams notes, Schlesinger's explanation of the "inexplicable" loss of the Soviet request "does not speak to the point of how the leaders could forget the request even if they lost the document."

When pressed on the matter of "communications," Schlesinger retreats to a second line of argument, namely, that none of these misunderstandings "made much essential difference," because Stalin suffered from "paranoia" and was "possessed by convictions both of the infallibility of the Communist word and of the inevitability of a Communist world." The trouble is that there is very little evidence which connects either Stalin's "paranoia" or Marxist-Leninist ideology or what Schlesinger calls "the sinister dynamics of a totalitarian society" with the actual course of Soviet diplomacy during the formative months of the cold war. The only piece of evidence that Schlesinger has been able to find is an article by the Communist theoretician Jacques Duclos in the April 1945 issue of *Cahiers du communisme,* the journal of the French Communist Party, which proves, he argues, that Stalin had already abandoned the wartime policy of collaboration with the West and had returned to the traditional Communist policy of world revolution.

Even this evidence, however, can be turned to the advantage of the revisionists. Alperovitz points out that Duclos did not attack electoral politics or even collaboration with bourgeois governments. What he denounced was precisely the American Communists' decision, in 1944, to withdraw from electoral politics. Thus the article, far from being a call to world revolution, "was one of many confirmations that European Communists had decided to abandon violent revolutionary struggle in favor of the more modest aim of electoral success." And while this decision did not guarantee world peace, neither did it guarantee twenty years of cold war.

Schlesinger first used the Duclos article as a trump card in a letter to *The New York Review of Books,* October 20, 1966, which called forth Alperovitz's rejoinder. It is symptomatic of the general failure of orthodox historiography to engage the revisionist argument that Duclos's article crops up again in Schlesinger's more recent essay in *Foreign Affairs,* where it is once again cited as evidence of a "new Moscow line," without any reference to the intervening objections raised by Alperovitz.

Sooner or later, however, historians will have to come to grips with the revisionist interpretation of the cold war. They cannot ignore it indefinitely. When serious debate begins, many historians, hitherto disposed to accept without much question the conventional account of the cold war, will find themselves compelled to admit its many inadequacies. On the other hand, some of the ambiguities of the revisionist view, presently submerged in the revisionists' common quarrel with official explanations, will begin to force themselves to the surface. Is the revisionist history of the cold war essentially an attack on "the doctrine of historical inevitability," as Alperovitz contends? Or does it contain an implicit determinism of its own?

Two quite different conclusions can be drawn from the body of revisionist scholarship. One is that American policy-makers had it in their power to choose different policies from the ones they chose. They could have adopted a more conciliatory attitude toward the Soviet Union, just as they now have the choice of adopting a more conciliatory attitude toward Communist China and toward nationalist revolutions elsewhere in the Third World.

The other is that they have no such choice, because the inner requirements of American capitalism *force* them to pursue a consistent policy of economic and political expansion. "For matters to stand otherwise," writes Carl Oglesby, "the Yankee free-enterpriser would . . . have to . . . take sides against himself. . . . He would have to change entirely his style of thought and action. In a word, he would have to become a revolutionary Socialist whose aim was the destruction of the present American hegemony."

Pushed to what some writers clearly regard as its logical conclusion, the revisionist critique of American foreign policy thus becomes the obverse of the cold war liberals' defense of that policy, which assumes that nothing could have modified the character of Soviet policy short of the transformation of the Soviet Union into a liberal democracy—which is exactly the goal the containment policy sought to promote. According to a certain type of revisionism, American policy has all the rigidity the orthodox historians attribute to the U.S.S.R., and this inflexibility made the cold war inevitable.

Communism really does threaten American interests, in this view. Oglesby argues that, in spite of its obvious excesses, the "theory of the International Communist Conspiracy is not the hysterical old maid that many leftists seem to think it is." If there is no conspiracy, there is a world revolution and it *"does aim itself at America"*—the America of expansive corporate capitalism.

Revisionism, carried to these conclusions, curiously restores cold war anti-communism to a kind of intellectual respectability, even while insisting on its immorality. After all, it concludes, the cold warriors were following the American national interest. The national interest may have been itself corrupt, but the policymakers were more rational than their critics may have supposed.

In my view, this concedes far too much good sense to Truman, Dulles, and the rest. Even Oglesby admits that the war in Vietnam has now become irrational in its own terms. I submit that much of the cold war has been irrational in its own terms— as witness the failure, the enormously costly failure, of American efforts to dominate eastern Europe at the end of World War II. This is not to deny the fact of American imperialism, only to suggest that imperialism itself, as J. A. Hobson and Joseph Schumpeter argued in another context long ago, is irrational—

that even in its liberal form it may represent an archaic social phenomenon having little relation to the realities of the modern world.

At the present stage of historical scholarship, it is of course impossible to speak with confidence about such matters. The question to which historians must now address themselves is whether American capitalism really depends, for its continuing growth and survival, on the foreign policy its leaders have been following throughout most of the twentieth century. To what extent are its interests really threatened by Communist revolutions in the Third World? To what extent can it accommodate itself to those revolutions, reconciling itself to a greatly diminished role in the rest of the world, without undergoing a fundamental reformation—that is, without giving way (after a tremendous upheaval) to some form of socialism?

Needless to say, these are not questions for scholars alone. The political positions one takes depend on the way one answers them. It is terribly important, therefore, that we begin to answer them with greater care and precision than we can bring to them now.

[XV]

The Foreign Policy Élite and the War in Vietnam

THANKS TO THE PENTAGON PAPERS, WE CAN NOW SEE THAT THE war in Vietnam is the latest and boldest gamble of the cold war crisis managers. The Pentagon papers are a vastly revealing study of the ways in which power is exercised at the higher levels of the American government by the group variously described as the power élite, the foreign policy establishment, or the representatives of the military-industrial complex.

The record of American involvement in Vietnam, as it emerges from the secret Pentagon study, gives concrete substance to these journalistic abstractions. It refutes the genial theory, developed and popularized over three decades by sociologists, political scientists, and historians of the "consensus" school, that the United States is a "pluralist" society in which the "countervailing" influence of broadly representative constituencies—unions, corporations, lobbies, citizens' organizations—prevents the excessive accumulation of power in any single sector of the body politic, while the "broker state" mediates among the claims of conflicting interests.

In the formulation of American policy in Southeast Asia, no conflicting claims had to be accommodated. Pluralism and countervailing power were nonexistent, Congress was silent, and the public was without effective representation of any kind. Working largely in secrecy, the policymakers found themselves unopposed and virtually unaccountable. It is precisely because their actions were so little shaped by domestic opposition that

American policy in Vietnam reveals so clearly the workings of the official mind.

The policymakers did not, of course, make policy in a vacuum. External conditions, including the military strength of the adversary, set limits to what they could accomplish. Moreover, they inherited from their predecessors not only a variety of foreign commitments but a certain way of looking at the world and at America's role in world history. The world-view of the decision-makers was shaped, during a period of five or six decades, in part by experiences common to most educated Americans. The sense that American culture had "matured" or "come of age," combined with lingering feelings of cultural inferiority to Europe, made them hunger for a larger American role in world affairs, while at the same time it led them to demonstrate that influence in the crudest possible manner. But the official mind was also shaped by the policymakers' consciousness of themselves as an emerging political élite, and especially by their long-standing struggle—against "isolationists," America Firsters, provincial business interests, and various liberals and radicals notoriously "soft" on communism—for a decisive role in the conduct of foreign relations.

In the course of these struggles, they developed not only a fascination with the trappings of power, but illusions of omnipotence and a messianic sense of having been called to the defense of the "free world" at a critical juncture in world history—habits of mind that conspired to draw them into an ever-widening tangle of international commitments, culminating in the disaster of Vietnam. The Vietnamese war must be understood, then, not as an isolated incident but as the end product of a long history of class rule. It cannot be blamed on a particular party or administrative clique, since both parties shared in making it, and the advisers most directly responsible for it built on the work of their predecessors.

Those advisers, whether they served Democratic or Republican presidents, were men of similar backgrounds and outlook. For a long time the policymaking élite has been drawn from an Eastern-based upper class educated at Ivy League colleges and law schools, entrenched in the Wall Street law firms and the major banks, and directly or indirectly connected, through a network of interlocking directorates but especially through its control of finance, to the giant manufacturing corporations. If one can speak of an American ruling class—big capitalists, high-level executives and managers, highly paid corporation lawyers, and heads of the military bureaucracy—this WASP-ish élite, strategically located at the heart of the economy and endowed with the advantages of genteel birth and what passes for cultivation, constitutes its most highly developed sector. Trained for public service and somewhat "cosmopolitan" in outlook, it regards itself as uniquely qualified for leadership, especially in foreign affairs. Its present dominance in this field, however, was only gradually and with difficulty attained.

The old-family commercial and financial élite—the nearest approximation in America to a national upper class—began to emerge in the last three decades of the nineteenth century, out of the regional élites that had maintained an uneasy dominance over politics and social life in the early republic. This new upper class created and preserved a sense of its own identity through institutions maintained for that purpose and through a policy of ethnic exclusiveness flexible enough to allow for the occasional absorption of outsiders like the Kennedys, the Baruchs, the Morgenthaus, and more recently the Moynihans and Kissingers.

Within the upper bourgeoisie as a whole, however, the national financial élite was only a single and by no means the dominant element. Entrenched local élites, based on land or old family businesses, distrusted its drive to expand the powers of the national government. A crude manufacturing and entrepreneurial element, greedy for quick wealth in a prospering economy and too newly arrived to appreciate the importance of class solidarity, resented its air of superiority and its internationalism. Manufacturers cared more for protection from foreign competitors than for expanding American influence abroad. Mark Hanna and McKinley did not share Theodore Roosevelt's enthusiasm for imperial adventures, and many American businessmen opposed the war with Spain and the acquisition of the

Philippines for the same reasons they opposed all disturbances of the public peace. The American bourgeoisie, such as it was at the turn of the century, understood very clearly its dependence on governmental favors—tariffs, subsidies, franchises, sound money—and it swiftly united to put down the menace of Bryanism. It was far from united, however, on questions of foreign policy. Manufacturing and local elements tended to resist costly armaments and the expansion of federal and executive power that was implicit in an aggressively activist policy abroad. Not until World War I swept the country into the current of world politics did the more cautious among the bourgeoisie reconcile themselves to America's assumption of global responsibilities. Even then, many of their reservations persisted, surfacing in the thirties and again, briefly, at the close of World War II.

Meanwhile, Theodore Roosevelt had infused new life into the fading seaboard aristocracies by exhorting them to dirty their hands in politics instead of engaging in genteel dissipations. Roosevelt and his colleagues—Henry Cabot Lodge, John Hay, Alfred Thayer Mahan—tirelessly lectured their peers on the importance of rising above a vulgar concern with trade, even as they proved themselves quite capable of defending the interests of American business. They talked much of destiny and mission, and those of their own class who took the message to heart did indeed begin to develop vigorous traditions of public service, a sense of their own superiority, and an ill-disguised contempt for the more cautious and conservative elements of the bourgeoisie.

Nevertheless the latter continued to play a major role in both political parties. The relapse into unimaginative conservatism under Taft showed that Theodore Roosevelt's attempt to revitalize the Republican Party had not been an unqualified success. Throughout the twentieth century, the "liberals" in the Republican Party—whose liberalism is defined largely by their support of an "internationalist" foreign policy—have had to contend with a rock-ribbed conservatism of the kind so ardently defended in the forties and fifties by Robert Taft, son of the President. State and local politics, and to some extent even congressional politics, have remained more responsive to local business interests than are the higher reaches of the administrative bureaucracy; and the Republican Party, infrequently successful in capturing the presidency, has been a congressional party much more than a presidential one. The Republican administrations of the twentieth century, alternating with periods of more stylish and adventurous rule, have typically had about them the flavor of the statehouse and the county courthouse. The Democrats, on the other hand, although they too have had to deal with stubborn parochialism in some sections of the party, have produced a series of celebrated "internationalist" presidents. As Republican orators never tire of pointing out, it is the Democrats who four times in the century have committed American troops to foreign wars.

Yet the difference in flavor between the Republican presidents and the liberal administrations of Wilson, Franklin Roosevelt, Truman, Kennedy, and Johnson should not obscure an underlying continuity of policy and outlook, even of personnel. Precisely because it had to contend against provincial conservatism in both parties, the foreign policy establishment needed all the more urgently to develop an élan of its own, to make itself indispensable at the middle and upper levels of the administrative hierarchy, and thus to achieve immunity from the shifts of partisan politics. As the most educated and politically conscious wing of the banking and commercial élite, the foreign policy establishment prided itself on its ability to take a bipartisan, truly national view of American interests. Gradually it managed to persuade the country that foreign affairs should be kept out of partisan politics; after 1945 this tradition was seldom challenged. The growing influence of the military, especially after World War II, only furthered the removal of foreign policy from party politics and hence from popular debate; for the military—with which the foreign policy élite in the late forties formed an effective alliance—had already established its own independence from outside scrutiny and control. Administration was replacing politics in many areas of government, but nowhere was this process carried to such lengths as in the making of foreign policy. Eventually the Pentagon, the State Department, the intelligence agencies, the top military men, and the high-level advisers in the White House came to constitute almost a government within a government, uniquely devoted to the pursuit of American world power.

The vicissitudes of domestic politics have had remarkably little effect on the course of American foreign relations. Since the time of Theodore Roosevelt, and especially since the time of Wilson, the main lines of American foreign policy have remained consistent: opposition to social revolution and the spread of communism; gradual displacement of the old European empires and maintenance of these empires under American auspices or client regimes; economic and political penetration of western Europe; and the attempt to make Western parliamentary democracy the model for world order.

The continuing tensions between the foreign policy establishment and the local and conservative elements of the bourgeoisie did, however, yield an important side-effect. They sharpened the former's sense of itself as a vanguard, willing to accept the risks and glory of world power, from which so many of their countrymen seemed inexplicably to shrink. Twice in twenty-five years the United States, under the direction of the foreign policy élite, came to the rescue of western Europe. On both occasions liberal administrations had to drag an unwilling and ignorant public, as they saw it, into facing up to the responsibilities of a great power. The struggle against isolationism in the thirties was particularly important, for it set new precedents for deviousness and secrecy. Fearful of rousing his political opponents, Franklin Roosevelt hesitated to ask Congress to move more than a step at a time toward the abrogation of the neutrality laws passed in the mid-thirties, while at the same time he and his advisers saw that Great Britain and the other European democracies could not hold out against fascism without American help. It was not simply a matter of defending the nations of western Europe against Hitler but of defending their colonies in the Far East as well.

In 1940 Roosevelt and Churchill entered into secret agreements which in effect committed the United States to defend British possessions in the Pacific should they come under Japanese attack. As it became clear, late in 1941, that the United States would soon be called upon to honor this commitment, the chief policymakers were faced with the formidable task of explaining and justifying it to the American public. At the last moment, Pearl Harbor came to their rescue.

World War II greatly enlarged the influence and prestige of the foreign policy establishment. Victory gave these men a feeling of invincibility. With Germany defeated, they believed that the time had come for what Secretary of the Navy James V. Forrestal called a "showdown" with the Soviet Union. Once again it appeared that the public, tired of war and drugged with wartime propaganda about the heroism of Russian resistance to Hitler, wished only to retreat into the humdrum daily pleasures of peacetime. Accordingly Forrestal, Stimson, Harriman, Acheson, Kennan, Dulles, Clifford, and other spokesmen of the foreign policy establishment in the critical years from 1945 to 1947 spared no effort in alerting the American people to the gravity, as they measured it, of recent international developments: Soviet expansion into Europe, the collapse of western Europe, a highly unstable situation in the Far East.

What is surprising, in retrospect, is not that some people turned a deaf ear to their summons but that the great majority accepted with little difficulty a surprising turn of events which not only redefined an ally as a hated enemy but also demanded a decisive repudiation of isolationism and committed the country to a global struggle against communism that had no foreseeable end. The foreign policy élite had discovered the art of crisis management, while the intellectuals, meanwhile, supplied a "tragic" view of the world, stressing the inconclusiveness of diplomacy and the impossibility of quick solutions, that made more palatable the assumption of commitments the consequences of which were impossible to predict. Crisis now succeeded crisis, each demanding a suitably heroic response.

By 1947, when the British announced that they were no longer able to defend Greece against internal subversion, Truman had no trouble getting congressional approval for a sweep-ing and open-ended commitment to contain Communist "aggression" wherever it presented itself. According to a con-temporary observer, the State Department regarded the British announcement as a delegation to the United States of "world leadership, with all its burdens and its glory." The architects of the Truman Doctrine believed that "a new chapter in world history had opened, and they were the most privileged of men."

Seven years later, the French withdrawal from Vietnam pro-voked a similar sense of crisis in the Eisenhower administration. The National Security Council had already decided, in August 1953, that "any negotiated settlement would mean the eventual loss to Communism not only of Indochina but of the whole of Southeast Asia." When it became clear that the French intended to withdraw, Dulles, Admiral Radford, and others pressed for direct American intervention.

The case of Vietnam, however, was complicated by the inabil-ity of the anti-Communist elements to establish even the sem-blance of a stable government. Vietnam exposed a problem which was inherent in the whole policy of containment but which had not yet become fully explicit. The containment policy assumed that communism spread by means of external "aggres-sion" and that its expansion, therefore, could be checked by giving military support to reliable anti-Communists. Except in western Europe, however, the only reliable anti-Communists proved to be reactionary politicians and generals unable to command popular support.

It followed that the logic of containment demanded in the long run an increasing commitment of American money, mili-tary advice, air power, and, finally, troops to anti-Communist regimes which could not survive without them. Containment had always carried within it the strong possibility of direct confrontations between Communist guerrillas and American military forces—confrontations from which it would be difficult to retreat and to which there would be no compromise solutions. Such confrontations were to be reckoned with whenever a client regime found itself faced with a strong and determined opposition at home. They had not occurred in Greece, because the Soviet Union chose to abandon the guerrillas; they had not occurred in the Middle East or in Latin America (except in Cuba) because internal oppositions were unable to wage a protracted struggle; while the Korean War ended in a stalemate largely because Communist pressure from the North was not matched by any corresponding pressures in South Korea itself.

In Vietnam, however, the United States had to deal not only with the reactionary governments of Bao Dai, Diem, and their successors, but with a determined political opposition capable, as it turned out, of transferring the struggle to the battlefield when that became necessary.

The case of Vietnam should have compelled a reassessment of the containment policy itself, since there was always a strong likelihood that involvement in Indochina would force the United States to carry containment to its logical and horrifying limit. As early as 1949 the State Department had withheld its support from Bao Dai on the grounds that "we cannot at this time irretrievably commit the U.S. to support of a native government which by failing to develop appeal among Vietnamese might become virtually a puppet government separated from the people and existing only by the presence of French military forces."

Later that year, however, the flight of Chiang Kai-shek from the Chinese mainland sent the Truman administration into a panic, as a result of which it recognized Bao Dai and sent economic and military aid to the French in Indochina. Dean Acheson explained that "the choice confronting the U.S. is to support the legal governments in Indochina or to face the extension of Communism over the remainder of the continental area of Southeast Asia and possibly westward."

Again in 1954, reservations about extending the American commitment were expressed by Congress, the Joint Chiefs of Staff (who noted that "from the point of view of the United States, Indochina is devoid of decisive military objectives"), and the National Intelligence Board (which predicted that neither the French nor the Vietnamese would be able to establish a strong government). The authors of the 1968 Pentagon study make the significant observation that "the available record does not indicate any rebuttal" to these warnings. Nevertheless, the Eisenhower administration committed itself to the support of Diem.

A pattern thus discloses itself at the very outset of American involvement in Vietnam, one that was to be repeated many times, on an ever-larger scale. In the face of abundant warnings that the political situation in Saigon was unlikely to improve, American officials clung to the hope that American intervention would somehow compensate for the weakness of Saigon. They can only have cherished this hope so blindly because the alternative—re-examination not only of American commitments to South Vietnam but of the containment policy itself—was too painful. To have undertaken such a re-examination would have exposed the policymakers to the charge of "losing" Vietnam to the Communists.

The absence of public debate, moreover, meant that such debate as there was would take place among those who shared the same premises and questioned only their application to Vietnam; or more typically, advocated their application to Vietnam on condition that Saigon give "guarantees" of its good intentions. These were easy enough to provide, particularly since American governments increasingly abandoned their half-hearted insistence on domestic reforms and asked merely that Saigon achieve "internal security"—more and better police, suppression of political opponents, and "the appearance" (as William Bundy, Assistant Secretary of State for Far Eastern Affairs, put it in a memorandum of September 8, 1964) "of a valid government." The degree to which American officials saw the problem of Saigon as a problem of "morale" shows the degree to which the American political élite, itself increasingly isolated from normal democratic procedures, had lost the capacity to think in political terms at all.

Eventually the government managed to convince itself that

Saigon's "morale" problems stemmed from uncertainty over the extent of American commitments. Thus William Bundy advised Dean Rusk on January 6, 1965, "that Saigon morale in all quarters is now very shaky indeed, and that this relates directly to a widespread feeling that the U.S. is not ready for stronger action. . . ." (As for the earlier insistence on domestic reforms, "the blunt fact," Bundy continued, "is that we have appeared to the Vietnamese . . . to be insisting on a more perfect government than can reasonably be expected"!) The instability of successive South Vietnamese regimes, originally an argument against intervention, was magically transformed into an argument for large-scale escalation.

The fact that these regimes were unable even to provide internal security nevertheless acted as a check on American commitments to Vietnam. Once it became clear that the United States had embraced the underlying policy objective of an independent, non-Communist South Vietnam, most of the military men pressed for a total commitment of American resources; civilian officials, however, held back. Even the political objective of the war remained somewhat fuzzy in their minds. Although in fact their policy demanded nothing less than the defeat of communism in South Vietnam—an objective, consistently reflected in the terms they offered Hanoi, which can best be characterized as non-negotiable demands—the civilian advisers tended to draw back from the implications of this commitment.

Sometimes they told themselves that the object of American policy was merely to avoid a humiliating defeat, forgetting that the only way to do so, once the basic commitment to Saigon had been made, and short of revoking that commitment, was to win a decisive victory. At other times they claimed that American policy sought only to give the South Vietnamese a chance to determine their own fate. In fact, however, a "Vietnamese solution" was unacceptable to the United States, since it was tantamount to defeat.

Shrinking from a firm and explicit commitment to victory— even though such a commitment was implied by every action of the American government since 1950—the civilian advisers by their own admission "gambled" on short-term measures, hoping that each would be the last. In the early sixties Herman Kahn provided a theory of escalation that served to rationalize this indecision. Thus the war escalated in stages, and American officials were able to conceal the ultimate costs not only from the public but from themselves. Willing to take military risks far beyond what was dictated by common prudence, they nevertheless shrank from the risk of a public accounting in which American objectives would be openly debated, Saigon's weakness exposed, and the price of victory made clear.

For all their pretentious rhetoric about the responsibilities of a great power, the policymakers were afraid to ask the public to pay the price of power, or even to admit to themselves how high that price had become. Adept at generating a sense of national emergency, they hesitated to ackowledge how serious the emergency was in fact becoming. The high-minded slogans of public service—"Ask not what your country can do for you; ask what you can do for your country"—concealed a refusal to intrude on the continuing celebration of American "peace and prosperity," the great barbecue of the fifties and sixties, with a demand for real sacrifices. Having lived through the war against fascism or been raised on its heady legend, many among the political élite inordinately admired Winston Churchill; but it was not for them to tell the people the worst and ask for their blood and tears. Instead, following a pattern set in the first years of the cold war, they combined global pronouncements with cautious requests for money and men, implying that each request would be the last. Their experience of the thirties and forties—rather, the lessons they mistakenly drew from that experience—had convinced them that the American people could not be trusted to rise to important occasions.

Perhaps American officials had private doubts about the importance of this particular occasion. In spite of intelligence reports that cast grave doubt on the validity of the domino theory, the policy élite continued to insist that Vietnam was vital to American security. They tended, however, to confuse security with prestige—"our reputation as a guarantor," as John Mc-

Naughton, Assistant Secretary of Defense, put it in one of his typically inconclusive memoranda. The underlying insecurity of the American élite—in part the product of a long tradition of American cultural inferiority—nowhere reveals itself more clearly than in its excessive concern with the trappings, as opposed to the reality, of power.

Time after time, the dominant consideration in any decision was how it would look. In November 1964, according to the record of a meeting of a select committee of the National Security Council, McNaughton and William Bundy argued that even if the bombing of North Vietnam failed to save South Vietnam, "we would obtain international credit merely for trying." The record says that at least one official, Secretary of State Rusk, dissented from this analysis. But almost everyone connected with Vietnam policy would have agreed with General Taylor's description of an American defeat, when he argued, in March 1968, against any change in policy. To abandon Vietnam, he said, was "to accept needlessly a serious defeat for which we would pay dearly in terms of our worldwide position of leadership, of the political stability of Southeast Asia, and of the credibility of our pledges to friends and allies."

When Johnson asked the C.I.A. if the rest of Southeast Asia would "necessarily fall if Laos and South Vietnam came under North Vietnamese control," the C.I.A. once again denied the validity of the domino theory but added that the "loss" of these areas "would be profoundly damaging to the U.S. position in the Far East" and would raise the prestige of China *vis-à-vis* the Soviet Union. The same obsession with prestige and "position," now dressed up in the jargon of games theory, spoke in McNaughton's memorandum to McNamara of September 3, 1964: "The relevant 'audiences' of U.S. actions are the Communists (who must feel strong pressures), the South Vietnamese (whose morale must be buoyed), our allies (who must trust us as 'underwriters'), and the U.S. public (which must support our risktaking with U.S. lives and prestige)." American policy experts seem, in short, to have permitted the sense of themselves as actors on a stage to overshadow other considerations, even questions of national security. "We are the greatest power in the world," said Walt Rostow, "—if we behave like it."

Isolated in so many ways from the American people, the crisis managers nevertheless betrayed a typically American conception of what it meant to behave like "the greatest power in the world": it meant to get tough, to bully and swagger. It was "essential," in McNaughton's words, "that [the] U.S. emerge as a 'good doctor.' We must have kept promises, been tough, taken risks, gotten bloodied, and hurt the enemy very badly." When George Ball, still working within the dominant assumption that "credibility" and prestige were decisive in the war, argued that the N.A.T.O. allies—whose respect meant so much to the American élite—would "be inclined to regard a compromise solution in South Vietnam more as new evidence of American maturity and judgment than of American loss of face," his sensible advice went unheeded.

Their confidence that bluster and a show of toughness would prevail led American officials into the fatal mistake of supposing that the North Vietnamese could be intimidated. The belief that superior size and strength always win, especially when accompanied by superior technology, made it difficult for officials to credit what the C.I.A. and other authorities repeatedly said, that bombing "had no measurable direct effect" on Hanoi's capacity to continue the war.

The American contempt for Orientals distorted even further the policymakers' perception of the situation. Racist assumptions made it easier to believe that the North Vietnamese would back down in the face of threats and the crude "carrot-and-stick" diplomacy of Ambassador Lodge. Repeatedly American planners spoke of "breaking the enemy's will." Thus the high-level bombing scenario devised in May 1964, while proposing terms which the Pentagon historians call "tantamount to unconditional surrender," assumed that only limited bombing of the North would be necessary to achieve these terms, providing the United States chose "targets which have maximum psychological effect on the North's willingness to stop insurgency." The bombing was accompanied by a note—the kind of note which it is difficult to imagine the American government sending to a European power—saying that American patience with Hanoi was "growing extremely thin." Unfortunately, Pham Van Dong showed himself, in the words of the Pentagon analysts, "utterly unintimidated."

We knew the war was monstrous; what we didn't completely grasp, until the Pentagon papers dispelled all doubts, is that it was utterly contemptible as well. The war was the work of little men who wanted very badly to be big men but were unwilling to pay the price. Hoping to achieve a notable victory on the cheap, they gambled on their ability to manipulate the "little guys" on the other side as easily as they manipulated their puppets in Saigon.

At every turn they made the elementary and unforgivable error of underestimating the adversary. They consistently disregarded the advice of their own intelligence agencies, who warned that the chances of success were small and the prizes not worth the risk. Wholly aware of Saigon's military weakness, they convinced themselves that an American military "presence" would magically impart strength to regimes which had lost the confidence of their own people. Posing as fearless defenders of democracy, they timidly shrank from a public reckoning in which (in the words of an interagency memorandum of June 10, 1964) "disagreeable questions" might have to be answered. They concealed their actions from Congress, the American people, and their own allies.

When necessary they resorted to outright lies, at once grave and petty, as when McNamara assured Congress in August 1964 that "our Navy played absolutely no part in, was not associated with, was not aware of, any South Vietnamese actions [in the Tonkin Gulf] if there were any"; or when Johnson, three weeks later, told the country that "we have tried very carefully to restrain ourselves and not to enlarge the war."

In the spring of 1965, when academic criticism of the war

began, McGeorge Bundy gave the professors "low marks" for raising the same questions that were being raised, it turns out, by the C.I.A.—questions about the accuracy of the State Department's interpretation of the war as "aggression from the North," about the efficacy of the bombing, about the stability of Saigon. What sort of marks are we to give Mr. Bundy himself, who, in the face of these same intelligence reports, advocated "sustained" and "continuous" bombing of North Vietnam on the grounds that it would rally anti-Communist elements in the South and "have a substantial depressing effect upon the morale of Vietcong cadres"; and who, two weeks before the fall of General Khanh, wrote that "we see no one else in sight with anything like his ability to combine military authority with some sense of politics"?

What marks shall we give Maxwell Taylor, who urged Kennedy to send ground troops in 1961 and assured the President that "the risks of backing into a major Asian war by way of SVN [South Vietnam] are present but are not impressive" and that "NVN is extremely vulnerable to conventional bombing, a weakness which should be exploited diplomatically in convincing Hanoi to lay off SVN"?

What marks shall we give General Wheeler, who blithely declared that "there appears to be no reason we cannot win if such is our will" but forgot to take into account the other side's will and capacity to match escalation with escalation?

What marks shall we give Walt Rostow, who consistently predicted that North Vietnam could be bombed into submission, and who told Rusk in May 1965 that Hanoi "now is staring at quite clear-cut defeat"?

What marks shall we give those who urged escalation in the face of their own stated misgivings? In January 1965, William Bundy saw only a "faint hope of really improving the Vietnamese situation," yet he advocated escalation on the grounds that "even on an outcome that produced a progressive deterioration in South Vietnam and an eventual Communist take-over, we would still have appeared to Asians to have done a lot more about it" than if the United States withdrew. This recommendation is matched in its vacuity only by McNaughton's memorandum of January 19, 1966, in which he urged more bombing and troops in spite of his belief that the war had become "an escalating military stalemate" and his prediction that "we will probably be faced in early 1967 with a continued stalemate at a higher level." Because the stakes now seemed too high for turning back, sharpened misgivings inspired the same course that foolish optimism had: escalation. It was left to Johnson to ask, much too late, the obvious question: "When we add divisions can't the enemy add divisions? If so, where does it all end?"

In one respect the Pentagon papers give a misleading picture of the war. Ending in March 1968, with Johnson's decision to suspend bombing and to remove himself from the forthcoming presidential campaign, they leave the impression that the government had learned from its mistake and now sought to extricate itself from the war. In fact the Nixon administration has attempted to achieve the same end as its predecessors—a non-Communist South Vietnam—through measures politically more acceptable to the American public: reduction of American casualties, removal of war news from the headlines, increased bombing. But although Nixon has postponed the final reckoning, he cannot indefinitely avoid the defeat that has been inherent in Vietnam from the beginning. Eventually Vietnam, what is left of it, will be unified under a Communist regime, and the humiliation of the United States, which American officials for two decades sought so desperately to avoid, will be complete.

Already the war has made us the most hated nation in the world. It has exposed terrible divisions within American society, alienated our youth, poisoned our culture, and contributed to a mounting economic crisis. It has brought to the surface the ugliest elements in American life and confirmed Ortega's description of the United States as "a primitive people, camouflaged behind the latest inventions." In Vietnam, the American stands once more revealed as "the [John] Paul Jones of nations," in the words of Herman Melville—"intrepid, unprincipled, reckless, predatory, with boundless ambition, civilized in externals but a savage at heart."

The war is more than a generalized expression of American culture; it is also the particular expression of a particular class which has for too long played the dominant role in our affairs. This was not a war thrust on the country by reactionaries or marginal elements; it was a liberal war, the culmination of twenty years of cold war carried out under liberal auspices and reflecting the traditions of a ruling class supposedly enlightened, mature, and superior to the grosser strains in American life. The pretensions of the political élite have been thoroughly shattered by this debacle, and if the American people have learned anything from it, they will not again turn to a Johnson or a Kennedy merely because he presents himself to the public as more moderate than a Goldwater or a Nixon.

The political élite itself has learned nothing from the war. Its spokesmen are drawing from recent experience the conclusion that what is needed is still greater secrecy in the conduct of foreign relations, together with tighter controls of the press. Confronted with the accumulated consequences of their own incompetence, they arrogantly maintain that the press is to blame for violating "national security." The real lesson of the Pentagon papers and the war is that our security can no longer be entrusted to men fatally removed from American life and as contemptuous of their countrymen as they are of the Vietnamese, whose country they have devastated in order to show the world American "leadership" in action.

[XVI]

Educational Structures
and Cultural Fragmentation

I

BEFORE THE NINETEENTH CENTURY FORMAL SCHOOLING WAS CON-
sidered indispensable only for those preparing for careers in
law, medicine, or the church, although others of course availed
themselves of it. Most people did not go to school at all—a fact
that has usually been taken to mean that the masses lived in
darkness and that the eventual achievement of universal education came about because the masses learned to demand it as
their birthright. Recent scholarship, much of it inspired by a
growing disillusionment with the school, calls this assumption
into question. It now appears that middle-class reformers played
a decisive role in the creation of the modern school system and
that they saw the school essentially as an instrument of social
control—the "civilizing" effects of education being closely associated, in their minds, with the need to discipline people whom
the dislocations of early capitalism threatened to render unruly
and rebellious. The coming of universal education did not so
much liberate the masses as subject them to bureaucratic custody.

The school in western Europe and the United States rose on
the ruins of apprenticeship and other informal institutions of
learning. Apprenticeship had been a broad and variegated institution, by no means confined to the manual trades. Among the
laboring classes apprenticeship was often a means, not merely of
transmitting skills, but of providing elementary instruction in
reading and arithmetic, in conduct and deportment, and in

other pursuits necessary for the assumption of adult responsibilities. The upper classes had their own form of apprenticeship, such as foreign travel or sending children to live with other families. Indeed the "putting out" of children was a universal custom in the pre-modern Western world; all classes practiced it, and it should be considered as the most prevalent form of apprenticeship in pre-industrial society.

In addition to this domestic apprenticeship and to the more familiar forms of craft apprenticeship that have survived, in debased form, into our own time, informal schools grew up, often in close proximity to the crafts. The most important were the schools run by scribes, which taught writing and arithmetic to girls as well as boys, to adults as well as children, and to people of all social classes. A painting by Holbein depicts such a school in progress, with an inscription on the master's sign that reads: "Whoever you may be, burgesses, artisans, labourers, women or girls, and whatever your needs, he who comes here will be faithfully instructed for a reasonable fee."

All these informal institutions of learning taught subjects that were later incorporated into primary and secondary schools. Formal schooling only gradually displaced and degraded this popular, secular education, secularizing itself in the process and steadily widening the scope of its claims until it asserted a monopoly not only of education but of cultural life in general. The system of universal compulsory education did not triumph without a struggle. As late as the middle of the nineteenth century, as Michael Katz has recently reminded us, it was only one of several alternatives, at least in the United States, and its dominance did not appear inevitable. Those who saw education as a form of charity, to be undertaken by private corporations in a spirit of *noblesse oblige,* shared with proponents of "democratic localism" a sharp suspicion of the new educational professionalism that was beginning to emerge. One of the localists, Orestes Brownson, predicted that "as soon as they can get their Normal Schools into successful operation, [educational bureaucrats] will so arrange it, if they can, that no public school shall be permitted to employ a teacher" not certified by themselves. Proponents of localism and variety opposed not only centralization and bureaucracy but the attempt to make education compulsory. They argued that a uniformity of belief and opinion could not be imposed on an unwilling people and warned that "the prejudices against this system of education are very strong." One of them said: "If we ever expect to root deeply this system in the affection of the people, we must make the system voluntary—entirely so. But if we force it upon the people, it will be taken with an ill grace, and will be made use of, if used at all, with reluctance and suspicion."

The same arguments were advanced by those who favored a third kind of education, which Katz refers to as "corporate voluntarism": a system of autonomous and competing academies, "aided but not controlled by the state." Educational systems, as one of them put it, "ought to be wisely suited to the character and condition of the people among whom they are introduced." The advocates of the common school, identifying themselves with the reformist surge of the 1830's and 1840's and seeing themselves as battling for progress and enlightenment against popular ignorance, replied to all these contentions that the people would never institute sound systems of education if left to themselves. "We were told that it was dangerous to force this system upon the people, when they are not prepared to receive it; but we never heard in any state, of the people asking for provisions on the subject of education, until they were offered." Reformers like Horace Mann and Henry Barnard argued, moreover, that education had tasks to perform far more important than instruction in academic subjects; it was for this reason above all that education could not safely be left to popular initiative. The school was to be seen as the agent of a general social reformation.

The rhetoric of the school reformers closely resembled that of the proponents of the asylum. Like the penal reformers and medical superintendents, they attributed crime and vice to the crowded conditions of urban life, to "deficient household arrangements" (in Barnard's words), to an excessive preoccupation with intellectual as opposed to moral culture, and to "civilization" in general. It is interesting to note that the two sets of reformers advanced identical critiques of existing educational structures. According to Edward Jarvis, one of the leading proponents of the insane asylum, the schools encouraged students to "look for success, honor, or advantages, which their talents, or education, or habits of business, or station in the world, will not obtain for them." The advocates of the common school proposed to remedy this fault by a rigorous "classification of scholars" according to age and ability and by shifting the emphasis of public education from "intellectual culture [to] the regulation of the feelings and dispositions, the extirpation of vicious propensities, the preoccupation of the wilderness of the young heart with the seeds and germs of moral beauty, and the formation of a lovely and virtuous character by the habitual practice of cleanliness, delicacy, refinement, good temper, gentleness, kindness, justice, and truth."

In both cases, reformers claimed that the success of the new system depended on removing their clients—students, madmen, or criminals as the case might be—from the pernicious influences that surrounded them and on subjecting them to regular discipline under the supervision of trained professionals. Tocqueville and Beaumont noted that "philanthropy has become for [the penal reformers] a kind of profession, and they have caught the *monomanie* of the penitentiary system, which to them seems the remedy for all the evils of society." The same thing could have been said of the founders of the common school. Having armed themselves with a strong professional pride—"the man who imagines himself a teacher, merely because he has seen others teach in a particular way, is just as much an empiric, as a pretender in medicine, who occasionally walks through the wards of a hospital"—they proposed to use compulsory schooling as a means of instilling work discipline, self-reliance, and "character." In soliciting public support, they appealed to the belief that schools under the proper leadership would facilitate social mobility and the gradual eradication of poverty or, alternately, to the hope that the system would promote order by discouraging ambitions incommensurate with the students' stations and prospects. The latter argument was probably more appealing to wealthy benefactors and public officials than the first. Both led to the same conclusions: that the best interests of society lay in a system of universal compulsory education which would isolate the student from other influences and subject him to a regular regimen; and that the system must be operated by a centralized professional bureaucracy.

The ideology of school reform shared another feature with the ideology of the asylum. It contained a built-in, ready-made explanation of its own failures. Once the principle of the common school and the asylum had been generally accepted and the memory of earlier customs had begun to fade, critics of the new system found it difficult to resist the logic of the position put forward by the custodians: that the admitted failures of the new institutions could be attributed to lack of sustained and unequivocal public commitment, particularly in the matter of funds, and that the only remedy for those failures, therefore, lay in bigger and better schools and asylums, better professional training, more centralization, greater powers for the custodians —in short, another dose of the same medicine. Toward the end of the nineteenth century the school, like the asylum, came under heavy public criticism. The schools were inefficient and costly; monotonous classroom drill failed to engage the pupils' enthusiasm; too many of the pupils failed. This criticism, however, in no way questioned the underlying premises of universal compulsory education; its upshot was a concerted drive to make the schools more "efficient." Joseph Mayer Rice, who had inaugurated the muckraking attack on the school system with a series of articles in the *Forum* in 1892, published in 1913 a tract called *Scientific Management in Education*. Here as in his earlier writings he stressed the need to remove education from political control. The application of this commonly held idea to education had the same consequences as its application to city government in the form of civil service reform, the city manager system, and other devices intended to end "political" influence and promote the introduction of "business methods." It encouraged the growth of an administrative bureaucracy not directly responsible to the public and contributed to the centralization of power.

The political machines which the new system displaced, whatever their obvious shortcomings, had roots in the neighborhood and reflected—although with many distortions—the interests of their constituents. The new educational bureaucrats, on the other hand, responded only to generalized public demands for efficiency and for an educational policy that would "Americanize" the immigrant—demands the educators themselves helped to shape—and therefore tended to see their clients as so much raw material to be processed as expeditiously as possible. Ellwood P. Cubberley voiced a widespread concern when he referred to the new immigrants from southern and eastern Europe as "illiterate, docile, [and] lacking in self-reliance and initiative," and argued that the task of the public schools was "to assimilate and amalgamate these people as a part of our American race, and to implant in their children, so far as can be done, the Anglo-Saxon conception of righteousness, law and order, and popular government, and to awaken in them a reverence for our democratic institutions and for those things in our national life which we as a people hold to be of abiding worth." Charles William Eliot of Harvard, in a speech to the National Educational Association in which he urged a fuller utilization of the "public school plant" as "the only true economy," insisted that educational reform "means a larger and better yield, physically, mentally, and morally, from the public schools."

The high rate of failure provoked the usual outcries of alarm. A recent critic of American education has boldly suggested that the unacknowledged function of the common school system is to fail those whom the higher levels of the employment structure cannot absorb; whose origins, in other words, consign them to economic marginality. Failure in school thus prepares a certain necessary part of the population for failure in life.[1] The

---

1. On this analysis, the current crisis in public education derives from the fact that failure is no longer functional. Since the number of unskilled jobs is rapidly diminishing, those who fail have no place to go and become permanent charges on the state. Many of them also become discontented and rebellious.

debates of the progressive period furnish support for this interpretation. Critics of the schools attacked the high rate of failure
while urging reforms that would inevitably perpetuate it. (The
continuing high rate of failure then served as the basis of
renewed appeals to the public, both for money and for additional powers for the educational bureaucracy.) In response to
the outcry about failure, systems of testing and tracking were
now introduced into the schools, which had the effect of relegat-
ing academic "failures" to programs of manual and industrial
training (where many of them continued to fail). Protests
against genteel culture, overemphasis on academic subjects,
"gentleman's education," and the "cultured ease in the classroom, of drawing room quiet and refinement," frequently coincided with an insistence that higher education and "culture"
should not in any case be "desired by the mob." The demand for
"educational engineering" and the elimination of "useless mo-
tions" led to the adoption of an "index of efficiency" of the kind
expounded by Leonard Ayres in his *Laggards in Our Schools,*
whereby a school's efficiency would be measured by the children's progress through the grades. "If we can find out how
many children *begin* school each year we can compute how
many remain to the final elementary grade. Such a factor would
show the relation of the finished product to the raw material."
Adoption of this principle reinforced the class bias of the educational system. Since children of immigrants and of rural migrants
to the city commonly entered school at a later age, the number
of "over-age" children did not necessarily reflect their failure to
make satisfactory academic progress. Failure henceforth would
be tied more firmly than ever to class and ethnic origin.

2

EVEN THE MORE LIBERAL IDEAS OF THE PROGRESSIVE EDUCATORS WERE
turned to the purposes of "efficiency"; when this proved impossible, they were ignored. John Dewey and his followers revolted
against unimaginative classroom methods, against the authori-

tarianism that was built into the school system in so many ways, and against the school's inability to make modern life intelligible. Except in private schools for the very rich, their good intentions have left few imprints on the educational system. Instead the rhetoric and ideas of progressivism were appropriated by educational bureaucrats for their own purposes. Ambiguities in progressivism itself facilitated this process. Like the advocates of efficiency, the progressives attacked impractical academic instruction, demanding what would be called today a more "relevant" education. They too exaggerated the influence of the school as an agent of social reform seeing education as a panacea for all the evils of industrial society. In the history of education in the twentieth century, higher as well as lower, it is often difficult to distinguish radicals from modernizers. Sharing with the advocates of efficiency a deep antipathy to genteel culture and perhaps to culture in general, the progressives had no secure philosophical basis from which to resist the perversion of their ideas in the practice of the public schools.

A concrete example—the much-discussed model system of Gary, Indiana—shows how the ideas of progressive and bureaucratic critics of education overlapped and how, when they did not, the progressive ideal of spontaneity and creativity lost out to considerations of bureaucratic efficiency. A new and rapidly growing industrial city with a large immigrant population, Gary embodied in extreme form the conditions confronting the school system as a whole. In 1907 William Wirt, a follower of Dewey, became director of the Gary schools and instituted what came to be known as the "platoon system," adopted thereafter by more than six hundred schools in over a hundred cities. The "platoon" or "duplicate" school, by providing shops, kitchens, laundries, laboratories, and gymnasiums in addition to conventional classrooms, and by using these facilities at all hours of the school day (and even on weekends and during the summers) could accommodate twice as many students as the conventional school. This feature of the Gary plan immediately commended itself to advocates of a more efficient use of the plant. Wirt himself explained his reforms in an article entitled "Scientific

Management of School Plants." An admirer of the system, writing under the title, "The Elimination of Waste in Education," argued that the new demands being placed on the public schools would lead either to false economies—inferior buildings and teachers, two shifts of children working half-time—or to reforms similar to those introduced at Gary, designed to "create a thoroughly modern school plant, equipped with every modern necessity; then to operate it according to recently developed principles of scientific management."

As a student of John Dewey, Wirt had other considerations in mind besides cost accounting; yet the terms in which he explained his general objectives, while consonant with much of progressivism, would have appealed also to those who were insisting that the school must concern itself with the "whole child." Enthusiastically endorsing the belief that the school "must assume the functions formerly exercised by the home and the small shop—the dis-integration of which throws the child on the mercy of the street," Wirt argued that "the traditional school, with children strapped to fixed school seats for nine hundred hours a year, and loafing in the streets three hours for one spent in school, is not prepared to develop good health, intelligence, industry, or reliability." Introduction of non-academic subjects was more than an economy designed to promote a better use of the plant; it also conformed to the popular belief that "it was the industrial training of children in the home and small shop," in Wirt's phrase, "that made children of the past generation reliable, industrious," and generally well behaved.

When Randolph Bourne visited the Gary schools in 1915, he saw them as the triumph of Deweyite principles. By incorporating industrial activities that had formerly taken place in the family and by running into the summer (though on a voluntary basis), the Gary schools served "as an extension of the home." Well equipped with every kind of facility, the system served as a community center, "a sort of town public university, attended by all classes of the population." Since the plant was maintained by the students themselves, the students "learned from doing," in the jargon of the day. "School life in Gary is, therefore, not a mere preparation for life, but a life itself." Conventional discipline could be dispensed with, "for Mr. Wirt finds that when children are busy and interested they do not have time to be mischievous. . . . They move freely about the building with the unconscious air of owning the school themselves." Noting that the academic classes were tracked "according to whether the children give promise of completing the school course in ten, twelve, or fourteen years," Bourne saw in this mechanism only a means of ensuring that "the brighter children are not retarded by the slower ones." He was impressed by the "helper" system, in which the older children helped to teach the younger ones, and by the easy way in which intellectual and practical instruction was combined. It is impossible to read some of his descriptions without sharing his enthusiasm or his hope that "the Gary school is bound to become the American public school of tomorrow," training "the type of mind most needed today—the versatile machinist, the practical engineer, the mind that adapts and masters mechanism." The following passage shows progressive ideals at their best; but it also suggests, inadvertently, why progressivism failed.

> I dropped into physics class, and found a dozen twelve-year-old girls and their nine-year-old "helpers" studying the motor-cycle. With that fine disregard for boundaries which characterizes Gary education, the hour began with a spelling lesson of the names of the parts and processes of the machine. After the words were learned, the mechanism was explained to them as they pored over it, and their memory of vaporization, evaporation, etc., called into play. The motor-cycle was set going, the girls described its action, and the lesson was over, as perfect a piece of teaching as I have ever heard. The intense animation of that little group was all the more piquant for having as a background the astounded disapprobation of three grave superintendents from the East.

As these last words intimate, it was neither the helper system, the relaxation of discipline, nor the hope of training "versatile mechanics" that accounted for most educators' interest in the Gary schools. It is saddening to read, side by side with Bourne's account, the study of the Gary system written three years later, under official auspices, by Abraham Flexner and Frank P. Bachman. These authorities urged that the "helper" system be "less freely and more discriminatingly used." With regard to industrial work, they judged it a defect of the system that "the tasks themselves are determined not by simple educational considerations . . . but by practical daily need in the school system or the home."[2] This criticism struck at one of the best features of the Gary system, the union of pedagogy and practice—a union which, as Bourne noted, gave the students a proprietary interest in the school and allowed a relaxation of discipline. ("It seemed really true that children, unless they were challenged to inventive wickedness by teachers' rules and precepts, were no more likely to spoil their school than a lawyer is likely to deface the panels in the library of his club.")

Heavily relying, at every stage of their inquiry, on recently developed systems of classroom testing, Flexner and Bachman concluded that although attendance was good, progress through the grades was unsatisfactory. "When compared with other cities, Gary is doing as well as they do, but probably no better, in advancing children through school."[3] The work, moreover, was "narrow in scope, empirical in method." It was a mistake to employ journeyman mechanics as instructors in the industrial arts, since "they are not apt to extract the intellectual elements from a given situation." Instruction in the household arts suffered from the same defect. "Written questions requiring the pupils to explain some of the fundamental principles of good

2. Again one is reminded of the asylum. Part of the meaning of "moral treatment," introduced into houses of confinement in the early nineteenth century, was the substitution of meaningless work—treadmills and the like and, in our own time, various forms of occupational therapy—for productive labor (however degraded), on the theory that all economic aspects of the asylum must be rigorously subordinated to therapeutic considerations.

3. This criterion, they insisted, was very important. "A common elementary school measure of whether or not children are where they should be on their way through the school is to determine whether or not they are entering or have completed the grade proper to their age. The significance of this measure lies in the fact that when school children fall too far behind their proper grade, they are likely to drop out even before completing the elementary course. . . ."

housekeeping—i.e., what are the essentials of a good meal, what are the main classifications of food, what determines the kinds of food needed—were for the most part meagerly answered." For the economies achieved by the Gary system, on the other hand, Flexner and Bachman had nothing but praise.

The fate of progressive education is already foreshadowed in this report. Those aspects of the Gary system that are demonstrably "efficient" will be retained and extended—tracking, lengthening of the school day, fuller use of the plant. The genuinely innovative features of the system, unable to produce satisfactory results according to the latest tests, will be unceremoniously dropped. Only the rhetoric of progressivism will remain—prattle about the need for "practical" education and "the proper development of the entire child."

3

THOSE WHO ATTACKED THE PUBLIC SCHOOLS IN THE NAME OF EFFI-ciency and utility did not spare the American university in their condemnation. Some of the most prominent critics of the common schools, like Charles William Eliot of Harvard and Charles Van Hise of the University of Wisconsin, were also instrumental in bringing into being the new "service" or vocational university. Their idea of a university that would put its modern facilities at the disposal of the community, emphasizing socially oriented research and vocational training over pure scholarship, bears a close resemblance to the ideas of school reformers in this period, both progressive and bureaucratic, who similarly wished to substitute "real life" for sterile intellectual pursuits (while in practice often upholding an intellectualism far more deadening than anything it replaced). The advocates of utility in higher education, like the public school reformers, saw education as an instrument of social reform, a means of overcoming the split between overspecialized industry and over-intellectualized schools. Just as the union of manual and mental instruction at the lower levels would revive one of the most desirable features of apprenticeship, so the introduction of a vocational and practical emphasis into higher education would help to bridge the gap between an attenuated "culture" fatally removed from practical life and an anarchic society badly in need of guidance and control.

The university was especially vulnerable to the charge of impracticality because it still retained the traces of its ecclesiastical origin: the ceremonial use of Latin, the classical curriculum, allegedly pointless ritual, a notable resistance to innovation. Institutions of higher learning were much slower than the rest of the educational system to absorb the lay culture that had always co-existed with the ecclesiastical culture schools in general had originally been designed to preserve. In the seventeenth and eighteenth centuries lay culture was revolutionized by new advances in science, political theory, philosophy, mathematics, and the arts; but almost every important discovery in these fields took place outside the universities and in many cases in open opposition to the universities. Scientific societies, private patronage, and other informal arrangements supported lay culture in its advanced forms just as apprenticeship, craft schools, and the family supported its more rudimentary forms. The university, on the other hand, still existed mainly to train young men bound for careers in medicine, law, and theology. This situation persisted well into the nineteenth century, only slightly modified by a new tendency to justify the traditional classical curriculum not for its intrinsic value but for the "mental discipline" students derived from it. By the 1870's, however, the classical curriculum was under vigorous attack not only by the proponents of utility but by a variety of other academic reformers.

At this point the history of higher education diverges from that of the public schools, precisely because in their drive to modernize the university the utilitarian reformers had to contend not only with a decaying classicism but with emerging academic interests equipped with competing programs of modernization. Advocates of "liberal culture" proposed to introduce the study of modern history and of modern literatures and languages. So far as this impulse was identified with polite gentility, it was itself old-fashioned, but in universities so long dominated by classical studies, it represented something of an advance. Much more formidable were the advocates of "research," who found increasing support among university faculties, particularly in the sciences and social sciences. As eager to identify themselves with modernity as the utilitarians, those who defined the university as a research center had the additional advantage of being well organized into professional organizations. Many of them had been trained in Germany, and they brought to academic discussions the prestige of German scholarship, then much admired. Above all, they spoke in the name of modern science. Their defense of pure research—of what Veblen was to call "idle curiosity"—carried great weight.

Unlike Veblen, however, most of the advocates of this position were unwilling to rest the case for "research" on "curiosity" alone. The defense of pure science itself rested on the material achievements of modern science. Thus Daniel Coit Gilman, president of Johns Hopkins during its formative period, defined the purpose of the university as "the acquisition, conservation, refinement and distribution of knowledge" and went on to argue that the university's pursuit of this goal should be subjected to no narrowly utilitarian test.[4] But Gilman did not leave the argument there; he added that applied mathematics had played an important role in developing steam locomotion, the telegraph, the telephone, photography, and electric lighting. "These wonderful inventions," he pointed out, "are the direct fruit of university studies." What is ominous about this defense of pure research is the assertion that although scientific "progress" is the purpose of the university, the results of that progress cannot be communicated to the public or even from one depart-

---

4. "If you persist in taking the utilitarian view and ask me what is the good of Mr. Glaisher's determination of the least factors of the missing three out of the first nine million numbers . . . I shall be forced to say I do not know; and if you press me harder I shall be obliged to express my conviction that nobody knows; and yet I know, and you know, and everybody may know, who will take the pains to inquire that the progress of mathematics underlies and sustains all progress in exact knowledge."

ment of the university to another, except in the form of "wonderful inventions." The whole controversy over pure and applied research presupposed an almost total fragmentation of culture.

Veblen's *Higher Learning in America,* published in 1918, stated the case for research in its most persuasive form. Savagely attacking both the service concept of the university, the popularity of which he attributed to the ascendancy of "pecuniary" influences, and the genteel tradition, Veblen argued for complete faculty control, separation of graduate and professional training from the liberal arts college, and acknowledgment of "disinterested" scholarship as the overriding purpose of the university. The partisans of pure research did not succeed in attaining these goals, but they had already left enduring imprints on higher education: the research seminar, the Ph.D. and publications as criteria of academic advancement, a new concept of academic freedom. The whole structure of graduate education, indeed, was largely the work of these scholars and reformers.

Conflicting pressures and interests formed the modern university, and the institution that emerged—the structure of which had been clearly defined by the time of World War I—rested on a series of compromises. The introduction of electives, together with extracurricular diversions of various kinds, helped to pacify the students. Throughout the eighteenth and nineteenth centuries American colleges endured chronic student disorders. If these abated somewhat in the late nineteenth and early twentieth centuries, it was partly because the discipline of compulsory chapel and class attendance, compulsory courses of study, and rigorous supervision of students' affairs was now relaxed somewhat, and because fraternities, athletics, and other such outlets played an increasingly prominent part in student life.

The elective system also represented a compromise between the demands of the undergraduate college and the research-oriented graduate and professional schools that were being superimposed on it. As Oscar and Mary Handlin have observed, "The hope that the lecture system would transform the teacher from a drillmaster into a creative scholar depended upon giving the professor enough latitude to present a subject he knew thoroughly and yet relieving him of students for whom attendance was an unwelcome task." Unfortunately the elective system also relieved the faculty from the need to think about the broader purposes of education—including the possibility that for many students attending *any* classes was an "unwelcome task"—and about the relation of one branch of knowledge to another. At the same time, the union of college and professional schools in the same institution preserved the fiction of general education, on which university administrators heavily relied in their appeals for funds.

A greatly expanded administrative apparatus now emerged not simply as one more element in a pluralistic community but as the only body responsible for the corporate policy of the university. The decision to combine professional training and liberal education in the same institution, and the compromises that were necessary in order to implement it, not only relieved the faculty of any responsibility for thinking about the underlying purposes of undergraduate education but rendered the faculty incapable of confronting larger questions of academic policy. These now became the responsibility of administrative bureaucracies, which grew up in order to manage the sprawling complexity of institutions that included not only undergraduate and graduate colleges but professional schools, vocational schools, research-and-development institutes, area programs, semi-professional athletic programs, hospitals, large-scale real estate operations, and innumerable other enterprises. The corporate policies of the university, both internal and external—addition of new departments and programs, cooperation in war research (beginning with World War I), participation in urban renewal programs—were now made by administrators, and the idea of the "service university" or multiversity whose facilities were theoretically available to all (but in practice only to the highest bidders) justified their own dominance in the academic structure. The faculty accepted this new state of affairs because, as Brander Matthews once said in explaining the attraction of

Columbia to humane men of letters like himself, "So long as we do our work faithfully we are left alone to do it in our own fashion."

4

THE BEST THAT CAN BE SAID ABOUT THE AMERICAN UNIVERSITY IN what might be called its classic period—roughly the period from 1870 to 1960—is that is provided a rather undemanding environment in which the various groups that made up the university were free to do much as they pleased, provided they did not interfere with the freedom of others or expect the university as a whole to provide a coherent explanation of its existence. The students accepted the new status quo because, as noted, they had plenty of non-academic diversions, and also because the intellectual chaos of the undergraduate curriculum was not yet fully evident, because the claim that a college degree meant a better job still had validity, and because in its relations to society the university seemed to have identified itself with the best rather than the worst in American life.

What precipitated the crisis of the sixties was not simply the pressure of unprecedented numbers of students but a fatal conjuncture: the emergence of a new social conscience among students activated by the moral rhetoric of the New Frontier and by the civil rights movement, and the simultaneous collapse of the university's claims to legitimacy. Instead of offering a rounded program of humane learning, the university was now seen to provide a cafeteria from which students were to select so many "credits." Instead of diffusing peace and enlightenment, it allied itself with the war machine. Even its claim to provide better jobs eventually became suspect.

It was no accident that the uprising of the sixties began as an attack on the ideology of the multiversity and its most advanced expression, the University of California at Berkeley; and whatever else it subsequently became, the movement represented, at least in part, an attempt to reassert faculty-student control over the corporate policies of the university—expansion into urban neighborhoods, war research, ROTC. Neither the anti-intellectualism so often associated with the student rebellion nor its underlying despair should prevent us from seeing that the whole development of the American university—its haphazard growth by accretion, its lack of an underlying rationale, the inherent instability of the compromises that attended its expansion—rendered such an accounting almost unavoidable.

Instead of bemoaning the loss of former glories (most of them illusory), we should ask whether higher education in the United States did not take a fundamentally wrong turn in the 1870's and 1880's, for which we are only now beginning to pay in full. What would have been the consequences of a stricter separation of professional training from undergraduate instruction? It is not easy to show that the union of the two has had a liberalizing effect on the professions; its main effect seems to have been to hasten the competitive upgrading of vocations to full professional status, as one group after another seeks the prestige of the advanced degree. Much of the recent clamor for relevance reflects an awareness that there is an increasingly remote connection between degrees and the training actually required for most jobs. The solution, however, starts not with changing the content of courses but with getting rid of the whole idea that courses—and colleges—are the only means to an education. The whole system of compulsory schooling needs to be reconsidered. Rather than trying to reform and extend the present system, we should be trying to restore the educative content of work, to provide other means of certifying people for jobs, and to hasten the entry of young people into adult society instead of forcing them to undergo prolonged training—training which, except in the older professions, has no demonstrable bearing on qualifications for work.

To review the gradual substitution of schooling for apprenticeship and other forms of experience by no means encourages the conclusion that the change was an improvement. The Handlins' recent study suggests that formal education in the early nineteenth century had only "marginal value" and that institutions of higher learning proliferated in this period not in response to genuine social or intellectual needs but as a result of "rhetoric, of inflated ambition and of sectarian bickering." Compulsory schooling triumphed largely because reformers and bureaucrats succeeded in convincing the public that adolescence was a social problem, to which detention in schools was the cure. It was only then that Americans fully accepted what the Handlins describe as "the belief that the school was the nation's only educational institution."

The displacement of apprenticeship by schooling led to a hardening of class lines, as educational advantages accumulated in the upper bourgeoisie and the professional and managerial strata. Another undesirable feature of the change, particularly as it concerned the lower schools, was that the working class abdicated control over apprenticeship—the process of qualification for work—to professional educators. It is significant that trade unions initially resisted the introduction of industrial education into the schools and capitulated only reluctantly, when they became convinced that the advantages of shifting the cost of vocational training to the schools outweighed the loss of their own control. In time not only the unions but vocational groups of all kinds not only acquiesced in but welcomed the assumption of vocational education by the schools and universities. By the 1930's Robert Maynard Hutchins could complain that "every group in the community that is well enough organized and has an audible voice wants the university to spare it the necessity of training its recruits." The effects of this shift on the school were as bad as the effects on society itself, not only because, as Hutchins pointed out, the competitive upgrading of vocations into professions threatened to downgrade the professions into vocations, but because the school system as a whole was called on to serve, in effect, as a source of vicarious experience; indeed as a substitute for experience. The point does not need to be belabored that educators have not followed Hutchins's sensible advice to "leave experience to life and set about our own job of intellectual training." It is more important to note that Hutchins himself refrained from exploring the implications of returning vocational training to the vocations. He took it for granted that prolongation of adolescence was inevitable in industrial society, that institutions of some sort must provide for this extended adolescence, that the school was best qualified to do so, and that in short "economic conditions require us to provide some kind of education for the young . . . up to about their twentieth year."

Like his great adversary John Dewey, Hutchins left uncriticized one of the central articles of American faith, the belief in the school as a panacea for social ills of every kind. He ends his own version of *The Higher Learning in America* with the completely conventional hope that educational reform will change "the character of our civilization." Like Dewey, Hutchins proposes educational reform (this time in a conservative version) as a substitute for social reform, hoping to restore order and meaning to modern life by restoring these qualities to the school. In fact the problem of education cannot be divorced from the larger problem of work. The structure of graduate and professional education cannot be changed without changing the structure of the professions themselves. As long as the worker or the professional regards his work simply as a means to provide himself with the compensatory satisfactions of a trivialized leisure—as a boring and monotonous routine over which he has no control, and the social consequences of which do not greatly concern him—so long will the educational system be geared to essentially industrial requirements.

[XVII]

The Social Thought
of Jacques Ellul

I

ALTHOUGH JACQUES ELLUL HAS WRITTEN ON THEOLOGY, LAW, AND
many other subjects, he is known in the United States principally
as the author of three sociological studies: *The Technological
Society, Propaganda,* and *The Political Illusion.* These works
alone, however, convey an imperfect impression of the force and
originality of Ellul's thought. What is valuable in his social writings takes on meaning only when one considers the ethical,
cultural, and philosophical position they are intended to support.
In itself, Ellul's analysis of modern society is unoriginal (except
for one or two sharp insights) and in some respects even misleading. Moreover, the work for which he is best known, *The
Technological Society,* is the weakest of his three sociological
treatises, although it is also the most ambitious. In large part, it
repeats what has already been said by Max Weber, by Veblen,
and by theorists of the managerial revolution, the "new class"
and "mass society."

Modern history, in this view, is the history of the rationalization of all phases of existence. Politics and statecraft, subjected to
the requirements of technique, become autonomous processes
unamenable to democratic control. Knowledge ceases to serve a
critical function, since the demands of technique lead thinkers to
make "a hard and fast separation between what is and what
should be," dismissing the latter as subjective and therefore

unscientific judgments of value. New methods of propaganda and thought control are developed to a high degree of efficiency, ensuring the continuing domination of technology. No longer the master of his destiny, man is reduced to an object, and society evolves inexorably toward a bland totalitarianism—a "worldwide totalitarian dictatorship," in Ellul's words, that "no obstacle can stop."

The bleakness of its pessimism distinguishes *The Technological Society* from its predecessors in twentieth-century sociology. Its central thesis does not. Neither does Ellul's attack on Marx, which draws heavily on conventional misrepresentations of Marxian theory.[1] Since the attack is directed not against Marx but against a caricature of his ideas, Marxian analysis of modern society is not seriously challenged by *The Technological Society,* any more than it is challenged by other theories of mass society. George Lichtheim once said of Weber's sociology of religion, hailed as a great conceptual breakthrough by Weber's admirers, that the entire elaborate structure "fits without difficulty into the Marxian scheme." The same holds for Ellul's theory of the "technological society." It is not for this that Ellul commands our attention.

His other works are another matter. Of particular importance are *The Political Illusion,* the recently published *Violence,* and a very early work, *The Presence of the Kingdom,* which anticipates most of the writings that have followed it. Published in France in 1948, *The Presence of the Kingdom* appeared in the United States in 1951 but received little notice. Only with its

---

1. According to *The Technological Society,* the last chance of revolution disappeared in the nineteenth century, when the revolutionary movement ceased to oppose technology with "spiritual forces" and adopted the materialist perspective as its own, thereby hastening the final triumph of economic man. "Proudhon and Bakunin had placed spiritual forces in rivalry with the economic order. Against them, Marx upheld the bourgeois order of the primacy of the economic. . . ." Unfortunately for this analysis, Marx never propounded any such thing as "dialectical materialism"—that was the contribution of Engels, who sought to establish the scientific credentials of Marxism according to the positivistic standard of scientific truth that had come to prevail at the end of the nineteenth century. Marx was not a determinist; he did not deny the element of human will in history; he made no easy assumptions about the inevitability of progress; nor did he equate social progress with technology.

in paperback in 1967 did it obtain a wider reading
hat time all three volumes of Ellul's sociological
ppeared in English translation. Yet the earlier book
moral and philosophical underpinnings of Ellul's
ys. Short and clear, it seems to have been written at
white heat. "In my description of the contemporary scene, behind each bare statement lies an experience; and I could support
each statement with concrete examples. To do this, however,
would require more leisure than my present circumstances permit, for the time is short." Modern society rushes toward a disaster that only revolution—"a radical transformation of our
present civilization"—can prevent; yet that same society is characterized by a "profound immobility," an "incapacity for revolution."

The Presence of the Kingdom is addressed to Christians, but it
raises questions that all radical intellectuals have to confront,
whether or not they approach them from a Christian perspective. The crisis of the faith is one aspect of the cultural crisis of
our time, and Ellul's plea that the church speak directly and
critically to social issues springs from the same concerns that
have led other intellectuals, working from secular premises, to
insist that culture must no longer be regarded as an activity
having no relation to politics, that artists and scholars must
abandon the pretense of neutrality, and that a new humanism,
in short, is likely to take shape only if it makes connection with
the struggles of exploited classes to change the world. In the
years since *The Presence of the Kingdom* first appeared, pleas
for culture to be "relevant" have once again become common
and even fashionable; but as the level of political militancy rises,
the advocates of cultural "commitment" have more and more
retreated to the position they held in the United States in the
thirties and which they have never ceased to hold on the European left—namely, that cultural radicalism means that intellectuals should enlist in the proletarian revolution (now seen as a
global uprising of the non-white, colonialized peoples). Ellul's
work, taken as a whole, constitutes a sustained critique of this
position, all the more effective, in some ways, for its being cast in

religious terms. When the newly militant church places itself at the service of "the revolution," Ellul believes that it ceases to bring anything specifically Christian (unless it is a particularly offensive type of sentimentality) to the understanding of modern society. Already foreshadowed in *The Presence of the Kingdom,* this theme in Ellul's thought emerges with great clarity in a most recent book, *Violence,* which was written in direct response to new-style Christian militants who argue, in the words of Richard Schaull, that the church "cannot stay out of the revolutionary struggle."[2] Ellul objects to this view on the grounds that it substitutes an appeal to the emotions for analysis and "confuses [the reader] as to the difference between socialism and revolution." He also points out that "to say that the Christian must participate [in revolutions] is to make revolution a value, even in a sense an absolute value"—in which case there is no longer any need for Christianity, all its own values having been subsumed under revolution. "Obviously, revolution is the overriding value, therefore the main argument; to be a revolutionary is more important than to be, or not to be, a Christian."

When Ellul himself exhorts the church to become "revolutionary," he does not mean that the church should place itself under the moral leadership of the proletariat or of any other revolutionary class. His reservations about revolution are strengthened by the belief that in the past—and especially in the recent past—revolutions have not brought about the liberating and democratic changes that were to have justified their vio-

2. The quotation from Schaull, cited in *Violence,* p. 53, comes from Schaull's "Revolutionary Change in Theological Perspective" in John C. Bennett, ed., *Christian Social Ethics in a Changing World* (1966). Schaull also contributed a lengthy essay on revolution to Carl Oglesby's *Containment and Change* (1967). There he attempts to qualify his position by arguing that "the most authentic revolutionary is one who can unite full commitment with a certain degree of detachment, who can keep a sense of humor that allows him to laugh at himself, and who can maintain a critical attitude toward all revolutionary thought and action" (*Containment and Change,* pp. 245–6). But this is mere rhetoric. How can "full commitment" co-exist with "a certain degree of detachment"? Either one is fully committed to revolution or one is committed to some other value. It is hardly necessary to add that Schaull's essay reveals none of the "critical attitude" to revolution that he recommends as standard equipment for the "authentic" revolutionary.

lence, terror, and suppression of opponents. Ellul's writings have always reflected a profound disenchantment not merely with advanced capitalist society in the West but with its socialist alternative. That capitalism and socialism are essentially identical is one of the constant themes of his work. "At bottom, the U.S.S.R. obeys the same rules as the U.S.A." This idea leads Ellul into serious mistakes, as I shall try to show later, but it does enable him to escape the illusion, so common among modern revolutionaries, that a change in political structures, without an attendant spiritual or cultural transformation, will bring about a genuinely democratic society. Ellul is one of the few contemporary radicals fully to grasp the cultural dimensions of the twentieth-century crisis. The most impressive passages in his books are those in which he speaks of people's helpless bewilderment in the face of mass communications, the assimilation of science to technique, the degradation of art, the collapse of values. He shows how the mass media subject people to a barrage of disconnected and therefore meaningless facts and how this makes critical reflection on politics impossible. "News succeeds news without ceasing. For instance, in the columns of the newspaper he will read one day about an affair which quickly disappears from the paper, and also from the brain of the reader. It is replaced by others; it is forgotten. A man gets used to living like this, without a present and without a past. He gets used to living in complete incoherence. . . ."[3] In *Propaganda,* Ellul explores in detail the disastrous effects of mass communications.

Neither science nor art provide any alternative to the prevailing chaos. On the contrary, science and art contribute to it: science, by divorcing itself from philosophy and becoming

3. The following succession of front-page headlines in the Chicago *Sun-Times* amply bears out Ellul's point about the complete absence of continuity in the media's treatment of events. December 10, 1969: "9 in Congress ask Nixon for Hampton quiz"; December 11: "Mitchell reveals Mafia rule of big IRS group"; December 12: "Massive tax-reform bill passed by Senate 69–22"; December 14: "Supreme Court stiffens Southern school edict"; December 15: "Nixon talk today: more Viet troop withdrawals"; December 17: "Budget of $842 million is voted by city council."

merely a higher branch of technology; art, by giving up any pretense to make statements about objective reality, thereby dissolving in "self-expression." Neither science nor art any longer communicate anything except, in the one case, information required to solve technical problems—and even this is conveyed in symbols accessible only to specialists—and in the other case, inner experiences uncommunicable by definition. Modern art, by opposing to technological domination a cult of the irrational, "guides us in the direction of madness." Faced with rampant disorder, men take refuge in the great "explanatory myths" of our time: "the bourgeois myth of the Hand of Moscow, the Socialist myth of the Two Hundred Families, the Fascist myth of the Jews, the Communist myth of the anti-revolutionary saboteur." These provide the only "means of intellectual coherence" in a world made meaningless by loss of continuity, loss of memory.

2

"IN NO OTHER CIVILIZATION HAS MAN BEEN SO TOTALLY REPRESSED." Unlike Herbert Marcuse, Ellul does not refer to the repression of libido. His vision of liberation is altogether different from that of the "Freudian left," which proposes to free man from all forms of external authority. Ellul holds to the idea that order and authority are necessary and even desirable; that conflicts with authority are a necessary part of education and of growing up in general; and that "there is no liberty," as he puts it in *The Political Illusion,* "except liberty achieved in the face of some constraint or rule." When he speaks of repression, Ellul refers to the manipulation of the citizen by the media and by the state, the destruction of private life, the subjection of every aspect of life to the requirements of the "social machine," as defined by those in charge of it. Ellul's conception of the cultural revolution that would be necessary to put an end to these forms of domination has little in common with the conception that prevails today, which derives not from Christian humanism but from Marcuse, Reich, Zen, Bob Dylan, the Beatles, astrology, witchcraft, and the occult. Ellul's perspective on culture enables him to see the modern obsession with personal liberation as itself a symptom of pervasive spiritual disorder. *The Presence of the Kingdom* ends with a plea for "a new style of life," since Ellul recognizes that a moral doctrine has power only to the extent that it creates a culture suited to the needs of those to whom it is addressed—in this case, the "proletarian" mass man. Elsewhere Ellul speaks of the need for groups of the faithful to find a way "to live on the edge of this totalitarian society." But his insistence on the need for privacy, order, and continuity ("every achievement, however humble it may be, is worthy of being preserved"); his praise of the family coupled with an attack on those who "reject love as a conflict or insist that the woman should ultimately be the same as the man"; and his belief that institutionalized tension should be clearly present in human affairs and that it is precisely the "adjustment" of all tensions that signals the approach of the "unitary society"—all this sets Ellul apart from those cultural radicals who seek salvation in drugs, sexual liberation, and communal living arrangements. Without disregarding their positive contributions, he sees that such solutions do not seriously menace the existing order. "It is good for city dwellers to go to the country. It is good that a marked eroticism is wrecking the sclerotic traditional morality. It is well that poetry, thanks to such movements as surrealism, has become really expressive once more. But these phenomena, which express the deepest instinctive human passions, have also become totally innocuous. . . . It is harmless to attack a crumbling middle-class morality." The ruling class itself has come to believe in the need to transcend the "archaic cultures [that] still corrupt human life"; and it announces its own emancipation from the "metaphysical and dogmatic mentality" by declaring that "all doctrines which draw their inspiration from abstract conceptions have already betrayed their fundamental incapacity to organize the human world." What can the cultural left, with its worship of direct experience and its revolt against reason, add to this indictment of humanist culture?

In his latest book, *Violence,* Ellul addresses himself directly to the hippie phenomenon. His idea of cultural renewal takes on additional clarity in contrast with that of the hippies. Their "splendid élan," he writes, "seems doomed from the start, because the hippies have no understanding of what their real place in society is." Attempting to challenge the technological society, they are in fact supported by it. "In reality, they are only the product of its luxuriousness." Moreover, they offer a diverting escape from boredom. "The hippies introduce color, youth, pleasure. To be sure, they are a bit shocking, but a society held together by boredom is more or less proof against shock." This is particularly the case when so many of the values of dissident cultures merely reaffirm, in extreme form, those of the surrounding cultures: subjectivity, the impossibility of verbal communication, salvation through technology (drugs), utopia as the absence of tensions and conflicts.

When Ellul speaks of the need for a "moral revolution," he clearly has in mind something quite different from either hippie nonviolent or revolutionary militance. The "moral revolution" does not consist of investing contemporary politics with passionate moralism. The only moral attitude toward politics, according to Ellul, is one of severe realism—one that tries to assess the probable consequences of political actions. Moralism interferes with this by contributing to the escalation of rhetoric; in the end, it merely provides additional fuel for the propaganda machine. In *The Political Illusion,* Ellul writes: ". . . [T]he insertion of values into the discussion of political acts is never more than just words. Liberty, justice, the right of peoples to self-determination, the dignity of the human person—these are no longer anything but pale justifications for social conformity. . . . Once invoked, they only serve to support an already existing political design. They become part of the propaganda apparatus. . . ." It suits the interest of the state to induce in the citizen a heightened state of political passion, and nothing serves this purpose so well as moral rhetoric, whether it comes from the state or from dissident movements themselves. Unlike many theorists of mass society, Ellul does not see political quiescence or "apathy" as the chief characteristic of the mass man. The mass man is "immersed in the immediate present, disoriented, incapable of true political reflection," but he by no means necessarily lacks political opinions. On the contrary, his opinions may sweep him into political engagement; he may become a militant partisan of some cause. But militancy only adds to the already overheated political atmosphere, and the violence to which it so easily leads helps to legitimize the counter-violence of the state. The absence of genuine tensions in the "unitary society" does not at all preclude violence; the recognition of this is one of Ellul's sharpest insights.

> Our French society has become a unitarian society from which tensions are practically excluded, or, more precisely, only one form of tension exists—political tension. . . . I know the reader will retort: "What more internal tensions do you want in a country than those we have already experienced! Tension between collaborators and the Resistance from 1940 to 1945 (with all its sequels), tension between French and Independent Algeria, between army and nation, between the OAS and the anti-fascist Left . . . we live in terrible and permanent tension, and cannot see that it is fruitful." The problem is that the conflicts we know today are exclusively of a *political* order. . . .
>
> [T]hese tensions, of which so much is being said, and which are tragic for us because every twenty years they must be paid for with human lives, are the more tragic because they are absurd and illusory. The only tensions that still exist are political tensions, but despite their hard and violent character, despite widespread commitment to them, despite some people's seriousness in the debate, they are false tensions, emptying into a void, dealing with nothing serious in the structure of our society, and incapable of producing any solution or basic innovation.

It is precisely because so little of real importance is at stake that political controversies generate such rhetorical excesses: there is no limit to what people can say, since their words have no last-

ing consequences. True, they sometimes have immediate consequences of the most appalling character; yet nothing changes as
a result.

3

IN WHAT SENSE IS POLITICS "ILLUSORY"?

Ellul insists that the most important questions in life are not
political questions; the illusion, then, lies in supposing they can
be solved by political means. I think Ellul pays too little attention to the ways in which the distribution of wealth and power
influences other questions. He does not regard the ownership of
the means of production, for example, as an important question.
If that seems short-sighted, it has to be conceded that the left has
raised this most important of political questions in a form that
could hardly be better calculated to *conceal* its importance.
Instead of arguing that socialization of the means of production
is one condition essential to the survival of civilized relations
among people, the left has presented it as the end of history as
we know it, the end of conflict, the beginning of utopia. One
trouble with this kind of thinking is that it discourages any
action or reflection in the meantime; all questions are dissolved
into questions of political strategy: What steps are necessary to
bring about the revolutionary apocalypse, after which universal
love shall prevail? In this sense it is certainly true that modern
politics raises no important questions. And in a deeper sense it is
true that the most important questions of all—for instance, those
concerning "the interplay between constraint and liberty"—are
not political and lose something—everything—when stated in
political language.

For Ellul, the most serious moral and social issues revolve
around relationships—parent and child, man and woman,
teacher and pupil, man and God—in which there is an irreduc-
ible element of tension. In modern society, however, tensions are
banished from all realms but the political. Thus in education,
"the contemporary orientation is that the child must learn with-

out pain, that it must have agreeable, seductive work, that it must not even notice that it is working, and that in class the teacher must be really a sort of game leader, a permissive leader with whom there is no conflict." But to assert that there should be no conflict between teacher and pupil "radically falsifies the child's participation in social life and keeps his personality from developing." It is just this conflict through which the pupil learns and grows, providing, of course, that "in this conflict the teacher knows that his role is not to bully, crush, or train children like animals. . . ."

When he cannot banish tensions altogether, the modern man translates them into political terms. What is currently happening in American education affords an excellent example of the point Ellul is trying to make. Rebelling against the blandness of permissive education, American students—and students in other countries as well—have succeeded only in politicizing the relation between student and teacher. In the new situation thereby created, every pedagogical question becomes a matter for negotiation, and bureaucratic machinery has to be created for this purpose—the very proliferation of bureaucracy that some students began by attacking as unnecessary and oppressive. Although the student protest originates, at least in part, in an awareness that education has become an empty ritual, students find it difficult—given the exclusively political vocabulary in which discussion of conflicts, in our society, is invariably cast— to identify the source of the trouble as the school's abdication of moral and intellectual authority. They themselves accept the prevailing view that relations between students and teachers should be free of conflict and that whatever conflicts do exist therefore have to be removed or regulated by political means. The existence of conflict, in a society where conflict has been defined as exceptional and undesirable, automatically becomes a political question to which political categories—injustice, exploitation, authoritarianism, "the student as nigger"—are applied. Students hold up as an educational ideal the "free university" in which students set the standards, pursue their studies without having to be judged by their teachers, and confront their teachers, in short, as intellectual equals. To the degree that academic life falls short of this ideal, students seek political machinery to regularize conflicts by limiting what they perceive to be the arbitrary powers of the faculty. Because it has become so hard to imagine forms of authority that arise not from the wish to dominate or exploit but from inherent inequalities between teachers and students, students perceive authority in political terms and attack their teachers, not for having so little confidence in their ability to teach anything and for showing so little commitment to the intellectual life, but for acting like "authoritarians" by denying students the right to "participate in the decisions that affect their lives." The student protest thereby reinforces the flabby permissiveness of American education, since most faculties are all too willing to accede to student demands with a great show of democratic good feeling—just as most middle-class parents, in the similarly politicized struggles that take place in the home (and in many cases serve as the preliminary to the struggles now taking place in the university), have found it easier to bargain and negotiate with their children than to uphold ethical standards in a world seemingly devoid of any rational principle of authority.

The relations between men and women offer another example of the politicization of every aspect of life. Formerly the sexual relation was regarded as a private one belonging to the realm of love and therefore immune from the intrusion of sanctions derived from the realm of power. Feminism represented, among other things, an attempt not only to democratize the relations between men and women but to get rid of conflicts by denying their biological basis. Feminists did not confine themselves to attacking discrimination against women in the public sphere or to limiting the legal powers of husbands—powers that were, indeed, highly arbitrary and that gave rise to a thousand injustices. Pushed to its furthest limits, the logic of feminism denied that biological differences between men and women were of any importance and maintained, therefore, that whatever conflicts originated in those differences could be eradicated or at least regularized through appropriate political means. Feminists proposed to reform the family so as to eliminate sexual roles or, when that proved impossible under existing conditions, to abolish the family altogether and to assign its child-rearing functions, which allegedly interfered with the economic independence of women, to the community. That the new system may provide a more "efficient" way of ordering sexual relations and of rearing children is not the issue; what matters is that feminists have rested their case on those grounds. One hears of the Israeli kibbutz, for example, that the advantage of the new arrangement is that the child sees his parents only in an "affectional" context, whereas toilet training and all other matters pertaining to discipline are entrusted to the socialized agencies of child-raising. The family is thereby spared the terrible conflicts, Oedipal and otherwise, that arise when affection and discipline are concentrated in the same individuals. At this point, however, one has to ask with Ellul whether it is not precisely the conjunction of love and constraint that enables a child to grow up and to accept the constraints of adulthood without losing the capacity for love. It is true that children do grow up in the kibbutz and in fact develop into remarkably "well-adjusted" adults; but it is just that, their "adjustment" and their "ability to work well with others," so highly prized in the kibbutz, that may provide an ominous foretaste of our future.[4]

4

ELLUL SEES THE EXPANSION OF THE PRIVATE REALM AS A NECESSARY defense against the tyranny of the political, but this does not

4. According to Bruno Bettelheim, the founders of the kibbutz movement misunderstood Freud to be saying that "parents should never have any but good times with their children." The same fear of ambivalent attachments, based in part on the same misunderstanding of Freudian theory, can be seen in the middle-class American family today, and children brought up in it seem to show some of the same characteristics that Bettelheim ascribes to the kibbutz: a strong attachment to the peer group; a marked fear of being alone; more or less complete alienation from the past (since "there is no permanence in human relations except with the peer group"); a strong concern with personal "authenticity" in relations with others, unmediated by conventional forms of politeness; and a lack of introspection and of a highly developed inner life.

mean that he wishes individuals to retreat into purely personal consolations. He is well aware that this is a "suicidal solution." When he argues that "a private vision" has to be the basis of political realism and that "private life itself must be re-established," he means something quite different from the search for personal fulfillment that indeed, in the form of compulsive consumption, pervades our highly politicized society. The "privatization" of life is quite consistent with the politicization of everything. Ellul proposes instead "to create positions in which we reject and struggle with the State, *not* in order to modify some element of the regime or force it to make some decision, but, much more fundamentally, in order to permit the emergence of social, political, intellectual, or artistic bodies, associations, interest groups, or economic or Christian groups totally independent of the state, yet capable of opposing it. . . ." In this way he hopes that it will be possible to restore "an autonomous vitality to certain parts of society"—for instance, by creating "an authentic new tension between the intellectual and political realms." These words clearly imply a defense of the existing autonomy, and an attempt to enlarge the autonomy, of such institutions as the family and the school, in the face of all pressures to politicize them. They do not imply, however, that people should pretend that what happens in those institutions has no bearing on larger social questions—that intellectual life, for example, has nothing to do with politics. Ellul is not advocating political quiescence. The reason for restoring the autonomy of civil society is precisely that this "would make possible a political life that would be something else than mere illusion." Ellul realizes, moreover, that to search for a new culture "is necessarily a corporate act" and that isolated individuals cannot "follow this path."

In one of his latest books Ellul addresses himself at one point to American readers who might be tempted to interpret his attack on "the political illusion" as an attack on every form of political action, or to misread his condemnation of the Soviet Union as a defense of free enterprise. He writes: *"I absolutely do not say that capitalism is better than socialism.* I firmly believe the contrary. *I absolutely do not say that defense of the poor through socialist movements is wrong.* I firmly believe the contrary." He wishes only to show that socialism and Christianity, in his words, are not the same thing—that revolution cannot be regarded as a value in itself. When he criticizes socialism, Ellul is criticizing one form the "political illusion" has assumed, whether one looks at the socialist regimes in the Soviet Union and elsewhere, at revolutionary movements in the West, or for that matter at those social democrats (particularly conspicuous in France) who have wholly assimilated the technocratic and managerial point of view and condemn capitalism only because it embodies certain lingering technological inefficiencies.

Nevertheless I think that Ellul's position would be much clearer if it were not so firmly rooted in the theory of the "technological society." In itself, the attempt to anchor moral and cultural perspectives in a hard-headed sociological analysis of modern society should elicit nothing but our admiration. It is precisely this attempt that makes Ellul's work interesting in the first place; without it, Ellul would be only another moralist. My quarrel is not with Ellul's long excursion into sociology, which was entirely proper and necessary, but with the particular sociological conclusions he has arrived at, particularly in *The Technological Society*—the work, as I have said, for which he is best known in the United States.

I have already referred to Ellul's hostility to Marxism, which he sees merely as one of the great myths of the twentieth century—those "explanatory myths" that explain nothing. There is no doubt that Marxism as a social movement—as distinguished from a theory of industrial society—has acquired many of the features of a mythology and that Ellul's reservations on this score have to be taken seriously. In *The Technological Society*, however, Ellul tries to ground these reservations in a counter-theory of the modern social order which tries to show that "capitalism did not create our world; the machine did." Here he attacks Marxism not as a revolutionary myth but as a body of analysis. Marxism is useless as analysis, according to Ellul, because the character of industrial society derives not from capitalism but from technology. In order to make a case for the decisive influence of the latter, he has to dispose of the objection that technique is a neutral force and therefore compatible with a variety of social systems, and that what matters is the class relations, deriving from production, that ultimately determine the uses to which technique is put. Much of *The Technological Society* is devoted to this task. Ellul tries to show that technique is "autonomous" and that wherever technological habits of thought come to prevail, they drive out every other consideration. For that reason it makes no sense to distinguish between technology and the use that people make of it. "In a sound evaluation of the problem, it ought never to be said: on the one side, technique; on the other, the abuse of it." Since every technical process is explicitly designed to solve a specific technical problem, there is only one appropriate use to which it can be put. "A man can use his automobile to take a trip or to kill his neighbors. But the second use is not a use; it is a crime. The automobile was not created to kill people, so the fact is not important." In other words, the fact that cars are not used for killing—not intentionally, at any rate—does not prove that men can make a moral use of technology if they so choose and that in the last analysis, therefore, it is "man who decides in what direction to orient his researches." On the contrary, "a principal characteristic of technique . . . is its refusal to tolerate moral judgments." It is inevitable that the same society that expends vast amounts of technological knowledge in prolonging life or in making it more comfortable will also perfect ever more efficient techniques for destroying it. The automobile and the hydrogen bomb are parts of the same social process, and it is impossible to choose one without choosing the other.

To put it another way: "There is no difference at all between technique and its use. . . . The use of the automobile as a murder weapon does not represent the technical use, that is, the one best way of doing something. Technique is a means with a set of rules for the game. . . . There is but one method for its use, one possibility." Like much else in *The Technological Society,* this argument seems curiously removed from everyday reality. If one considers the automobile a little more broadly, not just as a machine but as part of a total system of transportation, it is apparent that in advanced capitalist society the automobile is in fact, if not a murder weapon, an instrument of violence in its social effects. Especially in the United States, the human need for open space, clean air, and livable communities is systematically subordinated to the automobile's need for parking garages and superhighways; and these things occur even though the automobile strictly speaking is designed for transportation, not the destruction of cities. This situation does not arise because the automobile in its technical aspect requires the suppression of other forms of surface transportation and thereby forces urban life to organize itself around cars to the exclusion of almost everything else. It is capitalism, not technology, that requires these things. The automobile may be designed for one use and one use alone, but this fact in itself does not explain why the state, not only in America but increasingly in western Europe as well, has chosen in effect to subsidize the automobile industry (as well as the airlines) at the expense of other forms of transportation—and this in the face of the terrible consequences to which such a policy gives rise.

5

IT CANNOT BE CLAIMED THAT A SYSTEM OF TRANSPORTATION ORGANized around cars and planes is intrinsically more efficient than a system in which various forms of rail transportation would also play an indispensable role. It cannot even be claimed that the existing system derives, as might first appear to be the case, from the unquestioned superiority of airplanes over trains. Since airports have to be built far from the center of cities, and since the only access to these centers is over highways choked with cars, travel time between the major cities of the eastern seaboard, say, is not appreciably reduced by substituting air travel for surface travel. Even from a purely technical point of view, it would make more sense to restore an efficient system of rail transport than to continue to build airports and highways that will be obsolete by the time they are completed. (It is precisely this anticipated obsolescence, however, that makes them attractive.)

City and regional planners have proposed just such an alternative system of transportation. They point out, not only that railroads are more efficient than airplanes for local and regional travel and for the transport of goods, but that the existing system has social by-products too important to ignore; that is, it contributes to the destruction of cities, to suburban blight, and to the general "environmental crisis." Yet there is no indication that the ideas of these planners will prevail. On purely technical grounds they ought to prevail, quite apart from other considerations. No one listens, however. What accounts for this anomaly?

In part the answer lies in the rise of the aircraft industry, nourished by war.[5] Obviously the aircraft industry wields great economic and political power. Yet precisely because it depends so much more heavily on military spending than on its ability to dominate the domestic market, the aircraft industry cannot be regarded as the decisive element in the American transportation system. The decisive element is the automobile industry, which is, indeed, the heart of the American economy. Not airplanes but automobiles, buses, and trucks have reduced the railroads to bankruptcy and thereby destroyed their ability to compete with the airlines. The central question, then, is why the automobile industry has come to dominate the entire economy, and political life as well.

There are several reasons, none of which can be attributed to technique. First is the automobile's apparently insatiable appetite

5. The dominance of air power in modern warfare, incidentally, does not rest on its technical efficiency. Experience with strategic bombing has shown again and again that its military effects are vastly overrated. The airplane is not necessarily the most efficient method of mass destruction, but it is the most *expensive* method of mass destruction. War, obviously, is the purest form of waste, and aerial warfare is the most wasteful method of war.

for roads, parking garages, gasoline, roadside establishments of all kinds, and innumerable ancillary goods and services. No other industry has such seemingly unlimited capacity to stimulate so wide a range of other industries. In a consumer economy the automobile plays a role analogous to that of the railroad in a nineteenth-century economy oriented around heavy industry. In the second place, the automobile has established itself as the most appropriate and glamorous symbol of the consumer culture and the values it embodies: personal mobility and the private satisfaction of culturally induced needs and wants. But above all, the automobile industry is central to the American economy because it has developed to such a high pitch the deliberate planning of waste. The industry maintains itself not only by building obsolescence into the product in the form of shoddy workmanship but by deliberately inducing changes of fashion and taste. The success with which the industry early made the annual change of models a national ritual showed how advertising could be used as a form of propaganda—a means of sustaining an ideology and a culture organized around compulsive consumption.

Ellul is well aware of the metamorphosis of advertising into propaganda, but he does not see that the origins of this process lie not in the expansion of the state but in the need to make mass culture an adjunct of corporate planning—of the planned production of waste. It is true that the state plays a much larger role in the modern economy than it formerly did and that it has come to wield frightening powers of destruction. But the nearly total subjection of the cultural apparatus to the advertising industry and the corporations ought to alert us to the fact that the growth of the state has come about to serve the needs of the corporations, not to serve technology in the abstract. The relationship between the corporations and the state, moreover, is one-sided. The corporations relegate to the state activities on which the corporate system depends but which are unprofitable, while retaining for themselves the revenues created by the elaborate system of state regulations and subsidies. The state directly or indirectly trains scientists, technicians, and skilled workers; administers and finances welfare programs; sponsors urban renewal in the interests of the real estate developers and automobile manufacturers; subsidizes the huge amount of scientific research required by advanced technology; and grapples unsuccessfully with the sheer physical removal of ever-accumulating waste. But the profits made possible by these and similar public expenditures—above all by war—accrue to the corporations, while the state depends on taxation for its revenues. This one-sided interdependence of the corporations and the state leads to the much-discussed disparity between private affluence and public squalor—a characteristic feature of advanced capitalism which, however, is never mentioned in *The Technological Society*.

Faced with dwindling markets and the threat of chronic overproduction, mature capitalism increasingly depends on imperial expansion abroad and on the domestic production of goods that will be quickly superceded. "The capitalist system lives and thrives by waste." I have confined myself to the automobile industry because it is one of the best examples of this tendency, because it illustrates more clearly than others the social consequences to which it leads, and because Ellul himself introduces the example of the automobile in order to prove that technique obeys its own laws and "refuses to tolerate moral judgments." It would be possible, however, to cite many other examples of the importance of waste—the youth market, for instance, which has attained its present position in advanced economies largely because it is highly susceptible to changes of fashion and taste—and it would be possible, in every case, to show that the social disasters that Ellul attributes to technique are more accurately attributed to the distinctive character of advanced capitalist production. This emphatically does not mean that all the evils of the modern world can be charged to capitalism or that socializing the means of production would inaugurate the golden age. But it does cast a great deal of doubt on an interpretation of modern history that treats capitalism as "only one aspect of the deep disorder of the nineteenth century"—a disorder that originated in the triumph of technology.

6

IT IS NO ANSWER TO SAY THAT SOCIALIST COUNTRIES ARE COMING more and more to resemble capitalist countries in their use of propaganda and other totalitarian controls, as if this demonstrated the transcendent character of technique. This argument pays no attention to the historical setting in which socialist regimes have come to power in the modern world. It can be argued that a socialism of abundance in countries with firmly established traditions of political democracy would look very different from socialism in Russia, China, Algeria, or Cuba—economically backward countries in which political democracy has never taken firm root. It can be argued further that Western intervention in the twentieth-century revolutions in backward countries played some part, if not a major part, in forming those regimes into an authoritarian mold—for instance, by saddling them with a debilitating arms race. These arguments do not excuse Stalin's crimes against the Russian people, the suppression of freedom in Hungary and Czechoslovakia, or the liquidation of political opponents wherever socialist regimes have come to power. They do raise the question of whether socialism in backward countries is inevitably the same thing as socialism in advanced countries. The alleged identity of socialist and neo-capitalist regimes rests on a mechanical determinism that takes no account of historical variations.

The more extravagant claims made for this determinism—for instance, that it represents an alternative to Marxian theory— melt away under analysis. Deprived of these claims, the theory of the "technological society" offers insights either that are already present in Marxian theory or that fit into it without difficulty. Managerialism is merely the current version of capitalist ideology. If socialist countries share certain features with advanced capitalist regimes—and Ellul in any event has greatly exaggerated their similarities—that does not mean that there is an underlying identity between capitalism and socialism and that technique transcends both; it merely reflects the degree to which socialist regimes in undeveloped countries have had to draw on bourgeois models of industrialization. Given the shortage of technical personnel in undeveloped countries, reliance on bourgeois resources is inevitable. To conclude from this that socialism challenges capitalism only on the grounds of its technical inefficiency and that the most advanced elements among the bourgeoisie, indeed, have already conceded the argument and embraced socialism because it promises technically better results, makes it very difficult to understand why those very elements have resisted with such vigor and success the spread of socialism in the rest of the world.

The global struggle between socialism and capitalism, of which Vietnam is the latest and bloodiest phase, cannot be understood as a kind of factional dispute within the managerial class or, on the other hand, as the expression of mass antipathies whipped up by propaganda. At times Ellul pushes his critique of political illusions and propaganda to the point of saying that *all* politics are illusory. It is true that "the creation of political problems out of nothing is one of propaganda's most astonishing capabilities," but it does not follow that every political problem is the creation of propaganda. Ellul claims that it was "American anticolonialist idealism," presumably reinforced by propaganda, that forced the Dutch out of Indonesia and the French out of Vietnam, and that American involvement in Southeast Asia, therefore, "is the direct consequence of their action in disarming France." This account ignores several things. It was not the United States but Ho Chi Minh that "disarmed" France; far from urging the French to leave Vietnam, the United States tried to maneuver them into staying; and in fact the United States refused to sign the Geneva agreement because it did not want to be a party to the "disarming" of France. The main lines of American foreign policy have been clear and consistent: when the European powers were no longer able to hold the line against colonial revolution, the United States leaped into the breach. An interpretation that attributes all this to propaganda and "anticolonialist idealism" sacrifices historical accuracy to the internal consistency of a beautiful design.

Ellul's technological determinism adequately explains neither the structure of advanced capitalist society nor the foreign policies to which it gives rise. But the weakness of the social theory on which Ellul has tried to base his moral and cultural position does not undermine the position itself. At its best, his work helps us to make an indispensable distinction between the idea of socialism and the transcendent political myths that have been invoked to prove its moral necessity and/or its historical inevitability. His is the most thorough and convincing attack I know on the position that "revolution is *prerequisite* to reconciliation"—or if one prefers to state the issue in non-theological terms, that revolution is the prerequisite of cultural regeneration, of a genuinely civilized society. Ellul does not deny that there may be oppression that can only be ended through revolution; nor does he deny that revolutionary violence can sometimes clarify issues or create disorder "out of which (depending on how fluid the situation is) renewal may issue." What he does insist is that revolutionary violence must not be confused with the *creation* of order. Violence belongs to the realm of necessity; it is part of the natural order of things, whereas the proper object of politics is "the creation of a stabilized universe, an artificial universe (artificial in the sense that it is made by the skill of man), in which man recognizes forms and objects, assigns names and places, and creates a continuity with the help of (but also against) the fluidity of the universe." Out of violence, on the other hand, only chaos issues.

It must be emphasized that Ellul condemns violent revolution (while recognizing its inevitability in some situations—inevitability and justice are not the same), as a man of the left. "[I]f I attack the left in its common-places, that does not mean I am against the left. On the contrary, it is because I believe in values that only the left has stated, elucidated, and partially adopted (without acting on them), because the left has sustained the hope of mankind, because the left has engaged in the struggle for justice, that I cannot tolerate the absurdity of the present left. . . ." Such a position is difficult to understand for those who believe that to criticize the left is an "objectively" reactionary act. Because Ellul does criticize the left, and because he denies the primacy of politics, many radicals will regard him as a traitor to their cause. The real betrayal, however, is the radical intellectuals' subordination of their own work to political passions.

[XVIII]

Birth, Death, and Technology: The Limits of Cultural Laissez-Faire

INDIVIDUALISM HAS BEEN ESSENTIAL TO THE GROWTH OF LIBERAL democracy in the West. The essence of the democratic state is that it acts directly on individuals—rather than on corporations or estates—and that it treats all citizens alike; it is in this sense that the modern state represents the substitution of reason (embodied in the law) for force and favoritism. Based on law and on principles recognized as universally valid throughout a given society, and having at its disposal a monopoly of legitimate violence, the modern state from the beginning wielded formidable powers; yet at the same time its very existence presupposed the redefinition of many activities, formerly regarded as matters concerning the entire community, as essentially private affairs, with which the state had no right to interfere.

Economic life, for example, which had once been subjected to innumerable regulations, both local and national, came to be regarded, in the late eighteenth century, as a self-regulating mechanism requiring only that the state enforce the general rules of fair play and free competition. The business corporation, once recognized as a political as well as an economic institution, exercising delegated functions of government and thus subject to public control, was redefined in law as a private "person" with all the privileges and immunities of persons. Even the advent of welfare capitalism in the twentieth century brought with it no corresponding recognition of the public and political character of the corporation or of the social character of the labor it embodies. Labor, on the contrary, continues to be seen as a contract between the individual and his employer, not as the collective transformation of nature and self-realization of mankind as a whole.

The achievement of economic individualism, in the eighteenth and nineteenth centuries, was paralleled by the triumph of individualism in cultural life. Religion offers the clearest example. The principle of religious freedom, first officially recognized in Virginia in 1784 and later written into the Bill of Rights, meant that religious belief was henceforth to be regarded as a purely private affair, something between the individual and his maker. As in economic life, the development of individualism and of its counterpart, the rational state, had both positive and negative features. It undermined officially imposed religious conformity and set up the state as a guarantor of liberty of conscience, but on the other hand it obscured the social character of religion and weakened its power to offer a critical commentary on the conditions of social life. Whereas the churches had once claimed the right to speak with authority on the just price, on just wars, and indeed on all aspects of secular life, these matters were now widely held to be beyond the competence of religious authority. The church retired from its long struggle to change the world and concerned itself with purely spiritual affairs. It was only as individuals that evangelical Christians in the nineteenth century attacked slavery and other abuses; the churches, through their official silence, lent support to the status quo.

It was not to be expected that any area of life, even sexuality, would long remain exempt from this powerful drive for personal autonomy, this attack on all forms of personal dependence. If individualism meant the right to dispose of one's property and one's opinions with a minimum of outside interference, it also implied the right to dispose of one's person, even when exercising this right contradicted long-established usages. As early as the seventeenth century, certain moralists—in many cases the same people (often inspired by Puritanism) who were beginning to advance modern concepts of property and religious freedom—challenged the practice of arranged marriages, insisting that even daughters had a right to choose their husbands without parental intervention. The triumph of romantic love over external constraints became a standard theme of the bourgeois novel, in part at least because it embodied, in an exceedingly clear and durable set of symbols, the triumph of individual self-determination against the power of established institutions and external circumstances.

The idea of personal autonomy was identified with the concept of privacy and the assertion of the rights of the individual against traditional constraints, particularly those based on institutionalized hierarchy. Individualism had another aspect, and it is this second aspect that especially concerns us here. It was identified with a revolt against the constraints imposed by nature—that is, with man's increasing domination of nature through science and technology. Modern rationalism revealed itself not only in the rational state and in the vision of a social order based on universal reason but in the unprecedented advance of science; and in a culture that set an increasingly high value on privacy, self-dependence, and personal fulfillment, it was perhaps inevitable that the achievements of modern science should be seen, not as a new stage in man's collective self-awareness, but principally as another means to individual fulfillment and the satisfaction of personal wants. This tendency was particularly strong in the United States, where the material conquest and technological domination of the continent, instead of being undertaken as a great collective enterprise, remained an undertaking primarily of individual settlers, men and women dominated by the mystique of the self-reliant yeoman and the self-sufficient family farm. Older traditions of community survived in the practice of isolated groups like the Mormons, but for the most part the West—the most powerful symbol, throughout our early history, of man's expanding technological dominion over nature—was seen as offering unlimited opportunities for individual enterprise and for the untrammeled exercise of the individual will. In Europe, communal traditions were stronger. Even in Europe, however, the growth of scientific knowledge and of technological control over nature tended to be regarded as another phase of the individual's emancipation from age-old limitations—in this case, limitations imposed by economic scarcity, distance, disease and early death, darkness and cold; in short, "the natural limitations of earthly well-being." The development of science and technology was part of the same individualistic rationalism that was already dissolving traditional concepts of social and political relations; and if at times the results of technology were dismaying to those who remained sensitive to the disruption of communal ties and the rape of nature, in the long run they seemed to justify themselves because they added to the sum of material goods, brought increased comfort, and above all seemed to enlarge the area of personal choice. If it was not easy to show that the production of goods in unprecedented quantity, the mastery of distance, and the lengthening of life had created a richer social existence—if, indeed, the growth of classes and of bitter class antagonisms suggested the contrary—it seemed to be indisputable that they gave to the individual (or more accurately to individuals of the dominant classes) a hitherto unknown freedom to shape their own lives. The emerging concept of personal autonomy was thus bound up, not only with the idea of political and cultural freedom from institutional constraints, but with mastery over the biological conditions of existence.

The assertion of personal choice in the matter of marriage—an early example of the revolt against dependence—may be regarded as one of the first steps in the emancipation of women. This development shows with special clarity how closely the growth of individualism was tied to a revolt against limitations imposed by nature—in this case by the accident of sex. Of the various forms of hereditary discrimination which it has been the mission of liberal democracy to destroy, sexual discrimination was the most resistant to attack, not only because traditional attitudes went very deep but because discrimination in this area, more clearly than elsewhere, seemed rooted in nature. While man was involved in his great project of transcendence, women as a group remained tied to biological routine; and whereas the general tendency of modern history seemed to be toward the development of individuality, women remained, in Simone de Beauvoir's phrase, slaves to the species. By the middle of the nineteenth century, it was nevertheless unclear that biology should be allowed so completely to determine a person's life chances; or to put it another way, it was unclear that sexuality should any longer serve as a criterion for excluding a whole class of people from political and economic life. The growing movement for woman's rights, though for a long time it focused on the demand for the vote, also reasserted, more forcefully than before, women's demand for control of their own bodies. As some feminists were quick to point out, the emancipation of women implied not only the vote and the right to work but the right to bear children at one's pleasure.

It was here that the woman's rights movement intersected with modern technology. For it was technology alone that made the assertion of this new right plausible to middle-class women, many of whom were by this time increasingly familiar with various methods of contraception and free from religious scruples as to their use. Technological control over conception offered the most dramatic instance of an argument which by the latter part of the nineteenth century was becoming increasingly central to the feminist agitation—namely, that quite apart from considerations of political justice, technology itself had so altered the basis of existence as to make obsolete the traditional relationships between the sexes. Technology was not only a means to the liberation of women from unwished-for childbearing, and thus to women's self-fulfillment; it had to be seen as a determinant of history in its own right, indeed as a force which could not be resisted, and to which thought and social life must necessarily accommodate themselves. Feminist thought here reflects a more general change in attitudes toward technology: formerly regarded as a means of expanding the range of personal choice, it was now seen as a historical force in its own right, moving quite independently of human volition. According to late nineteenth-century feminists, technology had rendered sexual differences minimally important by abolishing the importance of sheer physical strength, both in industry and in politics. Machine production made manual labor increasingly unnecessary and thereby made obsolete objections to the industrial employment of women. Similarly, war was giving way to reason and universal peace—such was the optimistic late-Victorian view—and the argument that women should not vote because they could not bear arms no longer had any merit, if it ever had.

Lester Frank Ward, Charlotte Perkins Gilman, and Thorstein Veblen, among others, made this technological determinism central to the feminist position, arguing that the family itself had been superseded by technology—its economic functions by the factory, its educational functions by the school, and its biological functions by improved techniques of contraception and abortion. In 1929, Bertrand Russell published his little book *Marriage and Morals,* which summarized fifty years of the most advanced thought on these questions. Science, according to Russell, had destroyed religious superstitions surrounding the subject of sex, while technological improvements in contraception had removed the fear of pregnancy, formerly the basis of the Christian belief that extramarital sex was a sin, at least for women. There was no longer any reason to regard "sex relations which do not involve children" as otherwise than "purely private affairs." Modern marriage had only one purpose, to rear children; and even here, most of its functions, in particular those once associated with fatherhood, had "been taken over by the State." The father no longer provided protection or even support, since it was increasingly the "humanitarian sentiment of the community" that "the child should receive a certain minimum of care, even if he has no father to pay for it." Away from home during most of the day, fathers performed a negligible part in discipline, knowing their children mainly in "a play relation, without serious importance."

"It may be—and indeed I think it far from improbable—that the father will be completely eliminated before long. . . . In that case, women will share their children with the State, not with an individual father." In the face of this possibility Russell is curiously ambivalent. On the one hand, he thinks that the elimination of fatherhood, by doing away with the fierce possessiveness with which fathers defend their wives and children from the threat of attack, would remove one of the sources of war. On the other hand, "it would make sex love itself more trivial," would in fact encourage "a certain triviality in all personal relations," and would also "make it far more difficult to take an interest in anything after one's own death." The most interesting thing about Russell's book—and this is what makes it such a typical example of early twentieth-century attitudes toward the impact of technology on human relations—is that his reservations about the trivialization of sex and friendship are never admitted into the argument but exist only on its periphery. He assumes that the relentless progress of technology cannot be arrested short of an apocalyptic struggle in the dim future. When he considers the subject of eugenics—another step in the rationalization of child rearing, much discussed at this time—he is frightened by the possibility that the state will eventually assume complete control over procreation and the care of children, and he even foresees a time "when all who care for the freedom of the human spirit will have to rebel against a scientific tyranny," just as an earlier age had to rebel against ecclesiastical tyranny. But he sees no hope of acting effectively in the present to prevent these developments from working out to a cataclysmic confrontation in the future.

Here again we see a very common tendency in the prevailing thinking about science and technology, a contradiction that becomes increasingly glaring as science more and more impinges on the mysteries of love, birth, and death. The prevailing image of technological utopia begets the counter-image of technological nightmare—the appalling vision of a scientific totalitarianism, embodied in such anti-utopian novels as Aldous Huxley's *Brave New World* and George Orwell's *1984.* On the one hand we have a greatly exaggerated faith in the ability of science to solve all the material problems of life, and an exagger-

ated idea of the autonomy of science and technology as determining forces in history; on the other hand, these inflated
estimates of the power of science give rise to a hysterical fear of
scientific dictatorship. This fear, precisely because it is cast in the
form of an anti-utopian vision of the future, serves to postpone a
reckoning with science, while the sweeping quality of the scientific control it envisions serves to paralyze our will to act in the
present. At the same time it gives the illusion that the destructive
possibilities of science are at least being squarely confronted. The
anti-utopian and the utopian myths of science have a common
root in the assumption that science is an autonomous force,
rather than an instrument of the will of the human community,
and that its development is inevitable and irresistible.

In the absence of any public policy in these matters, scientists
continue to experiment with new means of liberating procreation from natural limitations. The latest experiments in the
artificial creation of living organisms presumably have profound
social implications; yet the discussion, such as it is, about extra-
uterine reproduction shows the same confusion that characterized earlier debates about contraception and its effects on the
family. The technical obstacles to the asexual reproduction of
human embryos, which could then be implanted either in the
womb or in an artificial placenta, do not appear to be insuper-
able. Robert G. Edwards and Patrick Steptoe of Cambridge have
already fertilized human eggs in the laboratory and produced
embryos; the next step is to implant them in the womb of one of
Dr. Edwards's patients, and the step beyond that, to develop an
artificial placenta.

Among other presumed advantages of this new technique, it
would allow scientists to determine the sex of embryos before
implantation and thus to offer parents a choice of gender in their
offspring. Beyond that, asexual reproduction would complete
the emancipation of woman from her age-old enslavement to
the race. According to Ti-Grace Atkinson, the artificial womb
would "de-institutionalize" sexual intercourse by eliminating its

"functional aspect." The last obstacles to the individuation of women will thus be overcome. A woman will be able to choose whether to have children or not (and to choose their sex), in either case without submitting to marriage or even to pregnancy and without sacrificing her career or her chances for personal fulfillment, let alone her youthful figure. With asexual reproduction established as "a truly optional method, at the very least," natural pregnancy might become an anachronism. In advocating "very concentrated research to perfect as quickly as possible this extra-uterine method of pre-natal development," Atkinson states a position that many feminists would probably regard as extreme. So far as radical neo-feminism seeks to persuade women that men are expendable, however, this is a logical extension of the neo-feminist argument. If men are expendable in bed—the explicit conclusion of many of the current attacks on the "myth of the vaginal orgasm"—why should they not be regarded as expendable in the reproductive process itself?

Underlying this discussion one can detect a number of familiar assumptions. Once again it is taken for granted that the progress of technology is inevitable and that although a program of "very concentrated research" would no doubt hasten its arrival, the day of the artificial womb is bound to come in any case. It is also taken for granted that the overriding objective is to enlarge the area of personal choice, in this case that of women, an oppressed caste. Those who see the artificial womb as an important part of woman's liberation either ignore or find unterrifying the possibility that unrestricted expansion of individual freedom simultaneously enhances the power of the state, in the case of asexual reproduction because the state would have to assume greater and greater control over the rearing of children. Those who hail the advance of technology ignore the crucial point: that although the application of technology to the control of procreation, beginning with primitive techniques of contraception and leading inexorably, it seems, to the artificial womb, has multiplied the choices open to those able to benefit from technology, this same process has had cumulative social effects beyond its effects on individuals; and it is precisely their magnitude and uncertainty that ought to convince us at last of the inadequacy of a laissez-faire attitude toward technological development and the desperate need for a social policy in these matters. The assumption of technological inevitability, however—which in turn is so closely bound up with the assumptions of liberal individualism—defeats every effort to formulate a policy, or even to insist that a policy is necessary.

The layman's undiminished enthusiasm for scientific advancement curiously coincides with rising doubts among scientists themselves. It is the leader of "The Feminists" who heralds the inevitable coming of the artificial womb and its beneficial effects, while the biologist James D. Watson, faced with the possibility of asexual reproduction and human cloning to which his own Nobel Prize-winning work has indirectly contributed, dares to raise the question: Is this what we want? Watson insists that "this is a matter far too important to be left solely in the hands of the scientific and medical community. The belief that surrogate mothers and clonal babies are inevitable because science always moves forward . . . represents a form of laissez-faire nonsense dismally reminiscent of the creed that American business, if left to itself, will solve everybody's problems." He urges the public to undertake a searching discussion of the issues and make up its own mind. This suggestion raises a number of interesting questions, and it should be noted that they are political rather than technological in their nature. What constitutes the public? Through what channels is it to make its wishes known? In view of the monolithic character of the media and the political system, do the people have an effective choice at all? What changes in the political structure would have to occur for the kind of discussion Watson envisions to take place, and to result in something more enduring than a new set of official platitudes?

Let us leave the no longer mysterious realm of love, sex, and childbirth, and turn to the questions that lie at the other end of the life cycle, questions about death. Here too it is doctors themselves who are beginning to have reservations about their increasing control over biology—in this case, their ability to keep patients alive longer than many of them want to live. In theory, the physician's responsibility is simply to keep the patient alive; in practice, doctors often commit euthanasia by turning off the machines that cruelly prolong life without being able to restore the body to health. Presenting a bland face to the public, the medical profession pretends to know nothing of such practices. It tries also to hide them from the patients themselves, in keeping with its longstanding rule that the dying patient should be the last to know the facts of his own case. There is increasing evidence, however, that the more sensitive spirits in the profession are beginning to find this official silence insupportable. It places on the doctor himself a burden that some find intolerable. In the days when most people died at home, the physician's role in the process was that of a trusted consultant; now he has become in many cases an executioner. For years the profession sought to establish jurisdiction over death, as over every other phase of the life cycle; but its very success in persuading or forcing the public to die in hospitals, surrounded by machines and attended by experts, has given rise not only to an exaggerated confidence in the hospital on the part of the public, but to baffling difficulties for the hospital staff, both philosophical and bureaucratic.

"Our hospitals," says a recent study, "are admirably arranged, both by accident and design, to hide medical information from patients." But this very secrecy creates difficulties for the staff, which is already overburdened with the problems of the living and is reluctant to waste valuable time on the dying. Hospitals try to deal with this problem by segregating the dying patient—a practice that is designed to let the patient know that his case is hopeless without actually telling him anything. To isolate the patient, however, also isolates the doctors who have to deal with him and makes their responsibility doubly burdensome and lonely.

Sometimes the doctor simply turns his back while the nurses allow the patient to die; but although a studied self-deception may sometimes help to soothe an uneasy conscience, even the medical profession balks at making it a way of life. Some doctors are beginning to question the wisdom of hospitalization in so-called terminal cases. Wouldn't it be better to send the patient home, if only to take some of the burden from the doctor's shoulders? Wouldn't it be wiser in general to give the patient a voice in his own future? Isn't the policy of silence self-defeating? There is talk of "natural" death—letting the patient die at his own speed, without the intervention of machines. Some hospitals have instituted seminars on "the dynamics of death and dying," designed to make doctors as well as patients face death without flinching.

According to a psychiatrist at Billings Hospital in Chicago, most of the doctors on the staff refuse to attend, evidently because they cannot see death in any form except as a crushing professional failure. In other words, the profession still conceives of its objective in technological terms—to prolong the life of the organism, regardless of circumstances—rather than as a work of mercy: to minister to the sick and the dying. Nevertheless the mere existence of seminars in "thanatology" suggests that the profession's conception of itself may be beginning to change. The same psychiatrist adds that even those doctors who manage to "cope" with the "failure" represented by the dying patient have more trouble facing these patients than the other members of the staff. In this connection it is interesting to read that "what is unique about Billings is the team concept that draws all paramedical personnel into the act, partly as a compensation for the reluctance of doctors to change their own attitudes." As the limitations of their own practice become clearer, doctors may be learning to value the paramedical elements of the profession and to understand that those in closer contact with patients have always played an indispensable part in the profession—indeed, if their work is considered as an errand of mercy, a part that is in some ways more important than that of the doctor himself. The recognition of the importance of "paraprofessionals" is one of the preconditions for a general restructuring of the professions. The upgrading of paraprofessional elements would have ramifying effects on professional life, helping to break down the monolithic structure of the professions and also making it possible for blacks, women, and others who have been discriminated against to enter without extended postgraduate training: an initial step toward genuine equality in employment. A recent study of women has argued that fewer women enter the professions in the United States than in Europe partly because the structure of professional careers in Europe is more open and fluid.

These signs of change, in what has become the most conservative of professions, may be the beginning of an important change in the professions in general. Considered in isolation, doctors' growing uneasiness about their own management of dying may seem insignificant. But there are signs of uneasiness elsewhere as well. Dr. Watson has reservations about cloning and insists that the question is too important to be decided by scientists alone. Other biologists have been saying the same thing about decisions to undertake research in biochemical warfare. Scientists in general are beginning to reconsider their traditional unwillingness to accept responsibility for the social consequences of scientific discoveries. The establishment of committees of "concerned scholars," the emergence of radical caucuses in various disciplines, the intense debates about social issues that are taking place at professional meetings and in schools where professionals are trained, may indicate a reawakening of the sense of corporate responsibility. It is true that questions of professional responsibility have sometimes been discussed in a superficial and even silly way, but it is important that they are being discussed at all. We may have reached the limits of a purely technological approach to professional work; or rather, the limits of that approach, which actually were reached a long time ago, may be growing clearer to professionals themselves. Certainly this is an outcome worth hoping for, and worth promoting by every available means, since a revolt against narrow professionalism and against professional irresponsibility—a revolt not against the professions but within the professions—is one of the necessary ingredients of a new anti-technological politics and culture.

Are we also beginning to understand the limits of liberal

individualism itself, which has furnished the political and cultural basis of the cult of technology? There cannot be a successful rebellion against the domination of social life by technology that does not incorporate a thoroughgoing criticism of liberalism, since the inevitability of technological development has always been defended on the grounds that it expanded the individual's freedom of personal choice. And until recently this was undeniably the case, at least for those able to avail themselves of the advantages of modern technology. It is only therefore when we find ourselves imprisoned in our private cars, marvelously mobile but unable to go anywhere because the highways are choked with traffic; when we find ourselves surrounded by modern conveniences but unable to breathe the air; provided with unprecedented leisure to fish in polluted rivers and swim at polluted beaches; provided with the means to prolong life beyond the point where it offers any pleasure; equipped with the power to create human life, which will simultaneously destroy the meaning of human life—it is only, in short, when we are confronted with the contradictions of individualism and private enterprise in their most immediate, unmistakable, and by now familiar form that we are forced to reconsider our exaltation of the individual over the life of the community, and to submit technological innovations to a question we have so far been careful not to ask: Is this what we want?

NOTES AND
BIBLIOGRAPHY

A WORD ABOUT THE TITLE OF THIS BOOK MAY BE IN ORDER. THIS TITLE, AND the quotation from Vico from which it derives, have evoked from several readers the inevitable reply (one might better call it a reflex) that of course Vico had it exactly backwards: it is the intrusion of human subjectivity into history that makes it impossible to understand "civil society" objectively, whereas the physical scientist can detach himself from the materials he studies, knowing that the processes he wishes to understand will not be altered by his own intervention.

Let us leave aside the difficulty that the argument about the objectivity of the natural sciences rests on an idea of science that scientists themselves discarded fifty years ago (for here too, it appears, the intervention of the investigator does indeed alter the processes observed, making complete certainty impossible). It is more important to understand how Vico's apparently naïve observation became one of the foundations of a philosophy of history far more profound than the naïve empiricism that has now so largely displaced it. For it was precisely the principle that the "world of nations" is intelligible because it is man-made, as restated by Hegel in the form of an assertion that "reality is not mere objective datum, external to man, but is shaped by him through consciousness," on which Marx based his attack on the mechanical materialism of Feuerbach and the eighteenth-century philosophers, according to which the so-called external world, in Marx's words, "is conceived only in the form of the *object* or of *perception,* but not as sensuous human activity, *practice* . . ." Eighteenth-century materialism, according to the *Theses on Feuerbach,* properly stresses the distinction between "sensuous activity" and thought; but it "does not conceive of human activity itself as an objective activity." The objective world, Marx insists, has to be seen as man's own self-creation, the product of his conscious intervention in nature and history, and the inability to recognize his own creation, accordingly, as the deepest sense of man's "alienation" from his own labor.

Instead of understanding the full implications of the fact that "circumstances are changed by men," men view even the social world as a kind of second nature, blindly obedient to external laws beyond human understanding and control. In the language of *Capital,* the social relations between men assume "the fantastic form of a relation between things."

In the latter book, Vico's principle provides an indispensable support for the Marxian critique of political economy, whose momentous "discovery, that the products of labour . . . are but material expressions of the human labour spent in their production . . . by no means dissipates the mist through which the social character of labour appears to us to be an objective character of the products themselves." Political economy—in many ways the successor of eighteenth-century materialism—accepts this identification between labor and its market value as a given, as a condition inherent in the nature of things, without subjecting it to the historical analysis that would reveal wage labor as a disguised form of forced labor, while at the same time disclosing the essentially social character of labor in general, which under capitalism appears merely as the satisfaction of individual wants.

Considerations of space prevent me from dealing with the perversion of Marxism itself into a positivistic science. What is important here is to insist that Vico's insight remains invaluable to the critical understanding of history (especially cultural history)—that is, to the approach to history that seeks not merely to understand it but to transform it—and that not only Marx but Michelet, Dilthey, Lukács, Croce, and many others have understood this and acknowledged their indebtedness to Vico. As Marx once wrote, when he noted the need for a "critical history of technology" that would do for human culture what Darwin's work had done for "Nature's Technology": "And would not such a history be easier to compile since, as Vico says, human history differs from natural history in this, that we have made the former, but not the latter?"

See Marx's first and third *Theses on Feuerbach* (1845) and *Capital,* vol. I (Modern Library edition), pp. 83, 85, 406, for the passages quoted, and Shlomo Avineri's *The Social and Political Thought of*

Karl Marx (1969), p. 68, for a paraphrase of Hegel's position, of which I have gratefully availed myself. Avineri's discussion of the issues treated here, in the section entitled *"Homo Faber,"* is the clearest I have seen. See also Herbert Marcuse, *Reason and Revolution* (1941); T. B. Bottomore's introduction and editorial notes to his edition of Marx's *Early Writings* (1964); George Lichtheim, *Marxism* (2nd edition, 1965); Jürgen Habermas, *Knowledge and Human Interests* (1971). The concept of "second nature" comes from Lukács; I am indebted to an unpublished paper by Russell Jacoby for clarification of this issue. For Giovanni Battista Vico's *The New Science,* see the translation by T. G. Bergin and M. H. Fisch (1961); the quotation in question is from ¶331. See also ¶236, where Vico remarks on "that infirmity of the human mind" whereby it "is naturally inclined by the senses to see itself externally in the body, and only with great difficulty does it come to attend to itself by means of reflection."

I. Origins of the Asylum

THIS ESSAY, HITHERTO UNPUBLISHED, WAS DELIVERED AS A LECTURE AT Vassar College on April 15, 1968, and again at the University of Missouri, April 27, 1968.

The quotation from Engels comes from a letter to Marx, December 15, 1882, cited in E. J. Hobsbawm's edition of Marx's *Pre-Capitalist Economic Formations* (1964), pp. 145–6.

There is a large body of historical writing on prisons, penal reform, insane asylums, and other places of confinement; but much of it reflects the "enlightened prejudice" criticized in this essay. Alice Felt Tyler, *Freedom's Ferment* (1944), a study of antebellum reform movements, includes chapters on the school, prisons, and various correctional institutions. The quotation in the text ("groping" toward modern practices) comes from p. 265 of the Harper Torchbook edition; see also p. 239 for the quotation from Horace Mann. Studies of American prisons include O. F. Lewis, *The Development of American Prisons and Prison Customs* (1922); Harry Elmer Barnes, *The Story of Punishment* (1930); Blake McKelvey, *American Prisons* (1936); N. K. Teeters, *The Cradle of the Penitentiary* (1935); N. K. Teeters and John D. Shearer, *The Prison at Philadelphia* (1957); and W. David Lewis, *From Newgate to Dannemora: The Rise of the Penitentiary in New York* (1955). See also Alexis de Tocqueville and

Gustave de Beaumont, *On the Penitentiary System in the United States and Its Application in France* (1833). For developments in England, see D. L. Howard, *The English Prisons* (1960) and Sidney and Beatrice Webb, *English Prisons Under Local Government* (1922), from the Archon Books edition of which (1963), p. 192, I took the quotation on imprisonment for debt. For helping me with this literature on prisons, I am grateful to Russell Menard, my research assistant at the University of Iowa.

On insanity, see Norman Dain, *Concepts of Insanity in the United States* (1964) and Gerald N. Grob, *The State and the Mentally Ill* (1966), from which I have quoted the passages on Woodward, pp. 66, 34, and 39.

A recent study of the origins of the common school system— Michael Katz, *The Irony of Early School Reform* (1968)—differs from the other works just cited in explicitly rejecting a progressive or Whiggish interpretation of the antebellum reforms. I have also referred to some of the recent polemics against the existing school system: Jonathan Kozol, *Death at an Early Age* (1967); Herbert R. Kohl, *Teaching the "Unteachable"* (1967); and Edgar Z. Friedenberg, *Coming of Age in America* (1965), from the last of which I have quoted passages on pp. 36, 33, 39, and 41.

My observations about racial attitudes derive largely from a reading of Winthrop Jordan's doctoral dissertation (Brown, 1960), later published as *White over Black* (1968); from conversations with George M. Fredrickson; and from Fredrickson's *The Black Image in the White Mind* (1971). Our article, "Resistance to Slavery," *Civil War History* (December 1967), pp. 315–29, reflects another aspect of our interest in the work of Erving Goffman and Gresham M. Sykes and its applicability to the history of slavery and racism.

As already indicated, it was that work which first led me to reject the Whiggish interpretation of the origins of the asylum. See especially Goffman's *Asylums* (1962), from which I have taken his formulations on p. xiii, and Sykes's *The Society of Captives* (1958). Later I was influenced by Michel Foucault's *Madness and Civilization* (1965) and by the review of this book by Steven Marcus in the *New York Review,* November 17, 1966, pp. 36–9, in which Marcus points out congruences between Foucault's study and the work of Philippe Ariès on childhood and the family, *Centuries of Childhood* (1962). The contemporary comments on Bicêtre are from Foucault, pp. 203, 297; the passages from Tuke are from the same source, pp. 252, 249;

and the lines from Ariès can be found on pp. 414–15 of *Centuries of Childhood*.

Two books by Thomas S. Szasz, *The Myth of Mental Illness* (1961) and *Psychiatric Justice* (1965) also challenge "enlightened" thinking about insanity. At the time the present essay was written, the great American vogue of R. D. Laing still lay in the future, and it was not yet apparent that the reinterpretation of madness might end by dissolving the very distinction between madness and sanity and by celebrating schizophrenia as the only sane response to a mad world. Lately there are signs that this madness too may be on the wane—see, for example, Leslie H. Farber's critique of Laing, "Schizophrenia and the Mad Psychotherapist," in Robert Boyers and Robert Orrill, eds., *R. D. Laing and Anti-Psychiatry* (1971)—in which case more serious work might now begin. A forthcoming dissertation by Roger Nash of Northwestern University, on ideas about and treatment of madness in the eighteenth and nineteenth centuries, will show among other things how the nineteenth-century reformers misrepresented colonial practice and conjured up an image of dangerous and homicidal lunatics that served as a rationale for confinement but undermined their own attempt to humanize madness. Another Northwestern dissertation (1972), by Peter Tyor, deals with treatment of the feeble-minded at the end of the nineteenth century but does not succeed in breaking out of the reform-to-custody formula, which has strangled so much historical writing on the asylum.

To my disappointment I find that this is also true of David J. Rothman's eagerly awaited study, *The Discovery of the Asylum* (1971). Nevertheless Rothman's book has two virtues that distinguish it from much of the writing on these subjects. It treats asylums in general, thereby relating changes in the care of criminals, the insane, orphans, and the poor to each other and showing them to be part of a larger historical movement. Moreover, it recognizes that colonial practices were in some ways more humane than the practices that replaced them. Colonial society distinguished not so much between deviants and "normal" people as between neighbors (the treatment of whom shows that insanity and crime were not regarded as automatically disqualifying a person for a useful role in society) and strangers, who were treated more harshly, usually by banishment. Since he understands the qualitative difference between colonial practices and later ones, Rothman is able to see how radical an innovation the asylum was.

In attempting to account for the "discovery" of the asylum, however, he falls back on an interpretative device that has already become as trite as the "status revolution" theory, which it resembles in its all-purpose applicability—namely, that the fluidity and mobility of American society gave rise to a pervasive fear of disorder, which vented itself on deviants, among others. This explanation makes it impossible to account for the very similar development of asylums in Europe in the same period. By linking the emergence of the asylum to the "critique of Jacksonian society" (p. 113), Rothman overlooks the reciprocal influences between American and European practices, which strongly suggest that the asylum arose out of conditions that were general in modern society rather than specific to the United States.

At one point Rothman observes in passing, in a discussion of almshouses, that local officials in the nineteenth century no longer found it possible to banish needy strangers, since "state regulations often prevented local communities from maintaining a high degree of insularity by prohibiting restrictions on interstate movement" (p. 204). This detail is worth pages of theorizing about "social disorder." It suggests that the invention of the asylum was related in quite specific ways to the elimination of local and regional variations and to the imposition on society of a uniform political and economic order—one of the preconditions of modern capitalism (and not, incidentally, a consequence of industrialism—another trite formula to which we may be tempted to resort in order to explain these developments). The creation of administrative uniformity influenced the development of asylums in another way: it made the distinction between townsmen and outcasts less meaningful than the distinction between those who were self-supporting and those who were not. The latter were now defined as deviant and confined in houses of "correction."

There is still another connection between uniformity and asylums. The new middle-class sensibility that was "revolted" by all kinds of differences in social condition can be fully understood only if we understand that the creation of a uniform political order—in other words, the creation of civil society in the modern sense, the abolition of distinctions not only between places but between persons as well—was the overriding political task of the great bourgeois revolutions of the late eighteenth century, which it took many more decades to complete.

II. Two "Kindred Spirits"

IN 1961 RICHARD J. HOOKER, MY COLLEAGUE AT ROOSEVELT UNIVERSITY, loaned me some manuscripts he had found in antique shops and second-hand bookstores, bearing on the history of women. One series consisted of twenty-four letters from Luella Case to Sarah Edgarton, running from 1839 to 1846, and two from Miss Edgarton to Mrs. Case. These letters, together with several others from Sarah to Mrs. Case that were published, with certain excisions, in the memorial by A. D. Mayo, *Selections from the Writings of Mrs. Sarah C. Edgarton Mayo* (1849), form the basis of the present essay, written in 1961 and published in *The New England Quarterly* (March 1963). I wish to thank Mr. Hooker for giving me access to these materials and *The New England Quarterly* for permission to reprint it.

The Edgarton–Case letters seemed to bear out certain ideas about nineteenth-century women that I had reached in collaboration with William R. Taylor, with whom I was working, somewhat sporadically, on a history of American women. In *Cavalier and Yankee* (1961)—a book devoted to quite different matters—Taylor had speculated in passing about the connection between the sentimental cult of the home and the antislavery movement. He argued that the repression of slaves also implied the repression of women and that the literary assault on slavery, especially in Harriet Beecher Stowe's *Uncle Tom's Cabin,* drew on the themes of the "sentimental revolution," attacking not merely slavery but, more generally, "the ruthless masculine world of business enterprise" (p. 309). (Helen Papashvily argues a somewhat similar thesis in her study of the domestic novel, *All the Happy Endings* [1956].)

In searching for an analytical framework for our projected study, Taylor and I were influenced by the restatement of the frontier thesis by Stanley Elkins and Eric McKitrick ("A Meaning for Turner's Frontier," *Political Science Quarterly* [September 1954], pp. 321-53, and [December 1954], pp. 565-602); by Elkins's *Slavery* (1959), especially the chapter on "The Dynamics of Unopposed Capitalism"; and by Oscar Handlin's essay "The Horror" in his *Race and Nationality in American Life* (1957). In these essays we thought we discerned a common tendency to treat the entire United States as a "frontier" of Europe and to see American society as characterized by extreme mobility and flux and desperately searching for a principle of order. This idea was perhaps not as trite in the early sixties as it became later; but as I have already tried to show, in notes to the previous essay, there is little to be said for it now. Although in the very broadest sense it is true that liberal capitalism, dominated by what C. B. McPherson has called the political theory of possessive individualism, created a social order lacking most of the traditional elements of cohesion, it is myopic to see this as a development peculiar to America or dependent in any way on the "frontier." Searching too eagerly for evidences of institutional decay, I took for granted in this essay the validity of clichés about the decline of the extended family and the loss of the family's functions, which have so long prevented scholars from seeing that the modern family represented not a decline from some hypothetical extended family (which tends to recede the more we pursue it backwards in time) but a reorientation of domestic life around the ideal of privacy.

Notwithstanding its lack of a sound interpretative framework, the essay nevertheless depicts a type of friendship that seems to have been very common among middle-class women in the nineteenth century, the existence of which suggests certain strains in the new-style domesticity that was emerging.

In addition to the sources already cited, the essay draws on C. C. Chase's sketch of Eliphalet Case in *Contributions of the Old Residents' Historical Association* (Lowell, Massachusetts), August 1889, pp. 124–7, 133–5, and October 1891, pp. 314–15; Eleanor Flexner, *Century of Struggle* (1959), p. 7, for the quotation on women's status; Randolph Bourne to Alyse Gregory, January 19, 1914, Bourne MSS, Columbia University Library, for the comparison between America and the continent; Antoinette Brown to Samuel C. Blackwell, December 14, 1855, Blackwell Family MSS, Women's Archives, Radcliffe College, for their marriage contract; Elizabeth Dwight Cabot to James Elliott Cabot, August 11, 1861, and August 18 [   ], Cabot Family MSS, Women's Archives, for details of their marriage; Bernard Bailyn, "Politics and Social Structure in Virginia," in James Morton Smith, ed., *Seventeenth-Century America* (1959), pp. 108–9, for statements about the colonial South; and Philip Rahv, introduction to *The Bostonians* (1945), pp. vi, xi, for discussion of "Lesbianism."

III. Divorce and the "Decline
of the Family"

THE QUOTATION FROM CALHOUN IS FROM THE THIRD VOLUME OF HIS *Social History of the American Family* (1919), p. 271. The historical study quoted on p. 36 is Nelson Manfred Blake, *The Road to Reno* (1962), p. 95. The quotation from Ariès is from *Centuries of Childhood,* p. 395. The excerpt from Olive Schreiner comes from *Woman and Labor* (1911), p. 104. The familiar lines from Lecky are quoted by Eva Figes, *Patriarchal Attitudes* (1970), p. 84. For Albert Ellis's ideas on courtship, see *The American Sexual Tragedy* (1954), especially chapter III. The present essay originally appeared in *The Atlantic* (November 1966), and in a very different version in *The New York Review,* February 17, 1966.

It is the mark of a subject in which historical analysis is still in a primitive state that even its chronology remains a subject of dispute. The strategy of the present essay was to revise the conventional chronology by arguing that the decisive changes in the history of the family took place in the seventeenth and eighteenth centuries, and not in the late nineteenth and twentieth centuries as a result of industrialization. If one were to pursue in more detail the relationship between the family and industrialism, one might see the bourgeois family as a precondition rather than as a consequence of industrialism. One might see the emergence of the privatized family, in other words, as part of a more general process of economic and political modernization, closely related to such analogous developments as the achievement of religious freedom (as a result of which religion, like marriage, was defined as a private matter) and the divorce between the state and "private enterprise"—in short, the divorce between the state and what at the end of the eighteenth century came to be known as civil society. This separation, the basis of modern political freedom, was the great achievement of the bourgeois revolutions in Europe and the United States and at the same time the underlying source of much of the tension and conflict in modern society. Its economic effect was to remove the obstacles to the unprecedented expansion of productive forces known as the industrial revolution. Because industrialism in its own right had profound effects on society, we often exaggerate its impact, seeing all of modern life in its shadow, when in fact the modernization of political and civil life had to take place *before* industrialism—at least in its bourgeois democratic form—could develop on any significant scale.

Sociological and historical study of the family has been almost wholly dominated by the myth of the industrial revolution and by a related idea, also mythic in its origins and function, namely, that the great event in the development of the family is the shift from the extended to the nuclear or conjugal form. The reason Ariès's work has had such a liberating effect on the study of the family is that it undermines both these ideas and thereby forces us to reconsider both the chronology and the nature of the changes that distinguish the modern family from its predecessors.

William L. O'Neill, in the first chapter of his *Divorce in the Progressive Era* (1967), has provided an excellent critique of the orthodox sociological clichés, drawing on Ariès, on the work of the revisionist sociologist William J. Goode, and also, to some degree, on the present essay. The work of assimilating these new perspectives, however, and of applying them to concrete problems in the history of women and the family, is still in its early stages; nor has the recent outbreak of neo-feminist historiography done much to dispel the confusion surrounding these subjects. Since the sociological clichés in question made their first appearance as armaments in the intellectual arsenal of the feminist movement—Calhoun's study, for example, is explicitly pro-feminist—it is not entirely surprising that they crop up with depressing regularity in Kate Millett's *Sexual Politics* (1970), in Shulamith Firestone's *The Dialectic of Sex* (1970), in the Figes book already cited, and in other recent studies written under the influence of women's liberation.

IV. The Woman Reformer's Rebuke

THIS ESSAY FIRST APPEARED IN *The New York Review,* JULY 13, 1967, pp. 28–32, and is reprinted by permission of the editors. The material on Carry Nation comes from Robert Lewis Taylor's *Vessel of Wrath* (1966), p. 19 ("angel on earth"); p. 20 ("incorrigible migrant"); p. 37 ("wagons and carts"); p. 117 ("bulldog"); p. 115 ("drunkard's grave!"); 121 ("motherly type"); p. 334 ("toughest proposition"); p. 324 ("rebuke, exhortation, warning"); p. 308 ("warm, down-to-earth gift"; "enigma of love"); p. 361 ("fought the good fight");

and p. 360 ("today's willingness to give in"). See also Carry Nation's autobiography, *The Use and Need of the Life of Carry A. Nation* (1904).

On Victoria Woodhull, see M. M. Marberry, *Vicky* (1967), p. 329 ("judgment of posterity"); and Johanna Johnston, *Mrs. Satan* (1967), pp. 214, 217 (doubts about Victoria's literacy, deriving from a contemporary, Benjamin Tucker); p. 133 ("yes, I am a free lover!"). Both these biographies draw freely from Emanie Sachs, *The Terrible Siren* (1928).

My treatment of Mrs. Eddy is based on her *Science and Health* (1912) and on Robert Peel, *Mary Baker Eddy: The Years of Discovery* (1966), p. 235 ("new way of shaping experience"); p. 268 (Mrs. Eddy on Quimby); p. 33 ("least qualified to make money"); p. 237 ("rebuke to their animal spirits"); p. 225 ("lonely woman past her prime"); p. 234 ("what is matter?").

The quotation from Donald Meyer's *The Positive Thinkers* (1965) can be found on p. 75.

V. The Mormon Utopia

THE FIGURES ON MEMBERSHIP COME FROM ROBERT MULLEN's *The Latter-Day Saints* (1966), p. 3. Quotations from Wallace Turner's *The Mormon Establishment* (1966) are taken from p. 4 ("in widening waves") and p. 56 (Mormons' low value on women). From Leonard Arrington's study, *Great Basin Kingdom* (1958), I have quoted the edition published by the University of Nebraska Press in 1966: p. 6 (Universalist opinion of the Mormons in Ohio as too "worldly"); p. 47 (Young on "commerce with the gentile world"); p. 352 (theocracy interfered with capitalism); p. 409 (role of the church in the modern Mormon economy); and p. 410 ("the remarkable thing about Mormon economic policy").

On Mormon recruitment in England, see Robert Bruce Flanders, *Nauvoo* (1965), chapter III, and two articles by M. Hamlin Cannon, "Migration of English Mormons to America," *American Historical Review* (April 1947), pp. 436–55, and "The English Mormons in America," *American Historical Review* (July 1952), pp. 893–908. On Joseph Smith, see Fawn Brodie, *No Man Knows My History* (1945) and Alice Felt Tyler, *Freedom's Ferment,* pp. 86–106. See also the latter, p. 108, on the connection between sectarianism and utopianism.

David Brion Davis analyzes the antecedents of Mormonism in "The New England Origins of Mormonism," *New England Quarterly* (June 1953), pp. 147–68; see also Whitney Cross, *The Burned-Over District* (1950).

John Humphrey Noyes's comparison of the Mormons and Shakers appears in a letter from Noyes to William Hepworth Dixon in the latter's *Spiritual Wives* (1868), vol. II, p. 182; his remarks on the role of monogamy in sexual disorders, in his own *History of American Socialisms* (1870), pp. 628–9. Professor Franklin H. Littell also draws a connection between the Mormons and Shakers in his introduction to the 1965 reprint of Charles Nordhoff's *The Communistic Societies of the United States* (1875), pp. xxii–xxiii: ". . . communities such as the Shakers and the Mormons had a special attraction to young women, and in some years took in several times as many female as male converts. . . . The Shakers, with their celibacy, and the Mormons, with their polygamy, offered a much better and longer life for young women than they could anticipate in the common social conditions of the society at large." This was also the view of the Mormon women interviewed by Jules Rémy in *A Journey to Great Salt Lake City* (1861); for the interview quoted in the text, see vol. II, pp. 101–6.

This essay appeared in *The New York Review*, January 26, 1967.

VI. The Anti-Imperialists, the Philippines, and the Inequality of Man

ON EXPANSIONIST IDEOLOGY, SEE, IN GENERAL, JULIUS W. PRATT, *Expansionists of 1898* (1936) and Albert K. Weinberg, *Manifest Destiny* (1935). For economic arguments in favor of annexation, see, for example, Albert J. Beveridge's *The Meaning of the Times and Other Speeches* (1908), pp. 37–46, and Lodge's speech in the Senate, *Congressional Record*, 56th Congress, 1st session, pp. 2628–9. For the argument that Filipinos were not ready for self-government, see Charles S. Olcott, *William McKinley* (1918), vol. II, pp. 110–11, and the National Edition of Theodore Roosevelt's *Works* (1926), vol. XIV, pp. 352–9. Teller's remark is in *Congressional Record,* 55th Congress, 3rd session, p. 969.

Representative statements of the anti-imperialist argument can be found in George S. Boutwell, *Party or Country?* (1900) and *Republic or Empire?* (1900); David Starr Jordan, *Imperial Democracy* (1899); George F. Hoar, *The Lust of Empire* (1900) and *No Constitutional Power to Conquer Foreign Nations and Hold Their People in Subjection Against Their Will* (1899); Richard Franklin Pettigrew, *Imperial Washington* (1922); Moorfield Storey, *Is It Right?* (1900); and Moorfield Storey and Marcial P. Lichauco, *The Conquest of the Philippines by the United States* (1928).

For Senator Daniel's reference to a "mess of Asiatic pottage," see *Congressional Record,* 55th Congress, 3rd session, p. 1430. Tillman's speeches can be found in the same source, pp. 1532, 1380, 1389, 836-7. According to Tillman's biographer, "His grievance, the real motive for his opposition, was the refusal of the Republicans to admit inconsistencies in their view of colored people. He wanted the Republicans to confess their conduct toward the colonials as frankly as he was confessing his toward the blacks." Francis Butler Simkins, *Pitchfork Ben Tillman* (1944), p. 355.

Gompers is quoted in opposition to annexation in an anonymous pamphlet, *Expensive Expansion* (1900), p. 9. Arguments similar to his can be found in James W. Stillman, *Republic or Empire?* (1900); Edwin D. Mead, *The Present Crisis* (1899); and George S. Boutwell in the *Annual Report* of the New England Anti-Imperialist League (1900), p. 18. Another anti-expansionist argument aimed at labor was that defense of the Philippines would require a large standing army, which labor would be taxed to support; see George F. McNeil in *Speeches at the Meeting in Faneuil Hall* (1898), p. 29.

For Schurz's alarm at the admission to citizenship of "creoles and negroes," see Frederic Bancroft, ed., *Speeches, Correspondence and Political Papers of Carl Schurz* (1913), vol. VI, pp. 6, 8-9; for the similar views of James L. Blair, see his *Imperialism, Our New National Policy* (1899), p. 18, which also contains his statement that "the two races could never amalgamate" (p. 23); for the views of David Starr Jordan, see *Imperial Democracy,* pp. 45, 48, 93, 97. Champ Clark's speech is in *Congressional Record,* 56th Congress, 1st session, p. 1520.

The argument that democratic institutions could not be adapted to the tropics appears, in various forms, in Schurz's *Speeches,* vol. V, pp. 481-4; in Samuel W. McCall, *Life of Thomas Brackett Reed* (1914), pp. 256, 258; and in the *Nation,* March 16, 1899, p. 196, which maintained that "our government was made for peaceable, industrious, homogenous, protestant men." For Charles Francis Adams on Indian policy, see his *Imperialism and the Tracks of Our Forefathers* (1899), p. 10.

For the vote on the treaty, see *Journal of the Executive Proceedings of the Senate,* 55th Congress, p. 1284.

When this essay was written, the entire literature on the anti-imperialist movement consisted of three articles: Fred H. Harrington, "The Anti-Imperialist Movement in the United States, 1898–1900," *Mississippi Valley Historical Review* (September 1935), pp. 211–30; the same author's "Literary Aspects of American Anti-Imperialism," *New England Quarterly* (December 1937), pp. 650–67; and Maria C. Lanzar, "The Anti-Imperialist League," *Philippine Social Science Review* (August 1930), pp. 7–41. In recent years the literature has been enriched, indirectly, by the publication of studies of the mugwumps by Geoffrey Blodgett, *The Gentle Reformers* (1966) and John G. Sproat, *The Best Men* (1968). The anti-imperialists themselves have begun to receive some attention, notably in Robert L. Beisner's *Twelve Against Empire* (1968). The most recent study is by Daniel Schirmer, *Republic or Empire: American Resistance to the Philippine War* (1972). This last, however, represents a real regression. It views the anti-imperialists through the filter of contemporary opposition to the war in Vietnam, treating them as principled critics of racism and stressing the link between the anti-imperialist movement and abolitionism. Moorfield Storey, one of the few anti-imperialists who did resist the racist currents of the time (a few years later he helped to found the NAACP) plays a disproportionate part in Schirmer's account. Storey was not representative of the movement, either in condemning racism or in urging support for Bryan in 1900—a step most of his colleagues were unable to bring themselves to take. As for the connection with abolitionism, I have stressed it myself, as did the anti-imperialists in their speeches and writings; but unless it is recognized that the antislavery impulse had now dwindled into a feeble defense of regional traditions, the significance of the connection—and the poignancy of the anti-imperialists' attempt to identify themselves with their revolutionary antecedents—disappears from sight.

Schirmer's book, together with other recent works written from neo-abolitionist, neo-populist, and neo-feminist perspectives, is part of a recrudescence of Whiggish and progressive historiography disguised as radicalism. Although this new left historiography contains needed criticism of the "consensus" school, it has not made a convincing reply to the critique of Whiggish historians that was formulated by the consensus theorists, particularly by Richard Hofstadter in *The American Political Tradition* (1948), *The Age of Reform* (1955), and *The Progressive Historians* (1968). As so often in the past, a new wave of historical revisionism, instead of absorbing and transcending the work of its immediate predecessors, threatens merely to reverse its political direction, substituting new heroes and, in this case, loudly proclaiming its own radicalism but leaving the underlying issues where they were before, or in some cases at a more primitive level of awareness.

This essay first appeared, in slightly different form, in the *Journal of Southern History* (August 1958).

VII. The Moral and Intellectual Rehabilitation of the Ruling Class

THIS ESSAY HAS NOT PREVIOUSLY APPEARED IN PRINT.

The idea that the old mugwump élite was displaced by the new industrialists is so widely held that it cannot be traced to any single source; probably it grew up in conjunction with the attack on the genteel tradition, which associated that tradition with a dying class. It is clearly present in many of the studies of the period written in the twenties, such as Thomas Beer's *Hanna* (1929) and his *Mauve Decade* (1926), and it is an undercurrent in the studies of Matthew Josephson, *The Robber Barons* (1934), *The Politicos* (1938), and *The President-Makers* (1940). It reappears in different form in the theory of the status revolution, which received its most authoritative statement in Richard Hofstadter's *Age of Reform* (1955).

Statements about the business élite in Philadelphia are based on E. Digby Baltzell, *An American Business Aristocracy* (1962), to which I am also indebted for information about the nationalization of the upper class. C. Wright Mills emphasizes the continuity of the upper class in *The Power Elite* (1956). For the bureaucratization of the business career, see William Miller, "The Business Elite in Business Bureaucracies," in the collection of essays edited by him, *Men in Business* (1952).

On upper-class anti-Semitism, see Baltzell's *The Protestant Establishment* (1964). See also Barbara Miller Solomon's study of the movement to restrict immigration, *Ancestors and Immigrants* (1956) and Oscar Handlin's essay, "American Views of the Jews at the Beginning of the Twentieth Century," *Publications of the American Jewish Historical Society* (June 1951), pp. 323–44. On the corporation as an ethnic preserve, see Moses Rischin's introduction to his anthology *The American Gospel of Success* (1965).

My discussion of the failure of the merger movement and the rise of "political capitalism" is heavily indebted to Gabriel Kolko, *The Triumph of Conservatism* (1963), although I do not agree with Kolko in identifying these developments with "conservatism." The ideology of corporate capitalism in this period, together with changing attitudes toward unionism, has been studied by James Weinstein, *The Corporate Idea in the Liberal State* (1969). On the efficiency movement, see Samuel P. Hays, *Conservation and the Gospel of Efficiency* (1959); Samuel Haber, *Efficiency and Uplift* (1964); and Raymond E. Callahan, *Education and the Cult of Efficiency* (1962). The paragraph on this subject and on the steps by which the capitalist mastered the technical details of production owes much to conversations with Leon Fink and Gregory Kealey and to a talk by David Montgomery at the University of Rochester, November 1971.

For data on the National Board of Medical Examiners and professionalization in general, I have relied on an unpublished paper by Stephen J. Kunitz of the University of Rochester. On professionalization, see also Robert Wiebe, *The Search for Order* (1967).

On the upper-class military ideal and the "strenuous life," see George M. Fredrickson, *The Inner Civil War* (1965) for a discussion of Parkman and Roosevelt, and Edmund Wilson's essay on Oliver Wendell Holmes in *Patriotic Gore* (1962). John P. Mallan, "Roosevelt, Brooks Adams, and Lea: The Warrior Critique of the Business Civilization," *American Quarterly* (Autumn 1956), pp. 216–30, treats this ideology as a genuine alternative to business ideology and more broadly to "liberal utopianism." It belongs to a general tendency prevalent in the fifties to uphold the "realism" of Theodore Roosevelt against the misguided idealism of Woodrow Wilson; see, for example, John R. Blum's *The Republican Roosevelt* (1954). Henry F. Pringle's *Theodore Roosevelt* (1931), vitriolic as it is, remains a more discerning appraisal. See Roosevelt's *Autobiography* (1913), p. 136, for his fight with the bully in the bar. For his plea for "the virtue that shall be strong," see his *Realizable Ideals* (1912), pp. 42–3. Details on the

1884 Republican Convention are taken from John A. Garraty, *Henry Cabot Lodge* (1953); see p. 78 for the quotation from Foraker. Roosevelt's attack on the mugwumps ("men of cultivated tastes") is in the *Autobiography*, pp. 162–3. For Lodge's speech to the businessmen ("Gentlemen, I have seen it constantly stated"), see his *Speeches and Addresses* (1909), p. 285; for his remarks about athletes and pioneers, see Garraty, *Lodge*, p. 206. Roosevelt's denial of the existence of classes in American society comes from the eight-volume edition of his letters edited by Elting E. Morison (1951), vol. I, p. 114.

The picture of Roosevelt as a masterly realist—first sketched by Herbert Croly in *The Promise of American Life*—not only exaggerates Roosevelt's understanding of events (to say nothing of his skill as a politician) but obscures the continuity between Roosevelt and Wilson. The tendency to exaggerate the importance of the conflict between these two Presidents is perhaps unavoidably encouraged by John Wells Davidson's otherwise useful collection of Wilson's 1912 campaign speeches, *A Crossroads of Freedom* (1956). For Wilson's policies as President, see Arthur Link, *Wilson: The New Freedom* (1956); and for the liberalized version of imperialism under Wilson, N. Gordon Levin, *Woodrow Wilson and World Politics* (1968). Gabriel Kolko's *The Politics of War* (1968) has influenced my understanding of the diplomacy of the second Roosevelt.

On neo-liberalism see, besides the works referred to in the text, Walter Weyl's *The New Democracy* (1912); the early writings of Charles A. Beard; and the works of Veblen, especially *The Theory of the Leisure Class* (1899), *The Theory of Business Enterprise* (1904), *The Higher Learning in America* (1918), and *The Engineers and the Price System* (1921). Adorno's critique of Veblen is in *Prisms* (1967); Mills's, in the appendix to *White Collar* (1951). A fuller treatment of Veblen would also have to consider the elements of populism in his thought and the differences between populism and neo-liberalism; this last question is dealt with, briefly, in my *Agony of the American Left* (1969).

My view of American culture in general owes a great deal to Van Wyck Brooks's *America's Coming-of-Age* (1915). In writing of the regional revival I have also drawn on the admirable studies by Alfred Kazin, *On Native Grounds* (1944) and Larzer Ziff, *The American 1890s* (1966) and on Bernard I. Duffey's extremely useful *The Chicago Renaissance in American Letters* (1954). The discussion of cultural problems in this essay obviously draws on many other sources as well, but these are too diffuse, and in some cases too intangible, to document here.

VIII. Is Revolution Obsolete?

THE FIRST SECTION OF THIS ESSAY DRAWS HEAVILY ON BARRINGTON MOORE, Jr., "Revolution in America?" *New York Review*, January 30, 1969, pp. 6–12, and on his book, *Social Origins of Dictatorship and Democracy* (1966). The reference to Louis Boudin is to p. 240 of his *Theoretical System of Karl Marx* (1907).

This essay originally appeared, in a somewhat different version, as an epilogue to a collection of essays edited by Roderick Aya and Norman Miller, *The New American Revolution* (1971), pp. 318–34, and was addressed specifically to some of the other contributions in that volume. In the first paragraph, references to the "world-wide revolution of modernization" and to the term "revolution" as including "unintended, incoherent change" are from the contribution by Manfred Halpern, while the reference to "permanent revolution" comes from the essay by Richard M. Pfeffer. The quotation from Eric Wolf on peasant revolutions is taken from an article Wolf contributed to a companion volume, also edited by Aya and Miller, *National Liberation: Revolution in the Third World* (1971), p. 57.

The statement that blacks and youth are "useless classes" was made by Franz Schurman in his contribution to *The New American Revolution*. Schurman argued that such groups could become the basis of a socialist revolution, and my argument here was an attempt to refute the positions advanced in his article. The last section of my essay was addressed to the contribution by Richard Flacks, which argued that socialism is inconceivable unless it comes to power as a majority movement, but went on to maintain that a socialist movement therefore cannot be expected to emerge until the population as a whole experiences "the irrelevance . . . of ideologies based on scarcity." An unpublished manuscript by Eugene Genovese and me, written in 1969—shortly before the present essay was written—made some of the same points made here. It argued for the uselessness of both the Leninist and social democratic traditions. It emphasized the legitimacy of the working-class demand for law and order, upheld the primacy of work against leisure, and defended (perhaps too unreservedly) the concept of professionalism. This is an appropriate place to acknowledge my obligation to Genovese's work, especially to his fine essay on Antonio Gramsci in *Studies on the Left* (March–April 1967), pp. 83–107.

IX. The Professional Revolutionary

THE USE OF PSYCHOANALYTICAL BIOGRAPHY TO DEBUNK, TO REDUCE A subject to the sum of his symptoms, is exemplified by such early studies as Preserved Smith's analysis of "Luther's Early Development in the Light of Psychoanalysis," *American Journal of Psychology* (July 1913), pp. 360–77—a work that is tellingly criticized by Erikson in his own *Young Man Luther* (1958); by L. Pierce Clark, *Lincoln: A Psycho-Biography* (1933); by Freud's *Leonardo da Vinci* (1916); and (undoubtedly the worst example of all), by the study of Woodrow Wilson written by Freud in collaboration with William C. Bullitt and published long after Freud's death, *Thomas Woodrow Wilson* (1967).

In a penetrating review of Erikson's *Luther* (*History and Theory*, vol. I, pp. 291–7), Donald Meyer has written of the difficulties in making the jump from biography to history, particularly when the biographer is dealing intensively with the subject's private life, while at the same time arguing convincingly that psychoanalysis is more useful in solving this problem than behavioral psychologies.

More generally one might consult, for interesting attempts to marry psychoanalysis to history, Kenneth Keniston's study of alienated youth, *The Uncommitted* (1965) and Robert Jay Lifton's analysis of the cultural revolution in China, *Revolutionary Immortality* (1968).

For an assessment of Erikson's career as a whole, see Robert Coles, *Erik H. Erikson* (1970).

The book reviewed here, *Gandhi's Truth*, was published in 1969 by Norton. The review appeared in *The New York Times*, September 14, 1969.

X. After the New Left

THE THEORIES OF POST-INDUSTRIAL SOCIETY CRITICIZED IN THIS ESSAY CAN be found in two essays by Daniel Bell, "Technocracy and Politics,"

Survey (Winter 1971), pp. 1–25, and "Post-Industrial Society, the Evolution of an Idea," *Survey* (Spring 1971), pp. 102–68. For further criticism of these theories, see Norman Birnbaum, *The Crisis of Industrial Society* (1969), in which it is also argued that the student movement can be regarded as an "anticipatory strike." The same contention is developed at some length in Alain Touraine, *Le mouvement de mai ou le communisme utopique* (1968); see also the same author's *Post-Industrial Society* (1971). For another version of the theory of the "new working class," see Serge Mallet, *La nouvelle classe ouvrière* (1963).

Randolph Bourne's concept of "trans-national America" is advanced in an article of that title in the *Atlantic* (July 1916), pp. 86–97, reprinted in Carl Resek, ed., *War and the Intellectuals* (1964).

The quotation from Max Horkheimer on the family comes from his "Art and Mass Culture," *Studies in Philosophy and Social Science,* vol. IX, 1941, p. 291.

Quotations from Michael Miles, *The Radical Probe* (1971), are taken from p. 262 ("ideological vacuum"); pp. 85, 270 (cultural *vs.* political rebellion); pp. 80–3 (Brzezinski); p. 268 (automation); pp. 104, 278–9 (the knowledge industry); p. 105 (sources of the student movement); pp. 92 ff. (industrialization of the university); p. 105 ("super-industrial society"); p. 65 (intellectuals *vs.* mandarins); pp. 275 ff., 282 (relation of the student movement to other groups); and pp. 284–5 (repressive decentralization).

Quotations from Michael Walzer, *Political Action* (1971), come from pp. 66–7 (marginality of citizen politics); p. 84 (yearning for a total ideological position); p. 61 (fund-raising); and p. 25 (electoral and pressure-group politics).

Quotations from Saul Alinsky, *Rules for Radicals* (1971), come from pp. 91–2 (role of the organizer); pp. 110–11 (conversation with Indians); p. xix (long hair); pp. 137, 146–8 ("bringing to heel," "downfall"); p. 119 (turning the plight into a problem); and p. 183 (proxy participation). Quotations from the Vintage edition of Alinsky's *Reveille for Radicals* (1969) are taken from pp. 214–15 (organization and identity; black power); p. 35 (need to see the worker as also a consumer and citizen); p. 175 (on the sense of participation); and p. 184 (on "rousing" people to "a higher degree of participation").

Robert A. Dahl's *After the Revolution?* (1970) has been cited as follows: pp. 82 ff. (primary democracy); pp. 34–8 ("competence"); pp. 115, 117–18, 120 (the corporation); p. 138 (consumer representation); p. 132 (self-management); pp. 134–5 (the worker as economic man); p. 136 (on the prospect that workers' attitudes toward work might change); p. 139 (external controls); p. 137 (on the "unworldliness" of certain views of worker control); and p. 117 (the structure of the corporation a technical question).

This essay originally appeared in *The New York Review,* October 21, 1971.

XI. Populism, Socialism, and McGovernism

THE INTERPRETATION OF POPULISM AS AN AGRARIAN FANTASY RECEIVED definitive statement in Richard Hofstadter, *The Age of Reform* (1955). For populism as proto-fascism, see Victor C. Ferkiss, "Populist Influences on American Fascism," *Western Political Quarterly* (June 1957), pp. 350–73, and Peter Viereck's essay on McCarthyism in Daniel Bell, ed., *The New American Right* (1955). On "paranoia" and "anti-intellectualism," see Hofstadter's *The Paranoid Style in American Politics* (1965) and his *Anti-Intellectualism in American Life* (1963).

The rehabilitation of populism was begun by C. Vann Woodward, "The Populist Heritage and the Intellectual," *American Scholar,* 1959–60, pp. 55–72. Walter T. K. Nugent attacked the equation of populism with anti-Semitism in *The Tolerant Populists* (1963); see also Norman Pollack, "The Myth of Populist Anti-Semitism," *American Historical Review* (October 1962), pp. 76–80, my criticism of this article in the same journal (April 1963), pp. 910–11, and my review of the books by Nugent and Pollack, *Pacific Historical Review,* 1964, pp. 69–73. In *The Populist Response to Industrial America* (1962), Pollack argues unconvincingly that populists and socialists were saying the same thing. Michael Rogin reviews the whole controversy over populism in *The Intellectuals and McCarthy* (1967).

Joseph Kraft's review of Jack Newfield and Jeff Greenfield, *A Populist Manifesto* (1972), appeared in *The New York Times,* March 3, 1972. For quotations from this book, see p. ix ("economic passions jettisoned a generation ago"); p. 12 (Weathermen, Panthers, Yippies); p. x ("legitimate grievances of blacks"); p. 214 ("concrete economic interests"); p. ix ("self-interest"); pp. 14–30, *passim* ("elitist" liberalism); p. x ("Shangri-La"); p. 139 ("police practices that hinder"); p. 218 ("attack on economic privilege"); p. 177 ("mode of technocratic thinking"); p. 10 (economic origins of racism); p. 21 (Truman campaign); and p. 12 (populist anti-imperialism). The quotation toward the end of the essay, on the new populism as a "movement," comes from p. 12 of the Newfield-Greenfield manifesto.

Recent Marx scholarship is greatly indebted to Shlomo Avineri, *The Social and Political Thought of Karl Marx* (1968); George Lichtheim, *Marxism* (1961) and *The Origins of Socialism* (1969); and David McLellan, *The Young Hegelians and Karl Marx* (1969). See also McLellan's introduction to the Harper edition of selections from Marx's *Grundrisse* (1971). Another section of this uncompleted and unpublished draft of *Capital,* written in the 1850's, has been brought out by International Publishers under the title *Pre-Capitalist Economic Formations* (1964), with the introduction by E. J. Hobsbawm alluded to in the text.

This recent scholarship is based in part on work of neo-Marxist theorists in Europe, active since the twenties but only beginning to be known in this country. George Lukács's *History and Class Consciousness,* originally published in 1922, appeared in an English translation published by the MIT Press in 1971. A selection of writings by Antonio Gramsci has been published by International under the title *The Modern Prince* (1967). Karl Korsch's *Marxismus und Philosophie* (1930) remains untranslated. For the work of the Frankfurt school—most of which is also untranslated—see T. W. Adorno, *Prisms* (1968); Herbert Marcuse, *Reason and Revolution* (1941), a study of Hegel and Marx; and the essays by Adorno, Marcuse, and Max Horkheimer in volume IX of *Studies in Philosophy and Social Science* (1941).

The literature on the history of socialist practice is enormous; it is enough to list some of the works on which I have most depended, for information if not always for interpretations. On Germany, see Carl E. Schorske, *German Social Democracy* (1955) and J. P. Nettl, *Rosa Luxemburg* (1966); on Europe in general, Carl Landauer, *European Socialism* (1959) and the works of Lichtheim, already cited; on Italy, John Cammett, *Antonio Gramsci and the Origins of Italian Communism* (1967) and Giuseppe Fiori, *Antonio Gramsci* (1971); on England, E. P. Thompson, *William Morris: Romantic to Revolutionary* (1955); on Russia, David Shub, *Lenin* (1948), Isaac Deutscher's studies of Stalin (1949) and Trotsky (1954, 1959, 1963), and E. H. Carr's multi-volume history, *The Bolshevik Revolution* (1961–   ); on the Third World, Leo Huberman and Paul Sweezy,

Socialism in Cuba (1969), Benjamin Schwartz, *Chinese Communism and the Rise of Mao* (1952), and Barrington Moore, Jr., *Social Origins of Dictatorship and Democracy* (1966); on the United States, Ira Kipnis, *The American Socialist Movement* (1952), David A. Shannon, *The Socialist Party of America* (1955), Howard Quint, *The Forging of American Socialism* (1953), Daniel Bell, *Marxian Socialism in the United States* (1967), James Weinstein, *The Decline of Socialism in America* (1967), and Irving Howe and Lewis Coser, *The American Communist Party* (1957).

For quotations from Michael Harrington's *Socialism* (1972), see p. 89 ("cooperators in the gigantic enterprise"); p. 108 (on the continuing relevance of Marx); p. 141 (Marx on "historico-philosophic" theories); p. 142 (Marx on Russia); p. 141 (Marx on Bakunin); p. 160 (Harrington on Lenin); pp. 166–7 (Lenin on Russia); p. 244 (Harrington on "barracks socialism"); p. 196 ("doctors" and "heirs"); pp. 72–3 (prewar socialism and "working class optimism"); p. 203 ("socialize the losses of capitalist incompetence"); pp. 208 ff. (discussion of Godesberg program); pp. 250, 260 ("invisible mass movement"); p. 124 ("AFL reversed its 1894 decision"); pp. 259–60 (quotation from Hofstadter); p. 115 (Marx on America); p. 118 ("dialectical irony"); p. 268 (Meany on socialism); pp. 266–7 (Humphrey campaign); p. 269 (Vietnam and "estrangement" between workers and intellectuals); p. 269 ("invisible social democracy"); p. 120 (on the relation between a higher standard of living and working-class radicalism); p. 283 ("priorities"); and p. 262 (on the popular front).

Hofstadter's analysis of the New Deal as opportunism is in *The American Political Tradition* (1948), chapter XII. The quotation from Gorz comes from his *Strategy for Labor* (1964).

This essay appeared in *The New York Review,* July 20, 1972.

XII. The "Counter-Culture"

THESE FOUR ESSAYS HAVE BEEN INCLUDED LARGELY FOR THE SAKE OF whatever documentary interest attaches to this volume. Highly polemical and written on very short notice, they reflect a need experienced by many intellectuals in the late sixties and early seventies—to defend liberal culture against theorists of the "counter-culture"—but they also suggest the difficulties of approaching this issue in a purely polemical way. Part of the trouble lies in the very elusiveness of the "counter-culture" and the inability of its exponents to provide any rounded statement of their own position—an inability that is probably inherent in the position itself, which scorns exposition, analysis, and criticism. Writers who claim to speak for the new sensibility or at least to describe it sympathetically, like Charles Reich, Theodore Roszak, and Philip Slater, actually seem to be speaking for and to an older generation in need of reassurance; and in many respects they are themselves out of touch with the movement they try to defend. To criticize these writers, therefore, is to criticize a peripheral phenomenon of somewhat doubtful importance. To ignore them, on the other hand, appeared in the late sixties to be an equally unsatisfactory alternative, since their books did give expression, however imperfect, to some of the cultural currents of the time.

Seeing in these books symptoms of a much deeper cultural malaise and appalled by the anti-intellectualism often associated with the new left—and more generally by a flood of irrationalism in modern society as a whole—those who still believed that a radical politics without critical reason was a monstrosity attempted, in effect, to construct an ad hoc defense of liberal culture, as in the manifesto on the "cultural crisis," that would still be distinguishable from a defense of liberalism as a political ideology. What is really required, however, is a more penetrating understanding of the "counter-culture" itself and of its social and cultural antecedents. Does the "new culture" represent merely the culmination of cultural modernism, as some have claimed—a democratization of the avant-garde? Or does it portend a regression to a more primitive consciousness? Increasingly events seem to point to the conclusion that it is precisely the premises of modernism that are being rejected in, say, rock music and street theater. If art traditionally has been an interplay between tension and its resolution, the new art banishes tension and seeks to dissolve all oppositions in direct, unmediated experience, non-verbal states of being, trancelike euphoria. Performers alternately assault their audiences, whipping up moods of subdued violence, and make "love" to them, in both cases hoping to merge the performance with "life" and to put both art and life safely "beyond interpretation." The audience is offended or, worse, titillated; it enjoys being verbally assaulted; it imagines itself instantaneously released from "bourgeois inhibitions." Relieved of the need to perform an act of imaginative identification, it is more passive than ever, while its lingering reservations about the new art are silenced by the fear that what is new must be necessarily significant. "Great art is always ahead of its time." The rhetoric of the avant-garde is pressed into the service of an esthetic with which it has little else in common, in order to clothe the contemporary artist in an inscrutable authority that he claims to reject but uses in many ways to intimidate his audience and critics.

One of the sources of the new sensibility is a crisis in modernism itself; accordingly criticism of the "new culture" that takes the form of a defense of modernism against anti-intellectualism falls far short of what the occasion demands. Modernism in the arts has carried subjectivity and stylistic complexity to the point of complete unintelligibility, from which the only escape seems to be a studied simplification or cultivated archaism—a return to the religious origins of drama, in music to simple rhythms and melody (*Carmina Burana,* the Beatles), in the visual arts to a search for objectivity that begins with paintings of soup cans and easily proceeds to the further assertion that everyday objects, unmediated by artistic intervention, ought themselves to be considered works of art (and paid for accordingly, when certified by the artist's signature). The search for meaning, which has produced forms increasingly dense and impenetrable, gives way to a flight from meaning. On the fringes of modern society, superstitions reappear—witchcraft, the occult, fundamentalist movements the undisguised authoritarianism of which offers a glimpse of the fierce passion for order underlying the seemingly anarchic rejection of form and structure in the arts.

Clearly the answer does not lie in a slavish observance of traditional forms, most of which have reached the point of exhaustion. The enshrinement of the classics in concert halls and museums on the one hand, together with increasingly esoteric and meaningless experimentation on the other, have brought "high culture" to the breaking point, and the search for clarity, simplicity, and directness often springs from the same instinct that has led many artists periodically to refresh their work in the stream of popular art without at the same time sacrificing their claims to be "serious." Part of the job of criticism today would seem to be to insist on the difference between attempting to give popular themes more lasting form and surrendering to the utter formlessness of the moment.

The essay on Charles Reich's *The Greening of America* (1970) appeared in *The Yale Law Journal* (March 1971); the review of

Slater, in the Manchester *Guardian,* September 9, 1971. A somewhat different version of the piece on ethnic particularism—another strand running through the "new culture"—was given as a talk to the Anthropology Department at Sir George Williams University, Montreal, on February 11, 1972. The statement on the crisis of contemporary culture was written in the autumn of 1970 as the prospectus for a proposed journal of historical and cultural studies, which never came to fruition. It incorporated suggestions by Eugene Genovese, Norman Birnbaum, Gerald Graff, Warren Susman, Herbert Gutman, and David Kettler.

Parts of this note appeared in a symposium on the "new cultural conservatism" conducted by *Partisan Review* and appearing in the July 1972 issue. For the theory that "all the new sensibility has done is to carry the premises of modernism through to their logical conclusions," see Daniel Bell, "Sensibility in the 60's," *Commentary* (June 1971), pp. 63–73. See also Michael Miles, *The Radical Probe* (1971), p. 271 ; "In many ways, the cultural left has simply recapitulated the history of modern art. . . ."

In the essay on ethnic particularism, the references to historical scholarship that suggests the resilience of pre-industrial cultures are to the work of E. P. Thompson—particularly *The Making of the English Working Class* (1963)—and his followers, and to the work (much of it unpublished) of Herbert Gutman on the history of the American working class. Conversations with Gutman have helped me to understand the importance of the Chicago school of sociology in giving scholarly support to the myth of the melting pot. See also Rudolph Vecoli's critique of Oscar Handlin's *The Uprooted* (1951)— a book the theoretical assumptions of which clearly derive from the Chicago school—in the *Journal of American History* (December 1964), pp. 404–17. The essay by John F. Szwed is "An American Anthropological Dilemma: The Politics of Afro-American Culture," in Dell Hymes, ed., *Reinventing Anthropology* (1973). Like a number of recent students of black culture, Szwed finds highly congenial the conclusions of Melville J. Herskovits, whose *Myth of the Negro Past* (1941) stressed the African origins of American black culture. For many years Herskovits's work was out of fashion; since the resurgence of black nationalism, it has been undergoing a revival.

On Harlem see, in addition to *The Autobiography of Malcolm X* (1965), p. 87 and *passim,* Gilbert Osofsky, *Harlem: The Making of a Ghetto* (1966) and Nathan I. Huggins, *Harlem Renaissance* (1971).

For the concept of the culture of poverty, see Oscar Lewis's introduction to *La Vida* (1966).

The quotation from Gramsci can be found in *The Modern Prince* (1967), p. 20.

XIII. "Realism" as a Critique of American Diplomacy

THIS ESSAY APPEARED IN *The Nation,* NOVEMBER 24, 1962. QUOTATIONS from Kennan's *American Diplomacy* (1951) are taken from p. 95 ("red skein"); pp. 100–1 (psychology of "unconditional surrender"); p. 101 ("more enduring, more terrible, and more destructive"); p. 100 ("forgotten art of diplomacy"); p. 103 ("all that we are really capable of knowing); and p. 61 ("people are not always more reasonable than governments"). Kennan's statement about the " 'how' as distinct from the 'what' of diplomacy" comes from his "Russia and the Versailles Conference," *American Scholar* (Winter 1960–61), p. 39.

The 1922 quotation on the First World War comes from a letter, Lincoln Colcord to Oswald Garrison Villard, March 20, 1922, in the Villard MSS, Harvard University Library. Lippmann's comments on the U-2 crisis are reported in the Washington *Post,* May 12, 1960; Kennan's, in the same place, May 27, 1960. For the first Kennan on unconditional surrender, see George Kennan to Robert Lansing, May 23, 1917, in the George Kennan MSS, Library of Congress. Lloyd George's comment on Russia is taken from notes of a meeting of the Council of Ten, January 16, 1919; see the Ray Stannard Baker MSS, Princeton University Library.

The distinction between ideals and self-interest in foreign policy, so fashionable in the fifties, was insisted on not only by Kennan but by Robert E. Osgood in his influential *Ideals and Self-Interest in America's Foreign Relations* (1953). For other works associated with the neo-realist critique of American diplomacy, see "Sources of the Cold War: A Historical Controversy."

XIV. Origins of the Cold War

SCHLESINGER TRIES TO "BLOW THE WHISTLE" IN A LETTER TO *The New York Review,* October 20, 1966, p. 37. He admits that this was "intemperate" in his "Origins of the Cold War," *Foreign Affairs* (October

1967), p. 23 n. This article also contains the argument summarized toward the end of my essay. On "failure of communications," see pp. 25, 41, 45; on the Soviet request for a loan, which was "inexplicably mislaid," see p. 44; on Stalin's "paranoia," pp. 49, 52; on the "sinister dynamics" of totalitarianism, p. 49; on the Duclos letter, pp. 43-4. The quotation herein on p. 228, about the inevitability of the cold war, comes from the same article, p. 52.

Churchill's hopes for world peace are quoted in Staughton Lynd, "How the Cold War Began," *Commentary* (November 1960), p. 379. Baruch's statement about the cold war, from a speech written by Herbert Bayard Swope, is quoted in Eric Goldman's *The Crucial Decade* (1956), p. 60.

For Lynd on Kennan, see his *Commentary* article, p. 387 n.; for his observation about Roosevelt's "sincere and idealistic concern" for eastern Europe, see. p. 383.

Quotations from Williams's *Tragedy of American Diplomacy* come from the revised edition published by Delta Books in 1962: p. 208 (balance of power after World War II; U.S. freedom of choice); p. 214 (Russians' sense of their own weakness); p. 236 (Acheson on the importance of foreign markets); p. 240 (Truman's plea for U.S. world hegemony); p. 242 (Crowley on the connection between markets and "good governments"); and p. 244 (the U.S. "overplays its hand").

Kennan's advice to promote the "mellowing" of Soviet power appears in his famous "X" article, "The Sources of Soviet Conduct," *Foreign Affairs* (July 1947), reprinted in his *American Diplomacy* (1951), p. 127.

Quotations from Gar Alperovitz, *Atomic Diplomacy* (1965) are taken from p. 22 ("symbolic showdown"); pp. 29, 33 (Truman's ultimatum); p. 21 (Roosevelt's interpretation of the Yalta agreements); p. 34 (Stalin's objections about Poland); p. 57 (Stimson's memorandum of May 16, 1945); p. 13 (Byrnes's advice); p. 67 (Churchill on the need for haste); p. 153 (Churchill on the "irresistibility" of the atomic bomb); p. 225 (Stimson on the importance of the bomb at the meeting of September 1945); and p. 278 (Stimson on embitterment of Soviet-American relations). For Alperovitz on the Duclos letter, see *New York Review,* October 20, 1966, pp. 37-8, which also contains his comment about the "doctrine of historical inevitability."

Oglesby's remarks about the "Yankee free-enterpriser" can be found in Carl Oglesby and Richard C. Schaull, *Containment and Change* (1967), p. 111; see pp. 132-3 for the quotation about the international Communist conspiracy. For a more extended discussion of the question raised here—the degree to which American foreign policy is irrational in its own terms—see "The Foreign Policy Élite and the War in Vietnam," pp. 232-49.

The appearance of Gabriel Kolko's massive study of the diplomacy of World War II and the cold war, *The Politics of War* (1968) and *The Limits of Power* (1972), confirms my belief that differences within the revisionist camp would soon reveal themselves; Kolko disagrees with Alperovitz on the role of the atomic bomb in the diplomacy of 1945 and on a number of other points. His discussion of the Duclos letter, however, adds new support for Alperovitz's interpretation. In general his volumes examine the connection between corporate interests and foreign policy and show how the connection presented itself to the policymakers, without, however, falling into the kind of economic determinism that sees every decision as a corporate plot and credits American statecraft with an uncanny, almost diabolical understanding of global politics.

This essay first appeared in *The New York Times Magazine*, January 14, 1968. A few sentences had previously appeared in my review of Alperovitz's *Atomic Diplomacy* in *The Nation,* September 6, 1965.

XV. The Foreign Policy Élite and the War in Vietnam

ANYONE PRESENTING A CLASS INTERPRETATION OF AMERICAN POLITICS should expect certain standard objections to be raised almost automatically. In letters to *The Columbia Forum* (Spring 1972), pp. 49-52, one reader accused me of advancing a "conspiracy theory" of American foreign relations, while another read me a lecture on pluralism, arguing that the concept of class is "monolithic" and also "moralistic"; urging me to pay more attention to interest groups, bureaucracy, and "structures" in general; and citing the existence of the antiwar movement itself as evidence of the vitality of the democratic process. This last suggestion is particularly repugnant. The demonstrations to which the writer refers were highly irregular and often illegal actions to which men and women were driven out of an agonizing realization precisely that pluralism was *not* working, and many of these men and women are still in jail or standing trial for having taken part in them. That the bitter resistance to the war marked a dissolution of the political consensus—not another vindication of it—was recognized by those who tried to club it into submission and by perceptive observers within the establishment, who were themselves anguished by its desperate character.

Paul Seabury has argued, also in the *Forum,* that "nine men in the Johnson administration made the basic decisions to escalate and prosecute the Vietnam war"—a conspiracy theory with a vengeance! According to Seabury, the backgrounds of these men do not fit my description of the foreign policy élite. "None listed themselves as Episcopalian in *Who's Who in America,*" "none went to private boarding school," only three graduated from Ivy League colleges, and "only one . . . came from a family of genteel, inherited wealth." In order for his argument to carry any weight, Seabury would have to overcome his delicacy about naming names; the anonymity of his list protects it from attack. Even so, his choice of conspirators seems curious, evidently excluding both William and McGeorge Bundy (Groton, Yale, Episcopalian) and Ambassador Lodge (Middlesex and Harvard). This exclusion we infer from the flat statement that "none went to private boarding school." Or did Seabury forget that *Who's Who* often neglects to list private schools and religious affiliations? (This information can usually be found, however, in such sources as *Current Biography Yearbook.*)

In any case, it is obvious that responsibility for the "basic decision" cannot be assigned with such precision. The search for the sources of power has to range both downward and backward. It cannot stop with the very highest reaches of government. Dean Acheson says in his memoirs that one cannot understand the State Department without understanding the great influence wielded by the division chiefs. The same principle applies to other agencies. It is a reasonable assumption—although one that I am not now in a position to document—that career men are more likely to be drawn from the upper class than Presidents and heads of departments.

Seabury's list, if it were to mean anything, would also have to include officials in the Truman, Eisenhower, and Kennedy administrations—men like Acheson (Groton and Yale), Dulles (Princeton and Wall Street), and many others, who made a series of commitments to Saigon which left Johnson with greatly diminished choices; in effect, with the choice to escalate or withdraw.

G. William Domhoff's *The Higher Circles* (1970), which I encountered only after writing the present essay, contains an informative essay on "How the Power Elite Makes Foreign Policy." After defining the power élite as the "political arm of the upper class," Domhoff shows in some detail how the Council on Foreign Relations, RAND, the university research institutes, the National Security Council, and ad hoc committees like the Gaither Committee have influenced foreign policy—for example, by promoting bipartisanship, providing a rationale for general rearmament in the late forties, reaffirming the American commitment to Indochina in 1954, and criticizing excessive reliance on nuclear weapons in the late fifties. (The Gaither Report, which had a marked influence on the New Frontiermen, is of prime importance in the development of Indochina policy, not only because it led to a fascination with counterinsurgency but because in de-emphasizing nuclear armaments it made possible the Soviet-American détente in Europe, one of the preconditions of massive intervention in the Far East.) Domhoff also demonstrates the upper-class dominance of these agencies, identifying the upper class by its great wealth and by "social indicators" like inclusion in the *Social Register,* membership in certain clubs, and attendance at certain private schools. Finally—and without this the argument would be of little interest—he shows that this same class controls the major corporations.

Domhoff's book, together with his more recent study *Fat Cats and Democrats* (1972), goes some distance toward meeting the criticism often leveled at C. Wright Mills's *The Power Elite* (1956)—that although Mills demonstrated the existence of an upper class, he failed to connect it with the actual process of decision-making. My analysis of the Pentagon papers is intended to serve the same purpose. That analysis is indisputably crude—I should like to think because our knowledge of American class structure is in general quite crude—but it can hardly be refuted by citing anonymous decision-makers, by pretending that it is a conspiracy theory, or by confusing resistance to the war with the normal workings of a "pluralistic" society.

The essence of the pluralist theory of American society can be found in two highly influential books of the fifties: John Kenneth Galbraith's *American Capitalism* (1952), which proposes the theory of "countervailing power," and Robert A. Dahl's *A Preface to Democratic Theory* (1956). See also Dahl's *Who Governs?* (1961). The "consensus" school of American historiography is perhaps best represented by Daniel Boorstin, *The Genius of American Politics* (1953) and the two volumes of his *The Americans, The Colonial Experience* (1958) and *The National Experience* (1965). See also Louis Hartz, *The Liberal Tradition in America* (1955).

For the State Department's reaction to the British withdrawal from Greece, see Robert Lasch, "How We Got Where We Are," *Progressive* (July 1971), p. 15. The National Security Council's statement on Vietnam, August 1953, comes from Neil Sheehan, *et al., The Pentagon Papers* (1971), p. 11. This edition, published jointly by *The New York Times* and Quadrangle Books, contains the text and documentation published by the *Times* in June and July 1971.

The State Department's 1949 statement on Bao Dai is taken from the same source, p. 10, as is Acheson's statement on Indochina, p. 10. See p. 45 of *The Pentagon Papers* for the Joint Chiefs' 1954 opinion that Indochina is militarily insignificant; p. 16 for the Pentagon historians' observation that such judgments went unrebutted; p. 367 for William Bundy's memorandum of September 8, 1964, on internal security in South Vietnam; and p. 349 for his memo to Rusk of January 6, 1965, on morale. This last memo, p. 350, also contains the reference to a "Vietnamese solution" and its unacceptability.

Herman Kahn's *On Escalation* (1965) reportedly influenced high policymakers in the Kennedy and Johnson administrations. The phrases, "Ask not what your country can do," etc., come, of course, from John F. Kennedy's inaugural address.

See *Pentagon Papers,* p. 442, for McNaughton's solicitude for "our reputation as a guarantor"; p. 335 for the November 1964 deliberations of the National Security Council on bombing; p. 613 for Taylor's description of defeat; p. 262 for President Johnson's query and the C.I.A.'s reply; p. 366 for McNaughton's memo on "relevant audiences"; p. 264 for Walt Rostow's boast; p. 448 for McNaughton's "good doctor" memo; p. 464 for Ball's dissent; and pp. 495, 480, 487–8, and 340 for assessments by the C.I.A. and other intelligence groups on the futility of bombing.

For "carrot-and-stick" diplomacy, see pp. 264, 398; for "breaking the enemy's will," pp. 340, 404, 417; for terms "tantamount to unconditional surrender," p. 257; for the bombing scenario of May 1964, p. 257; for the "thinness" of American patience with Hanoi, p. 276; for American failure to intimidate Pham Van Dong, p. 277.

The interagency memorandum of June 10, 1964 ("disagreeable

questions"), appears on p. 265; McNamara's lie about the Tonkin Gulf incident, on p. 273; Johnson's lie about not enlarging the war, on p. 320; McGeorge Bundy's advocacy of bombing, on pp. 433 and 435–6; his statement about Khanh, on p. 402; Taylor's reassuring memo to Kennedy, on p. 148; Wheeler's reassurance, on p. 475; and Rostow's prediction of imminent North Vietnamese defeat, on p. 458.

For William Bundy's advocacy of escalation in the face of his own pessimism, see pp. 350–1; for McNaughton's memo of January 19, 1966, on "escalating military stalemate," see p. 503; for Johnson's heartfelt complaint, p. 579.

A good account of the Nixon policies, which cuts through the mystery of "Vietnamization," is Daniel Ellsberg's *Papers on the War* (1972).

Ortega's characterization of Americans comes from *The Revolt of the Masses* (1930), chapter XIV; Melville's, from *Israel Potter* (1855), quoted in F. O. Matthiessen, *American Renaissance* (1941), p. 444.

This essay appeared in *The Columbia Forum* (Winter 1971); I am grateful to Erik Wensberg, editor of the *Forum,* for many comments and criticisms that forced me to clarify the argument.

XVI. Educational Structures and Cultural Fragmentation

THIS ESSAY INCORPORATES PASSAGES FROM TWO PREVIOUSLY PUBLISHED articles: "The Good Old Days," *New York Review,* February 10, 1972, and "Educational Structures and Cultural Fragmentation," in John Voss and Paul L. Ward, eds., *Confrontation and Learned Societies* (1970); but most of the material is new and hitherto unpublished.

The material on apprenticeship and other informal educational arrangements is based largely on Lawrence Stone, *The Crisis of the Aristocracy* (1965); Philippe Ariès, *Centuries of Childhood* (1962); and Edmund S. Morgan, *The Puritan Family* (1948). For mid-nineteenth-century educational reform in the United States, I have relied principally on Michael B. Katz, *Class, Bureaucracy, and Schools* (1971). For the material on asylums, see David J. Rothman, *The Discovery of the Asylum* (1971). The quotation from Beaumont and Tocqueville comes from the 1964 reprint of their *On the Peni-*

tentiary System in the United States, p. 80. For the introduction of useless work into the asylum (footnote 2), see Michel Foucault, *Madness and Civilization* (1965).

The statement about educational professionalism ("the man who imagines himself a teacher . . .") is taken from Katz, p. 36.

For the attack on the schools at the turn of the century, see Lawrence A. Cremin, *The Transformation of the School* (1961) and Raymond E. Callahan, *Education and the Cult of Efficiency* (1962). The quotation from Cubberley is in Cremin, p. 68; the quotation from Eliot on the "public school plant," in Callahan, p. 127. Other quotations bearing on efficiency, scientific management, etc., come from the same source, pp. 16, 50, 62, 102. On the efficiency movement and progressive school reform in general, see also Joel H. Spring, *Education and the Rise of the Corporate State* (1972). On the high school, see Edward A. Krug, *The Shaping of the American High School* (1964).

For the argument that failure has been the "function" of public education, see Colin Greer, *The Great School Legend* (1972).

I have discussed Dewey's ideas at some length in *The New Radicalism in America* (1965), chapters 1 and 5, and have judged it unnecessary to add to that discussion here.

Randolph Bourne's articles on the Gary system appeared as a series in *The New Republic,* March 27, April 3, April 10, April 24, and May 1, 1915; see also his "The Gary Public Schools," *Scribner's* (September 1916). This last contains an introduction by Wirt, from which I have quoted the lines about the school as a substitute for the family and shop. Bourne's articles were later published as *The Gary Schools* (1916), with an introduction by Wirt. The Flexner-Bachman study, *The Gary Schools: A General Account,* was published in 1918 by the General Education Board, which commissioned it. My quotations are taken from p. 116 (helper system); p. 129 ("the tasks are determined by practical daily need"); pp. 180–1 (attendance); p. 135 ("the work is narrow in scope"); p. 129 (journeyman mechanics); and pp. 145–6 (household arts). For Wirt's article on "Scientific Management of School Plants," see *American School Board Journal* (February 1911). The article on Gary's success in "eliminating waste" was written by John Franklin Babbitt for *Elementary School Journal* (February 1912), and is quoted by Callahan, p. 131.

On the university I have found invaluable Laurence R. Veysey's

The Emergence of the American University (1965), which analyzes the conflict between four ideals of higher education—"mental discipline," "utility," "liberal culture," and "research." The quotation from Gilman in footnote 4 appears in Frederick Rudolph, *The American College and University* (1962), p. 273. The quotations from Oscar and Mary F. Handlin are from their *Facing Life: Youth and the Family in American History* (1971), p. 204 (elective system); p. 115 ("rhetoric, ambition, bickering"); and p. 155 ("nation's only educational institution"). This work also contains useful material on apprenticeship. Another helpful book on the university, especially on the competitive upgrading of vocations, is Robert Paul Wolff's *The Ideal of the University* (1969). On the irrelevance of higher education to job qualification, see Ivar Berg, *Education and Jobs: The Great Training Robbery* (1970).

Quotations from Robert Maynard Hutchins, *The Higher Learning in America* (1936), are taken from p. 36 (community pressure for vocational training); pp. 68–70 ("leave experience to life"); pp. 14, 61 ("economic conditions require us"); and p. 119 ("character of our civilization").

The writings of Ivan Illich—see especially *Deschooling Society* (1971)—were prompted by conditions in Puerto Rico, Mexico, and other countries where the construction of a common school system is just beginning, and where there is therefore still hope of reversing a wholesale commitment to compulsory schooling. The situation in advanced industrial countries is clearly more complicated, and "deschooling" can no more be regarded as a panacea than schooling. Merely in forcing us to reconsider the inevitability of the school, however, Illich, together with Paul Goodman (see especially his *Compulsory Mis-education*), has performed a major service for the history of education—the first fruits of which can already be seen in the books by Katz, Greer, and Spring. Finally it should be noted that this new work itself is already coming under attack from students of working-class culture, who object to the notion that public education was foisted on the American working class without its consent and who see in this view another example of a general tendency to regard the working class as passive and invariably acted upon rather than actively creating its own history. Much of the work of the next generation of social and cultural historians will probably be addressed to controversies of this kind.

XVII. The Social Thought
of Jacques Ellul

The Technological Society APPEARED IN 1964 IN A TRANSLATION BY John Wilkinson. It was followed in 1966 by *Propaganda*, translated by Konrad Kellen and Jean Lerner, and in 1967 by *The Political Illusion*, in Kellen's translation. All these books were published by Alfred A. Knopf. Since 1967, a whole series of Ellul's books have either appeared in English for the first time or been issued in inexpensive editions. The most important are a paperback reprint of *The Presence of the Kingdom*, translated by Olive Wyon (Seabury Press, 1967); *A Critique of the New Commonplaces*, translated by Helen Weaver (Knopf, 1968); *Violence*, translated by Cecelia Gaul Kings (Seabury, 1969), and *Autopsy of Revolution*, translated by Konrad Kellen (Knopf, 1971).

Quotations not already identified are taken from the following sources.

Part I: Lichtheim on Weber (George Lichtheim, *Marxism* [2nd edition, 1965], p. 385 n.); "the time is short" (*Presence of the Kingdom*, p. 138); "profound immobility" (*Presence*, p. 35); critique of Schaull (*Violence*, pp. 53–4); U.S.S.R. and U.S.A. (*Presence*, p. 36); "living in complete incoherence" (*Presence*, p. 101); irrationality of modern art (*Technological Society*, hereafter *TS*, p. 404); "explanatory myths" (*Presence*, p. 102).

Part II: "so totally repressed" (*Presence*, p. 77); liberty and constraint (*Illusion*, p. 212); subjection to the "social machine" (*Presence*, p. 78); "new style of life" (*Presence*, p. 145); "on the edge of this totalitarian society" (*Presence*, p. 60); every achievement worth preserving (*Presence*, p. 56); "woman should ultimately be the same as man," "adjustment," "unitary society" (*Illusion*, p. 215); "crumbling middle-class morality" (*TS*, pp. 416–17; see also *Commonplaces*, pp. 4–8); ruling-class attack on abstractions (*TS*, p. 414, quoting Alain Sargent); hippies (*Violence*, pp. 120–1); "moral revolution" (*Illusion*, p. 224 n.); "the insertion of values . . . is never more than just words" (*Illusion*, p. 94); "immersed in the immediate present" (*Illusion*, p. 75); "unitarian society" and tensions in France (*Illusion*, pp. 220–1).

Part III: tension and teaching (*Illusion*, p. 211). For the kibbutz, see Bruno Bettelheim, *Children of the Dream* (1969), pp. 36, 74 n., 97, 122, 130, 171, and 262.

Part IV: "suicidal solution" (*Presence*, p. 103); "private life must be re-established" (*Illusion*, p. 205); associations "totally independent of the state" (*Illusion*, p. 222); "authentic new tension between the intellectual and political realms" (*Illusion*, p. 223); "a political life that would be something else than mere illusion" (*Illusion*, p. 223); search for new culture a corporate act (*Presence*, p. 149); "I firmly believe the contrary" (*Violence*, p. 32); "capitalism did not create our world" (*TS*, p. 5); "it ought never to be said" (*TS*, p. 96); technique's refusal "to tolerate moral judgments" (*TS*, 96–7); automobile as a murder weapon (*TS*, pp. 97–8).

Part V: "capitalist system lives by waste" (Louis Boudin, *The Theoretical System of Karl Marx* [1907], p. 246); "deep disorder of the nineteenth century" (*TS*, p. 5).

Part VI: "propaganda's most astonishing capabilities" (*Illusion*, p. 213); U.S. policy in Vietnam (*Violence*, p. 90 n.); "reconciliation" prerequisite to revolution (*Violence*, p. 73); violence and "renewal" (*Violence*, p. 133); violence and necessity (*Violence*, pp. 91, 127); "artificiality" of society (*Illusion*, p. 53); "I believe in values that only the left has stated" (*Commonplaces*, p. 21).

Ellul's views on revolution, alluded to in Part I and throughout, are amplified in *Autopsy of Revolution*. For his theory of mass communications, see *Propaganda*, which I do not deal with here because I have already reviewed it in *The Nation*, April 4, 1966.

This essay appeared in *Katallagete* (Winter–Spring 1970).

XVIII. Birth, Death, and Technology

LEST MY ATTACK ON INDIVIDUALISM, HERE AND ELSEWHERE, BE CONFUSED with the panicky collectivism recently advocated by, among others, B. F. Skinner in *Beyond Freedom and Dignity* (1971), I hasten to add that it owes nothing to behavioral psychology or to the technological utopia that Skinner upholds as the alternative to individualism. For a criticism of Skinner's book with which I am in agreement, see Richard Sennett's review in *The New York Times*, October 24, 1971.

The phrase, "natural limitations of earthly well-being," comes from the Norton Library edition of Johan Huizinga's *In the Shadow of Tomorrow*, originally published in 1936, p. 109. For man's "transcendence" and woman's "imminence," see Simone de Beauvoir, *The*

Second Sex (1953), a profound and moving work that has very little in common with the neo-feminist outpourings referred to elsewhere in this essay.

On technological determinism and feminism, see Lester Frank Ward, *Dynamic Sociology* (1883) and *Pure Sociology* (1903); Charlotte Perkins Gilman, *Women and Economics* (1898); and Thorstein Veblen, *The Theory of the Leisure Class* (1899). Quotations from Russell's *Marriage and Morals* are taken from the Grove Press edition, p. 112 ("purely private affairs"); p. 121 ("taken over by the State"); p. 122 ("humanitarian sentiment of the community"); p. 123 ("play relation"); pp. 126-7 (elimination of fatherhood); and pp. 127, 137 (trivialization of personal relations).

Technical information about cloning and asexual reproduction can be found in Edward Grossman's "The Obsolescent Mother," *Atlantic* (May 1971), pp. 39-50, which also contains a very subtle parody of the argument for the inevitability of technological progress. See also, not only for technical details but for a scientist's reservations, Willard Gaylin's article, "We Have the Awful Knowledge to Make Exact Copies of Human Beings," *New York Times Magazine,* March 5, 1972, pp. 12 ff. For Watson's reservations, see his "Moving Toward the Clonal Man," *Atlantic* (May 1971), pp. 50-3.

The quotations from Ti-Grace Atkinson are taken from her "The Institution of Sexual Intercourse," in *Notes from the Second Year: Women's Liberation* (1970), pp. 42-7. For similar views, see Shulamith Firestone, *The Dialectic of Sex* (1970). On the vaginal orgasm, see Anne Koedt, "The Myth of the Vaginal Orgasm," *Notes from the Second Year,* pp. 37-41.

On dying, see David Dempsey, "Learning How to Die," *New York Times Magazine,* November 14, 1971, pp. 58 ff., which includes the quotation about hospitals' concealing information from patients (from a study by Barney G. Glaser and Anselm L. Strauss, professors at the University of California Medical Center in San Francisco) and the information about seminars in "thanatology" at Billings Hospital. See also David Sudnow, *Passing On: The Social Organization of Dying* (1967).

The study alluded to at the end of footnote 1 is Page Smith, *Daughters of the Promised Land* (1970).

Excerpts from this essay appeared in *The Hastings Center Report* (June 1972).

INDEX

A NOTE ABOUT THE AUTHOR

CHRISTOPHER LASCH was born in Omaha, Nebraska, in 1932. He attended Harvard University (B.A. 1954) and Columbia University (M.A. 1955, Ph.D. 1961), and has taught history at Williams College (1957–9), Roosevelt University (1960–1), the University of Iowa (1961–6), and Northwestern University (1966–70). Since 1970 he has been Professor of History at the University of Rochester. Winner of Harvard's Bowdoin Prize in 1954, he was held both the Erb Fellowship (1955–6) and the Gilder Fellowship (1956–7) at Columbia University. Mr. Lasch is the author of *The American Liberals and the Russian Revolution* (1962), *The New Radicalism in America* (1965), and *The Agony of the American Left* (1969). He has contributed many articles to *The New York Review of Books* and to other periodicals and journals. He now lives in Avon, New York, with his wife, the former Nell Commager, and their four children.

A NOTE ON THE TYPE

THIS BOOK was set on the Linotype in *Granjon*, a type named in compliment to Robert Granjon, but neither a copy of a classic face nor an entirely original creation. GEORGE W. JONES based his designs for this type upon the type used by Claude Garamond (1510–61) in his beautiful French books, and Granjon more closely resembles Garamond's own than do any of the various modern types that bear his name.

Robert Granjon began his career as typecutter in 1523. The boldest and most original designer of his time, he was one of the first to practice the trade of typefounder apart from that of printer. Between 1557 and 1562 Granjon printed about twenty books in types designed by himself, following, after the fashion of the day, the cursive handwriting of the time. These types, usually known as "caractères de civilité," he himself called "lettres françaises," as especially appropriate to his own country.

The book was composed, printed, and bound by
H. Wolff Book Mfg. Co., Inc., New York, New York
Typography and binding based on a design by
GUY FLEMING

DATE DUE